IS THERE LIFE WITHOUT MOTHER?

IS THERE LIFE WITHOUT MOTHER?

PSYCHOANALYSIS

BIOGRAPHY

CREATIVITY

LEONARD SHENGOLD

NEW YORK AND LONDON

First published 2000 by Analytic Press, Inc.

This edition published 2015 by Routledge
711 Third Avenue, New York, NY 10017, USA
2 Park Square, Milton Park, Abingdon, Oxon, OX14 4RN

First issued in paperback 2015

Routledge is an imprint of the Taylor & Francis Group, an informa business

Copyright © 2000 by The Analytic Press

All rights reserved. No part of this book may be reproduced in any form: by photostat, micoform, electronic retrieval system, or any other means, without the prior written permission of the publisher.

Typeset in Adobe Sabon 10.5/12.5 by CompuDesign, Charlottesville, VA

ISBN 13: 978-1-138-00979-0 (pbk)
ISBN 13: 978-0-88163-336-8 (hbk)

I dedicate this book on parents to siblings:
to Esther and Paul,
Edith and Lou,
Helen and Eddie.

[He] suffered from the Primal Curse, which is not—
as the Authorized Version suggests—
the knowledge of good and evil, but the
knowledge of good-and-evil.

—E. M. Forster, "The Longest Journey"

CONTENTS

Acknowledgments xi

PART I: Biography, Creativity, and Pathology

Chapter 1. Biography: Another Impossible Profession 3

Chapter 2. Artistic Creativity 11

Chapter 3. Clinical and Literary Examples 23

Chapter 4. The Primal Parent: A Patient's Cry 29

PART II: Literary Lives

Chapter 5. Jules Renard: Soul Murder in
Life and Literature 39

Chapter 6. Trollope: His Life and Creativity 61

Chapter 7. School Days and After:
Disorder and Early Sorrow, and Recovery 85

Chapter 8. Trollope's Writing Method 101

Chapter 9. Daydreaming in the Service of
Creativity and of Sexuality 117

Chapter 10. Identity and Fiction: Father and Son 129

Chapter 11. Identity and Fiction:
The Nuances of Resentment 135

Chapter 12. What Was Trollope Like? 147

Chapter 13. Trollope's Love for His Characters 159

Chapter 14. Trollope's Death 169

Contents

—— x ——

Chapter 15. Trollope with Mother.........................173

PART III: Conclusion and Epilogue

Chapter 16. Conclusion and More Literary Examples......187

Epilogue   Multiple Personalities.......................203

References 207

Index 213

Acknowledgments

I am grateful to many people. My wonderful and patient wife has read every word of my manuscript drafts and supplied counsel that was always helpful and almost always accepted. My son, David Shengold, one of my polymath children, has corrected facts and grammar in some of my chapters. Gladys Topkis, my friend and gracious, gifted, psychoanalytically proficient editor at Yale University Press (alas, now retired), was characteristically generous with her good advice, general wisdom, and great copy editing. John Kerr, my new, welcome, and empathic editor at The Analytic Press, made creative and excellent recommendations for rearranging my first draft of this book. He also advised clarifications of cloudy patches of prose and ideation and suggested transitions for badly connected subjects; most of these I not only agreed with but learned from. Eleanor Starke Kobrin of The Analytic Press was a wonderful helper and guide. Paul Schwaber discussed, usefully and kindly, a paper on Trollope based on part of this book at a conference at Yale honoring Gladys Topkis. Two friends, Paul Gray and Shelley Orgel, made valuable suggestions that are referred to in the text; two others, Austin Silber and Vann Spruiell, read parts of the manuscript and offered useful criticism and recommendations. Ian Graham graciously granted me permission to mention his clinical presentation at a meeting of the Toronto Analytic Society.

I am indebted to the many excellent biographies of Anthony Trollope—those of Michael Sadleir (1945), James Pope-Hennessy (1971), C. P. Snow (1975), R. H. Super (1988), Richard Mullen (1992), and, especially those by Victoria Glendinning (1992) and N. John Hall (1991), also the editor of Trollope's *Letters* (Hall, 1983a, b). I have profited from Richard Mullen and James Munson's (1996) *The Penguin Companion to Trollope*, from the fine articles about Trollope by Henry James (1883) and Jonathan Raban (1987), and from Teresa Ransom's (1995) and Pamela Neville-Sington's (1997) admirable biographies of Frances Trollope. I greatly enjoyed reading all—well, nearly all—of Anthony Trollope. Discovering Jules Renard through the chance reading of a selection from his *Journal* was a revelation. I wish my French were good enough to translate the entire *Journal*, an autobiographical masterpiece, into English (only a small selection from the 17 volumes in French has been published in English translation).[1] I have presented in various places a part of my chapter on Renard and invariably have aroused interest in him on the part of the English-speaking people in the audience. I hope this book will help motivate someone qualified to do the translation.

---

1. Gore Vidal (1990) is one of the few contemporary writers who has expressed his enthusiasm for Renard and his *Journal*, which Vidal calls Renard's "marvelous notebook" (p. 168).

PART I

Biography, Creativity, and Pathology

Chapter 1

BIOGRAPHY
Another Impossible Profession

> *Novelists have omniscience; biographers never do. . . . The biographer may be as imaginative as he pleases—the more imaginative the better—in the way he brings together his materials, but he must not imagine the materials.*
>
> —Leon Edel
> Writing Lives. Principia Biographica

Anthony Trollope (1883) wrote in and of his autobiography, "That I or any man, should tell everything of himself, I hold to be impossible" (p. 1). When writing another's biography, it is even more impossible to tell everything. Trying to find out and tell as much as one can about another person is a risky business that when done best requires—for biographer or psychoanalyst alike—tact, self-knowledge, and humility on the part of the author or the analytic interpreter. Psychobiography, which involves making considerable use of psychoanalytic knowledge and theory, is perhaps an even greater challenge. Lytton Strachey, who dabbled with a psychological approach, set the tone of biographies for decades after the publication of his first "best seller," *Eminent Victorians* (1918). He wrote in the preface to that book:

> [The biographer or the historian] will row out over that great ocean of material and lower down into it, here and there, a little bucket, which will bring up to the light of day some characteristic specimen, from those far depths,

Chapter 1

to be examined with a careful curiosity. Guided by these considerations, I have written the ensuing studies. I have attempted, through the medium of biography, to present some Victorian visions to the modern eye. They are, in one sense, haphazard visions—that is to say, my choice of subjects has been determined by no desire to construct a system or to prove a theory, but by simple motives of convenience and art. I have sought to examine and elucidate certain fragments of the truth which took my fancy and lay to my hand. To quote from a Master—"*Je n'impose rien; je ne propose rien; j'expose*" ["I impose nothing; I propose nothing; I expose"] [quoted by Holroyd, 1994, p. 420].

The wicked Strachey was himself the Master who had made up this quotation, "which critics were to assume came from Voltaire" (p. 420). As for the sentiment itself, no one can be sure that his choices were not determined by a need to construct a system or prove a theory—a need that would involve some basic aggressive or libidinal desire (or both) kept outside of conscious awareness.

In an earlier book review, Strachey attributed another fabricated quote to Livy, who (Strachey falsely stated) had written that he "would have made Pompey win the battle of Pharsalia, if the turn of the sentence had required it." Strachey, serious alongside the mockery of this characteristic variety of in-joking, added:

[Livy] was not talking utter nonsense, but simply expressing an important truth in a highly paradoxical way—that the first duty of a great historian is to be an artist. The function of art in history is something much more profound than mere decoration. . . . Uninterpreted truth is as useless as buried gold; and art is the great interpreter. It alone can unify a vast multitude of facts into a significant whole, clarifying, accentuating, suppressing, and lighting up the dark places with the torch of the imagination. More than that, it can throw over the historian's materials the glamour of a personal revelation, . . . and its value ultimately depends upon the force and quality of the character behind it [quoted in Holroyd, 1994, pp. 419–420].

Biography: Another Impossible Profession

Presumably the reliable character of the writer is all (Strachey is surely thinking of himself). But attempts to approach both current and historical "truth" do indeed depend on the predominantly reliable character of the biographer or the historian, or, in the case of my discipline, the psychoanalyst and the patient. And neither psychoanalysis nor biography is a field for scientific exactitude, although trying to achieve the impossible goal of gathering, establishing, and evaluating "fact" should, contra Strachey's tongue in cheek, not be abandoned in the service of art or any other tendentious goal—as far as one can help it. Complexity demands compromise; we must try to establish comparative certainties alongside the awareness that we are surrounded by uncertainties.

A psychoanalyst, in contrast to most biographers, who frequently have a dead or an uncooperative subject, at least has direct access to a patient's attempt to tell his story (as it is currently represented in his mind) by way of attempts at free association. Free association supplies patterns of unknown trends that can come to light as well as of characteristic distortions and elisions of conscious and unconscious material, involving, to use psychoanalytic jargon, *defenses* and *resistances* against the flow of emotion. These can be worked over in the course of time by analyst and patient and, it is to be hoped, modified. If the analysis works, what is insistently felt in relation to the analyst will, in time, bring to the present—through the transference and projection of feelings—some of the hidden basic conflicts of the patient's past. The psychoanalytic process involves the extended working over of the patient's defenses and resistances, transferences and projections as they gather emotional life in the verbal interactions and concentration on the flow of the relationship between patient and analyst. The artifacts and narratives available for applied psychoanalysis and for most biographers come at a remove from the subject, and inferential conclusions remain untested by the psychoanalytic process.

On the other hand, the biographer/researcher can, as the psychoanalyst cannot, actively seek out and make use of documents that might prove to provide corroborating "facts." An artist's work is itself a record that has been worked over by the artist's conscious awareness of shaping form and content. Works of art, like all human psychic productions, can transmit the creator's intentional conscious as well as cryptic unconscious communications.

Chapter 1

The cigar is also a cigar. But the psychoanalyst, who does not have firsthand contact with the artist as he (or she) does with a psychoanalytic patient, obviously has no more privileged access to certainty here than has anyone else. Psychotherapists may be more able to apply skills for informed speculation about what is unconsciously being communicated in works of art. These skills develop from innate perceptive abilities as well as from practice at picking up the unconscious tendencies of patients. Whether this is an advantage or a disadvantage in writing or reading biography depends on the tact and judgment of the observer in dealing with observations based on conjecture. Such conjecture always involves the observer's biases; reliability cannot be ascertained. Compensating for these prejudices depends on what can at best be only partial knowledge and mastery of one's unconscious predilections. The observer—from whatever discipline—needs honesty, self-knowledge, a gift for discrimination, Strachey's "a careful curiosity," and humility in relation to recovering historical truth. Writers of biography should be aware, as they attempt to interpret the life of a human being from his or her writings—as should psychoanalysts working with their patients' associations—of the subtle implications of George Gissing's statement, "The only true biography is to be found in novels" (quoted by Holroyd, 1994, p. 606). This partial truth implies the need to tolerate, work, and work well with uncertainties.

And the biographer is always there in some major way in the biography he fashions; the psychoanalyst is always there in some major way in the work of the psychoanalysis. Edel (1985) writes, "[The biographer] is far from anonymous. He is present in his work as the portrait painter is present in his" (p. 31). The art, sound judgment, and reliable character of the biographer can contribute more to the creation of a good biography than an inherent interest in the life and importance of the person evoked and described in it.

And yet what we can be certain about must not be ignored. "Novelists have omniscience. Biographers never do" (Edel, 1985, p. 15)—an overstatement. Virginia Woolf (1932) writes that, whereas the imagination of the novelist is relatively free, that of the biographer is tied. She criticizes her old friend Lytton, then dead, and praises his *Queen Victoria*, a book he had dedicated to

Biography: Another Impossible Profession

her. In that book, she wrote, "He treated biography as a craft. In the *Elizabeth and Essex* he flouted its limitations" (p. 223). That book's Queen Elizabeth, she thinks, lacks the feel of reality that Strachey had given Queen Victoria or the fictional reality of a great Shakespearean character. She reproaches him both for a relative failure in his art and for not anchoring his narrative enough on facts. In his foreword to *Queen Victoria*, Strachey wrote, "Authority for every important statement of fact in the following pages will be found in the footnotes." Of course, allegations of authority do not always make for "facts," but the note shows that Strachey was trying for historical accuracy as well as for art. "Facts" about Elizabeth's life were, of course, harder to find and establish than were facts about the Queen, who had died when Strachey was 21.

The biographer should strive to be tied to the facts. But what are facts? The biography of Sir Thomas More by his son-in-law, William Roper, who undoubtedly knew him well, is still an idealized portrait by a perhaps not too discerning and certainly positively prejudiced witness. The dates and most of the happenings may or may not be "facts"; mistakes are always possible. Roper's selections, omissions, and interpretations are inevitably contaminated by distortion motivated by his probably sincere need to see his father-in-law as good and right. Perhaps he also needed to deny forbidden hateful feelings that could have made for wishes to expose the parent-figure's weaknesses and sins. Those with or without personal knowledge of the individuals they have chosen to write about will be influenced by their own identifications, projections, and transferences directed onto the biographical subjects. This inevitable imposing of the author's inner conflicts and imagos[1] will produce both conscious and unconscious prejudices, positive and negative, of many varieties. The resultant biography is bound to be (to some extent) a palimpsest—the "facts" and their interpretations here thickened, there eroded—created by the confluence of the results of conflicting wishes within the biographer's mind.

Biographical biases can be predominately aimed in a derogatory and destructive direction, sometimes with an obviously

---

1. An imago is an internalized mental representation of another, usually a parent or a parent-figure. A biographer can, unconsciously, project a representation of self or other onto the subject of his study and his book.

conscious intention to distort and vilify. Shakespeare's *Richard III*—not a biography but an "historical" play and indubitably a work of creative art—was probably accepted by its contemporary audience as valid history and biography. The author either wanted or felt he had no choice but to serve and please Queen Elizabeth by portraying King Richard, the man whom her Tudor grandfather had killed and replaced, as a cruel and murderous criminal and usurper. Therefore Richard, despite descending from the reigning York dynasty, would have had no moral right to the crown. Propaganda, not truth, was undoubtedly intended—although the playwright may have simply, and perhaps relatively innocently, been continuing a long-established, politically motivated calumniation created by earlier chroniclers and playwrights in order to establish the legitimacy of the reigns of the Tudor monarchs. In any case, such tendentious purposes were transformed into a great play, and Richard III into a great villain, by Shakespeare's magical artistic creativity. Despite the continuing controversies of historians about the actual nature of King Richard's character and deeds, it is the fictional portrayal imagined and constructed by Shakespeare that we remember.

There is a depiction of the relationship between the Victorian explorer and author Richard Burton and his wife in a recent biography by Mary S. Lovell, (1998) that is very different from the relationship described by other biographers of Burton (for example, Brodie, 1967; McLynn, 1993). Lovell portrays Richard and Isabel Burton as having had a primarily loving and sensual marriage following their romantic courtship. This depiction challenges the view of other biographers who have depicted Burton as predominantly running away from his wife and from his dependency on her and stressing Isabel Burton's being driven by impulses both to idolize and to castrate her husband. In these Burton biographies envious hatred and revenge have been interpreted as the chief motivations for her censoring, mutilating, or burning his prurient unpublished writings and documents left in her care after his death. One biographer seems to like and defend Isabel, the others to dislike and attack her. The reader of these biographies finds conflicting elucidations of "facts" and "truth." The differences may be endlessly debated; it is possible that they will simply turn out to be unresolvable by "evidence" in the form of certainties that would settle contradictory interpretations. It can be salutary to conclude that one cannot settle on what actually

Biography: Another Impossible Profession

happened in such cases. (I do not know enough to say that such a conclusion would be proper in relation to the Burtons.) Remaining in doubt about people in the past can be analogous to what the psychoanalyst sometimes has to settle for when a patient makes a charge of having been abused as a child by an adult, an accusation that cannot be resolved with certainty in spite of long and thorough mutual analytic work. Sometimes the best that both patient and analyst can do is suspend disbelief in the possibility of abuse. To do so is better than adopting what may for some people be a false sureness in the course of trying to "establish" historical truth (see Shengold, 1999).

Freud wrote to Lytton Strachey after the publication of the latter's *Elizabeth and Essex* in 1928:

> I am acquainted with all your earlier publications, and have read them with great enjoyment. But the enjoyment was essentially an aesthetic one. This time you have moved me deeply, for you yourself have reached greater depths. You are aware of what other historians so easily overlook—that it is impossible to understand the past with certainty, because we cannot divine men's motives and the essence of their minds and so cannot interpret their actions. Our psychological analysis does not suffice even with those who are near us in space and time, unless we can make them the object of years of the closest investigation, and even then it breaks down before the incompleteness of our knowledge and the clumsiness of our synthesis. So that in regard to the people of past times we are in the same position as with dreams to which we have been given no associations—and only a layman could expect us to interpret such dreams as those. As a historian, then, you show that you are steeped in the spirit of psychoanalysis. And, with reservations such as these, you have approached one of the most remarkable figures in your country's history, you have known how to trace back her character to the impressions of her childhood, you have touched upon her most hidden motives with equal boldness and discretion, and it is very possible that you have succeeded in making a correct reconstruction of what actually occurred [quoted in Holroyd, 1994, p. 615].

Chapter 1

10

This was high praise, which Strachey appreciated. But whether the reconstruction can be called "correct" is, alas, subject to unresolvable doubt. Freud here stressed his reservations—knowing how much we do not know.

Chapter 2

ARTISTIC CREATIVITY

To Generalize is to be an Idiot. To Particularize is the Alone Distinction of Merit—General Knowledges are those Knowledges that Idiots possess.

What is General Nature? is there such a thing? What is General Knowledge? is there such a thing? Strictly Speaking All Knowledge is Particular.

—William Blake
"Annotations to Sir Joshua Reynolds' Discourses"

I want to stress how much I do not know about artistic creativity and its relation to trauma and pathology, as well as (with more hubris) how much is not known generally. A genius like Freud is always worth reading on any subject, and there are works and isolated insights about art and artists by him and other psychoanalysts that are valuable and even brilliant. Some analysts have shown a talent for literary appreciation and have avoided reductionism, and good use has been made of literary examples that illustrate or even enhance psychoanalytic clinical findings. But, in my opinion, applied analysis has not been one of the glories of psychoanalytic writings. (There has been brilliant writing about creativity by psychoanalysts, such as Ernst Kris ([1953]) and, more recently, John Gedo and Gilbert Rose, but I feel that the valuable insights of the latter two are not primarily derived from psychoanalysis, although they use its lexicon.)

Freud appreciated how much he had learned and could learn from literary artists like Shakespeare and Goethe and philosophers like Schopenhauer and Nietzsche. But Freud's (1908) initial published ideas about artistic creativity were reductive and faulty, as were those of his followers. In the early psychoanalytic literature, understanding the artist tended to be equated with connecting his creative product with neuroses and complexes. The work of art was relegated to being a substitute for the gratification of some instinctual need, and artistic creations were equated with daydreams. Creativity was viewed primarily as stemming from conflicts and deficits, from pathology. In "Philoctetes, The Wound and the Bow," Edmund Wilson's (1929) essay on creativity, influenced by Freud, the author chose Philoctetes as a symbol of the creative artist, the hero's stinking and unhealing wound motivating him to perfect and exercise his extraordinary powers as an archer.

There is some truth in this kind of linkage: trauma, misfortune, deficit can give rise to an impetus toward achievement and excellence. One sees many victims of child abuse and deprivation (of what I have called soul murder [Shengold, 1989, 1999]) and persons born with deficiencies spurred on to adaptation and mastery. Motivation is one prerequisite for creativity, but it is not the source of its power or nature. Wounds can (although not all do) motivate but do not account for the excellence of the bow or for the archer's skill in using it. We need to explore psychic health, not primarily psychopathology, in order to understand the ability to transcend and transform neurotic motivation adaptively and especially creatively. Lionel Trilling (1945) pointed this out specifically in relation to literature. Creativity is a kind of superhealth, made up of inherent and acquired gifts (which also include nonneurotic sources of motivation); the gifts can exist alongside—intertwined with and motivated by—pathology. Pathology and fantasies and realities of a traumatic past can, of course, also furnish much of an artist's subject matter, but to what extent there is a compulsion to deal directly with traumatic circumstances of the artist's past and what form it takes vary with each individual.

The origin of health remains a comparative mystery; health is perhaps largely, but surely not entirely, to be attributed to heredity. Inherited powers seem very important, but conscious will is certainly involved. Some are born creative, some achieve it, and some may have it thrust upon them. One finds various combinations of inherited creative potential, a preponderance of enhancing rather than inhibitory family and environmental influences, a will to mastery that is stronger than fear of achievement, and favorable accidental circumstances.

Good psychological therapists become experts in psychic pathology—conflicts, inhibitions, traumatic damage, deficiencies. Psychic pathology frequently inhibits, and even prohibits, giftedness and creativity, in everyday life as well as in artistic and scientific achievement. Insights about creativity should stress art as mastery, whatever art's variable and unclear relationship to psychic pathology. Charles Lamb (1833) said this in his essay "Sanity of True Genius" which is a refutation of the idea that literary genius is based on madness. His view of the work of a great artist takes genius far beyond daydream: "The true poet dreams being awake. He is not possessed by his subject but has dominion over it. . . . He ascends the empyrean heaven, and is not intoxicated" (p. 167). Great art increases our grasp of psychological and external reality. A similar view was expressed by the excellent poet Elizabeth Bishop, whose mother spent most of her adult life in an asylum and whose dear friend and fellow poet Robert Lowell suffered from periodic manic–depressive psychosis. In an interview, Bishop was talking about her beginning to teach the writing of poetry at the University of Washington in 1966:

> I've already start[ed] worrying about some of my students. Going insane is very popular these days, and it frightens me to see so many young people flirting with the idea of it. They think that going crazy will turn them into better poets. That's not true at all! Insanity is a terrible thing! I've seen it first-hand in some of my friends, and it is not the "poetic" sort of thing that these young people seem to think it is. John Clare did not write glorious poetry while he was in the asylum, I'm glad to say [quoted in Monteiro, 1996, p. 41].

I have a predominantly negative opinion of current psychoanalytic views and understanding of creativity.[1] There is so much that needs to be "particularized" (to return to this chapter's epigraph

---

1. And of our views of creative adaptation: for example, neurotic motivation can and does result in good marriages as well as bad ones.

from Blake), so much that we do not know. Applied psychoanalysis has generally been the province of amateurs, in both the best and the worst sense. Amateurs love what they are preoccupied with, but they can also be naive. To deal with art and psychoanalysis with the flexibility and integration necessary to permit insight requires knowing a lot and, even harder, knowing how much one does not know—specifics, not just generalities.

In my view, what we do not know about psychic health and pathology, and specifically about their relation to artistic creativity and greatness in literature and the visual arts, is at least as important as what we do know. There is no one "true" way to read *Hamlet*, although some readings are more important than others. The optimal balance between what is known and what is not known is also required when a therapist tries to grasp the many dynamic, complex, and often contradictory ways in which a patient has psychically registered his past and patterned his present. These are reflected in the repetitive themes from his associations (e.g., the text) that appear after emotional involvement with the analyst has given rise to real psychoanalytic work, after the analyst is able to interpret successfully the dynamically powerful emotional revivals from the past called, in the psychoanalytic lexicon, transferences and resistances. We do the best we can, realizing that this means being able only to *approach* complete understanding and historical truth. Great humility is called for. Freud's disciple Hanns Sachs said of psychoanalysis as an exploration of the mind, "Our deepest analyses are no more than scratching the earth's surface with a harrow" (quoted in Gitelson, 1973, p. 250). Of course, there are some artists whose harrows can scratch as deep as or even deeper than ours do. Trollope at his best was one of these. And Trollope himself stated something of the limitations inherent in knowing other human beings, even when they are writers who left revelatory records of themselves that would not be expected of most of us, certainly not of most postal employees. Trollope (1883) wrote:

> That I, or any man, should tell everything of himself, I hold to be impossible. Who could endure to own the doing of a mean thing? Who is there that has done none? But this I protest—that nothing that I say shall be untrue. . . . It will not, I trust, be supposed by any reader that I have

intended in this so-called autobiography to give a record of my inner life. No man ever did so truly, and no man ever will [p. 365].

He could have added, "No man ever can." But one can try, and inherent incompleteness and distortion do not invalidate the greatness of some autobiographies.

The novelist and critic C. P. Snow (1975) wrote about Trollope's miserable childhood: "We . . . can be grateful for [his] bad luck. It probably helped endow him with the specific insight, the delicate fluid empathy, which made him the finest natural psychologist of all nineteenth-century novelists" (p. 9.) Note that Snow seems to have viewed Trollope's psychological mindedness as "probably" being enabled by his miserable childhood—which I feel can be credited only with supplying the motive for a writer's use of his or her talents. Motivation does not endow or ensure creative ability or genius. The motivations toward mastery evoked by pathology and misfortune are, of course, always partly compromised by conflicts that also inhibit and distort creativity and creative talents.

In 1944, the American poet and critic Randall Jarrell wrote a letter about his friend the poet and novelist Robert "Red" Penn Warren. He called Warren a good man who "manages his life by pushing all the evil in it into the poems and novels." For Warren, Jarrell (1985) said, "Poetry is a therapeutic device, the most wonderful one you could want, but the best poetry isn't that" (p. 116). And Jarrell too believed that pathological motivation does not account for the creativity. He continued, "I don't think anything short of my theory can explain how anybody as intelligent as Red, anybody that can write the best parts of his poetry, can write and be satisfied with the worst part of his poems and novels" (p. 117). (Jarrell felt this way also about the pathologically and too personally motivated parts of the poems of a younger poet he very much admired, his friend Robert Lowell.)

Here is a statement of the importance of what we do not know, also from Randall Jarrell (1958):

> The truth, as everybody knows, is sometimes complicated or hard to understand; is sometimes almost unrecognizably different from what we expected it to be, is sometimes

difficult or, even, impossible to accept. And literature is necessarily mixed up with truth, isn't it?—our truth, truth as we know it; one can almost define literature as the union of a wish and truth, or a wish modified by truth [p. 295].

Being able to contribute some "particulars" in the impossible quest for truth requires creative power, which is inevitably, the human condition being what it is, mixed with deficiency, trauma, and neurosis.

THE RELATION OF PSYCHOPATHOLOGY TO TALENTS AND CREATIVITY

I have referred to the rich field for exemplification for clinical and theoretical exegesis that can be offered by the biography and fiction of creative writers. Writers openly display and articulate in their work their psychological insights and the psychopathology of themselves and others. Wittingly and unwittingly, they—in great contrast to the rest of us—both publicly reveal and publicly conceal. That combination can give the false impression that artistic creativity is based on pathology, a notion that I have inveighed against. This impression is all the more likely since, from the viewpoint of the psychoanalyst, some of the mechanisms of creativity seem akin—sometimes transformed, sometimes identical—to mechanisms that can be seen in clinical phenomena. These similarities have led to various psychoanalytic theses about creativity.

Freud (1937) wrote, "Every normal person, in fact, is only normal on the average. His ego approximates to that of the psychotic in some part or other and to a greater or lesser extent" (p. 235). Freud implied here, I believe, the importance of what I have called the delusions of everyday life. Freud was defining the functioning of an ordinary person's mental life as able to make use of, as well as be inhibited by, some of the mechanisms that resemble those employed in pathologically regressive or psychotic states of mind (that is, both for better and for worse). Arnold Cooper (1993) points out that aspects of paranoia can be seen in the regressions that accompany all psychoanalyses—even of those patients who do not in any obvious respect seem to be suffering from persecutory psychosis. One might speak, given the universality of the mechanism of projection (unconsciously attributing to another what is a characteristic of one's self), of the paranoia of everyday life. It is implicit in Freud's statement, as well as in Cooper's, that psychotic-like functioning is apparent in artistically creative persons as well as in ordinary individuals and their everyday creativity. Everyday creativity would involve using what Freud (1900) called primary-process thinking—unconscious infantile mental mechanisms—condensation, displacement, symbolism, and so on, which he described as exemplified both in normal (dreams, jokes and wit, slips of the tongue) and in pathological (neurotic symptoms) phenomena. Primary-process thinking continues throughout life to underlie and intertwine with the more logical, ordinary, conscious secondary-process thinking.

Ernst Kris (1953), an art historian who became a distinguished pupil of Freud, in a book that contained 20 years of articles about creativity and art, wrote of artistic creativity as involving:

> Inspiration—the "divine release from the ordinary ways of life," a state of "creative madness" (Plato), in which the ego controls the primary process and puts it to its service—[is to be] contrasted with *the opposite*—the psychotic condition in which the ego is overwhelmed by the primary process [p. 60].

Kris's concept here involved something essential to the concept of sublimation; he called it regression in the service of the ego—the transformation of what could appear to be pathological into a healthy and creative instrumentality. Something central to "the opposite" is in creativity able to be controlled and employed to a very different end. But how? And why?

Princess Marie Bonaparte, a patient of Freud's and later his close friend, is said to have declared that Freud stated in a conversation with her that psychoanalysis is a sublimation of paranoia. (Sublimation is used in psychoanalysis to indicate the ability to modify a pathological drive or tendency in order to turn it to an adaptive purpose.) The anecdote, doubly or triply removed—it was told me by Paul Gray, who heard it from someone who had conversed with Marie Bonaparte—is, if not *vero*, surely *ben trovato*. Freud (1916–1917) described the dynamics involved in contrary mental intentions resulting in a compromise that comes through

Chapter 2

as a "slip"—a parapraxis. He wrote, somewhat apologetically, that psychoanalysts work

> from small indications, as we are constantly in the habit of doing in the present field, [and this] brings its own dangers. There is a mental disease, "combinatory paranoia," in which the explanation of small indications like these is carried to unlimited lengths, and I would not of course claim that conclusions built on such foundations are invariably correct [pp. 66–67].

This statement implies that the "small indications" picked up by psychoanalysts can also, if not "carried to unlimited lengths," be quite correct. This would, of course, tend to be true if the paranoia can be sublimated. (I am again indebted to Paul Gray[2] for pointing out this passage to me. "Combinatory paranoia" was a term Freud used for paranoia in his early years, first referred to in an 1896 paper; later he would simply say "paranoia" or "dementia paranoides" (Freud, 1911).

I feel that Freud was saying something here about empathy and imagination. We all require at least a modicum of empathy to get on with others, although there are extreme forms of pathology that can deprive human beings of it almost completely. There are those, like psychoanalysts and writers of fiction and biography, whose work requires a great deal of empathy with other people. They not only need to have profound and subtle talents for observation and understanding of others but also must be able to put themselves in the mind and place of these others. They must perform and perform well what Robert Fliess (1942) called a "partial identification" with other people—he defined this as sampling

---

2. Paul Gray, having read my 1995 book, *Delusions of Everyday Life*, was aware of my interest in the connections between pathology and its transformations to ordinary everyday and artistic creativity. He pointed out Freud's allusion to "combinatory paranoia" and told me of the purported quotation attributed to him by Marie Bonaparte. I hope Paul Gray will fulfill his promise to give his own account of this fascinating and mysterious relation of psychopathology to creativity. He may well be able to help more than I can to indicate how to explore the healthy and superhealthy aspects of our mental functioning whose complete and satisfactory exploration may ultimately require some radical discovery or approach pointed out by a mind like Freud's.

what it is like to be in the shoes of that other person. Such an identification requires the ability to project aspects of the psychic representations of oneself and of meaningful other people onto patients or fictional characters or biographical subjects without losing perspective. In paranoia this projection occurs pathologically, without proper boundaries and checks. (So does the creation of "alter" characters by those who suffer from "multiple personality syndrome"—a form of pathology that shows a kind of creativity that resembles that of a novelist.) "Sublimation" implies possessing the power to use projection, as well as primary process, benignly and with flexibility and control (consciously or preconsciously)— and, one hopes, also with tact and wisdom. But, of course, how this power is gained is not yet either determined or understood— some have it and some don't.

It seems to me to be a complication that all of us tend to read artistic works in our own ways, consciously and unconsciously looking for or transferring or projecting our own package of psychopathology onto what we read. Some psychological healers may be even more prone to this tendency, since it is our *metier* to look for pathology—and we have not been trained, and may lack the know-how and the theoretical background, to pursue health and gifts with comparable facility.

It follows, so I repeat my belief, that the key to creativity lies within the mystery—the how? and why? and where from?—of inborn and acquired gifts and talents. The great French writer Jules Renard, of whom the reader will hear more, said of himself, in a characteristic mixture of exaggerated humility and honesty: "I have neither memory nor intelligence, and I am an artist only as a result of a lot of training, but I receive certain impressions with such intensity that in this I can measure up to the greatest men" (quoted in Bogan and Roget, 1964, p. 81).

I will break off this discussion by quoting Trollope (1879a) on the mystery of a writer's creative gifts and powers. The passage is from a short biographical book on Thackeray, whom he considered the greatest English novelist of the 19th century. Thackeray had at first wanted to be a graphic artist. He turned from illustrating to writing after he had lost all his money.

> If a man can command a table, a chair, a pen, paper, and ink, he can commence his trade as a literary man. . . . A

man can make the attempt though he has not a coat fit to go out into the street with; or a woman, though she be almost in rags. There is no apprenticeship wanted. Indeed there is no room for such apprenticeship. It is an art which no one teaches; there is no professor who, in a dozen lessons, even pretends to show the aspirant how to write a book or an article. If you would be a watchmaker, you must learn; or a lawyer, cook, or even a housemaid. Even the cab-driving tyro must sit for awhile in the box, and learn something of the streets, before he can ply for a fare. But the literary beginner rushes at once at the top rung of his ladder. . . . That he should be able to read and write is presumed; and that only. So much can be presumed of everyone, and nothing more is wanted. *In truth nothing more is wanted—except those inner lights as to which so many men live and die without having learned whether they possess them or not.* . . . The temptation is irresistible, and thousands fall into it. How is a man to know that he is not the lucky one or the gifted one? Among the unfortunate, he who fails altogether and from the first start is not the most unfortunate. A short period of life is wasted, and a sharp pang is endured. But he who has a little success, who succeeds in earning a few halcyon, but ah! so dangerous guineas, is drawn into a trade from which he will hardly escape till he be driven from it, if he come out alive, by sheer hunger. He hangs on till the guineas become crowns and shillings—till some sad record of his life, made when he applies for charity, declares that he has worked hard for the last year or two, and has earned less than a policeman in the streets or a porter at a railway. It is to that that he is brought by applying himself to a business which requires only a table and chair, with pen, ink, and paper. *It is to that which he is brought by venturing to believe that he has been gifted with powers of imagination, creation, and expression* [pp. 10–12; italics added].

The inner lights, the gifts of the "powers of imagination," are a mystery. One's ways of making use of these gifts are subject to critical analysis; the source of the gifts themselves remains unknown.

Artistic Creativity

I will end by taking up a question that may be on the reader's mind: why deal with applied analysis at all? Since biography is so difficult and applied psychoanalysis is fraught with pitfalls, why am I devoting more space in this book to literary than to clinical examples? For several reasons: above all, confidentiality considerations make furnishing verbatim clinical details impossible. At best, some disguise or distortion is needed, and fictionalizing means falsifying. Although that can be minimized, it is a break with the psychoanalyst's essential task of trying to be as truthful as possible. Some compromise is necessary when using clinical material, and yet it must be used in writing and teaching; this makes for an impossible goal as part of what Freud has pointed out is an impossible profession. One cannot write freely and factually about current patients who might recognize themselves, because to do so can interfere with what is going on in the clinical work of the patients' analyses. With completed cases, it may still be impossible to keep out crucial details that might make them recognizable; this is especially true for well-known or famous people. Moreover, pondering and exploring the difficulties inherent in biographical and historical work and writings has its own value for the clinician. These difficulties have their own general implications for understanding what we can know about people that apply to what can be known through clinical psychoanalysis. Psychoanalysis deals with influencing and, above all, enabling patients to explore and attempt to become responsible for what can and what cannot be known of their individual biographies and histories.

A positive reason to write instead, tactfully and modestly (that is, without false certainty), about extraordinary people who have a gift for literary expression is that such exceptionally endowed people are able to verbalize the manifestations of psychic dynamics better—more richly and evocatively—than most of us can.

Chapter 3

CLINICAL AND LITERARY EXAMPLES

Goodness is not natural. It is the stony fruit of reason. One has to grab oneself by the skin of one's ass to drive oneself by force to the least good action.
—Jules Renard, *Journal* (my translation).

Before launching into my illustrations of what "Life Without Mother" means, I want to pause to briefly delineate my term for child abuse and deprivation, soul murder (see Shengold, 1989, 1999 for a history of the term and its full definition), and to explain further why I am writing this book.

SOUL MURDER

Some lack of care and even torment is inevitable in the course of growing up. Soul murder is my term for the abuse and neglect of children by adults that was intense and frequent enough to inhibit the children's subsequent emotional development. What they had suffered continued to dominate their unconscious fantasy life and motivations owing to their having become subject to the compulsion to repeat the cruelty, violence, neglect, and sexual overstimulation of their past.

My patients, healthy enough to sustain intensive therapy or psychoanalysis, ran a psychopathological range from neurosis to

Chapter 3

what in a few might be called psychosis. They also varied in their possession of strong and healthy characteristics (emotional flexibility, ability to love and work, talents, creativity). Soul murder is a crime rather than a diagnosis. Human beings are infinitely complex and cannot be reduced to diagnoses; nor are they made uniform by having undergone similar traumatic events—only complete murder accomplishes complete dehumanization. My patients were all different, despite certain predictable similarities. [Being made to bear too much—overstimulation—is the essence of trauma, which evokes overwhelming anxiety and rage in a relatively helpless child. With neglect and understimulation, the frustration of basic needs also results in rage and intense sexual craving; this is reactive overstimulation. Abuse and neglect—both too much and too little—produce similar effects. In either instance, "too-muchness" requires and evokes massive psychic defenses that result in deadening emotion and impulse. Repeated abuse and neglect lead to deindividualization and dehumanization.] Henrik Ibsen, in more than one of his plays, mentioned soul murder, which he defined as killing the joy in life in another human being. Here Ella Rentheim is addressing John Gabriel Borkman:

> You have killed the love of life in me. Do you understand what that means? The Bible speaks of a mysterious sin for which there is no forgiveness. I have never understood what it could be; but now I understand. The great, unpardonable sin is to murder the love of life in a human soul. . . . You have done that. You deserted the woman you loved! Me, me, me! What you held dearest in the world you were ready to barter away for gain. That is the double murder you have committed! The murder of your own soul and of mine! . . . It is you who have sinned. You have killed all the joy of life in me [Ibsen, 1896, p. 272].

Children who are beside themselves with overexcitement, rage, and anxiety have an imperative need for external help. When the tormentor/seducer is a parent, the child must often turn for rescue to the very person who was the abuser. The other parent is usually either absent or an unconscious (and frequently a masochistic) abettor, or both. If the adult abuser is not a parent, the child's rage is still directed at the parent, generally at the mother, for having allowed the abuse to occur.[1]

Every child urgently needs good parenting and will cling desperately even to fragments of realistic benevolent parental functioning to fashion what is often the delusion of having had a concerned loving parent. Such a delusion, which can exist alongside bitter hatred and accusation toward the parent, arises out of need for a caring rescuer. This is clearly shown in George Orwell's (1948) prophetic novel, *1984*, in which the "hero," Winston Smith, ends up "loving Big Brother," who has destroyed his soul.

The most destructive psychological effect of child abuse is the need to hold on to the abuser by identification (an unconscious becoming like him or her); this is part of a compulsion to repeat the experiences of abuse—as tormentor (enhancing sadism) and as victim (enhancing masochism). The child who is abused seems often to take on the guilt of the crime—which the abuser may or may not feel. This guilt frequently takes the form of masochistic provocativeness and a need for punishment. There may have been actual brainwashing by the abuser, which supplements a pathologically intense need of the confused child to doubt or deny what has occurred. The pathological compulsion to repeat traumatic events—an inevitable part of human nature whose existence is so hard to accept—results in the passing down of child abuse and its consequent hate, hatefulness, and deprivation of joy from one generation to the next. This legacy results in the tragedy that abused and deprived children, when they become parents, tend—sometimes despite conscious resolutions never to do so—to abuse and deprive their own children; the impulses are there and all-too-frequently the actions too.

LITERARY "CASE HISTORIES"

This book features studies of the life and some of the works of two great authors, Anthony Trollope and Jules Renard. I use these

---

1. When presenting papers on soul murder in various places, I was at first surprised to hear comments by leaders of therapeutic groups for women who have been sexually abused by their fathers that they seem more angry at the mother who did not protect them than at the father who actually was the abuser. This ought not to be a surprise to the reader of a book titled *Is There Life Without Mother?*

literary "case histories," in addition to a clinical one, to illustrate the continuing power of the early parent on development into adult life. In Trollope this power is relatively hidden; in Renard it is obvious. There have been many excellent biographies of Trollope; my research has been applied to them as well as to his writings. My interest in the great novelist was instigated by my reactions to Trollope's (1883) *An Autobiography*. I then read and reread his writings. This has been one of the main pleasures of writing this book. Jules Renard is a great French writer, largely neglected in the English-speaking world at present. It is a shame that his works—novels, plays, essays, and journals—are for the most part out of print (but not in France) or have not been translated in Britain and America. I have done my inadequate best to read in and translate from the French when the English translations seemed not quite right or I could not find any. I hope I have not made too many errors. In the longer excerpts from his novel *Poil de Carotte*, I have by and large used the translation of Ralph Manheim, who has, I think, captured the tone of Renard (1894b) very well.

The previous two chapters involve excursions (relevant to Trollope and Renard) into speculations about artistic creativity and biography. But my emphasis on literature and creativity has a clinical purpose: to illustrate a universal human burden based on the initial complete dependency of human beings that I have characterized by the question, "Is there life without mother?" Some version of this question (sometimes it is as or more applicable to a person's father) was actually asked by a patient I describe here. Feeling that the question is there to be explored in every intense psychological investigation, I have chosen it as the title for this book. One of the basic principles of psychoanalytic theory and, since Hughlings Jackson, of neurological theory as well is the genetic principle: the earliest somatic and psychic developmental events—the latter featuring early parenting—have an inordinate determining influence on the future maturation of every individual's body and mind, including their mysterious interconnections.

In this book I am not illustrating ordinary dependence on parents; rather, I am stressing the unusual but not rare case of an adult for whom the central need for a parent has remained urgent and primary. The question "Is there life without mother?" becomes clinically relevant when it dominates a person's life and work. Such unfortunates are (or feel threatened to become) deprived of a separate identity and inhibited in the capacity to love others, and this lack may be obvious or relatively hidden. Among the afflicted would be most victims of attempts at soul murder. But not all the people I am writing about are soul murder victims, although I feel that most soul murder victims would be among them. The preponderant influence of parental pathology can be present in relation to many different kinds of parents: monsters, like Renard's mother; absent parents; parents who are disturbed enough to regard their children as parts of themselves; psychotic, psychopathic, and addicted parents; neglecting parents; frightened, weak, and inadequate parents; indifferent and hateful ones. There are also other and sometime inexplicable reasons for this kind of preoccupation with parents; for example, being born with or acquiring (as a result of trauma) major structural or functional deficiencies can call forth the same insistent cry for, and lifelong dependence on, mothers, who, however good and caring they may be in reality, cannot fulfill their children's needs any more than soul murdering parents do. (I, of course, am not trying to base the complicated mysteries of psychopathology or of psychic health exclusively on the relationship with parents, but it seems to be the most important environmental influence on healthy or pathological psychic development.)

I am saying something that every psychologically minded person can know and observe, but I feel its clinical relevance is often blocked by the resistance in all of us to the idea of a bad or pathological parent. Underlying this resistance is the terror we all harbor of the loss of a good and vitally needed parent. Dependency on parents is central to our identity. Loss of the parent and loss of parental love are two of the main psychological situations of danger that, according to Freud, are basic to our conscious and unconscious motivations. I have observed that my most difficult and resistant patients (they are not necessarily the sickest ones) resist change primarily because they are terrified of losing the inner psychic presence of parents, without whom they feel they cannot survive. To some extent this is true of all of us—so we all tend to feel something of the force of the question, "Is there life without mother?" In large part loss is feared because aggression and murder are part of our nature and part of our earliest experience.

Chapter 3

This is true whether we explain it as the result of an innate aggressive instinctual drive (Freud) or as the result of inevitable frustrations at the hands of parents, society, and Mother Nature (Freud would agree; it is not controversial). The impact of murderous aggression leads us all to our individual versions of a psychic trap of infancy and early childhood—the double bind of wishing to get rid of the very parent (later, parents) without whom we feel we cannot live. People psychologically dominated by the intensity of their preoccupation with their parents, like the patients and writers I am referring to in this book, expect that any change, even one consciously longed for, will mean dreadful loss. These people cling to their parents with a combination of becoming like them, submitting to them, or compulsively defying them (negative submission).

In all of us, regressions, reactions to inevitable traumata and deterioration, can bring back both the intense needs and the murderous aggressive feelings of early life. Awareness that one can also feel there is no life without mother can evoke anxiety and resistance, blocking insight in the minds of therapists as well as of patients. I think this resistance is illustrated in a double slip in the announcement of a lecture I gave based on part of this book: "Is There Life Without Mother?" by Leonard Shengold, author of *Soul Mother* and *Soul Mother Revisited*. (My witty colleague Shelley Orgel said to me when he read the notice, "Soul Mother! Oh yes, the Bessie Smith story.") In the slip *Mother* has, twice, displaced *Murder*. This unconscious call on mother neatly illustrates one of the main theses of this book.

Chapter 4

THE PRIMAL PARENT
A Patient's Cry

Mother is the name for God in the lips and hearts of children.
—William Thackeray, *Vanity Fair*

We all have or have had mothers and fathers who left indelible traces in the course of our maturation and experience, traces that added to and modified the mysterious inherited givens with which we were born. With the possible exception, or near-exception, of identical twins, no two of us are exactly alike. Our minds contain uniquely digested and distorted dynamic versions of the mother and father figures with whom we have interacted and identified.

The concept of the primal parent is an important theoretical one. The earliest mothering figure is not always literally the mother. The primal parent is Robert Fliess's (1956; also see Shengold, 1989) term for the earliest representation in the child's mind of an all-important parental other. The primal-parent imago is a metaphorical construction for the partly internalized, perhaps partly inherited dynamic parental presence in the infant's developing mind—we know that something is there but not how to picture it. It derives its power and character from the pervervid needs and emotions of the infantile unconscious mind. At this early time, according to theory as refined by infant observation, all appears to be black or white emotionally, either blissfully good or terribly bad. These alternating contradictions in clamorous feelings threaten to allow for no compromise, moderation, or mutual

Chapter 4

existence—each intensity can temporarily cancel out the opposite. These contradictory feelings would amount to, and may be the mythopoeic origin of, paradise juxtaposed with hell. Fortunately the opposing intensities are interspersed with blank or comparatively peaceful interludes.

During this earliest period of psychic development, the mind emerges out of chaos and fusion and eventually comes to a separate identity. The mental universe during infancy is for a considerable time reduced to, and therefore subsequently reducible to, a giant parental figure that begins to bring order out of chaos and a nascent, gradually enlarging figure of the separating self. These primal representations of primal parent and self perhaps at first coalesce out of parts and pieces, in the infant's mind, the newer and more vulnerable (subject to regression) self-representation increasing as the parent representation is slowly reduced. I do not want to sound authoritative here; it must be emphasized that despite all our speculations based on theory, and infant observations influenced by theory, we do not know and perhaps will never know the precise details of what occurs within the child's mind during the first year of life. These primal mental representations can henceforth proceed in dynamically varying combinations, moving predominately sometimes forward toward separation of the self, but also, at least occasionally, regressively back toward merger with the parent.

In the course of development, initially the separated-out mother and then the father, emerging slowly and piecemeal, are registered in the mind. Gradually the rest of the outside world—at first centering on the infant's body, family, and family surroundings—is registered in the mind; here the nursery has become the universe. In this maturational sequence, the mother- and then the father-figure acquire tremendous power. For both boy and girl, the father can, but does not always, eventually take over from the mother, at least for a while, as the principal—in contrast to the primal—psychic registration of the parent. But the earlier primal parental mothering figure remains in the unconscious mind, and it can be reactivated in situations of extreme need. It never disappears, and in the sense of its potential return in emergencies we probably cannot live without it. But its (usually partial) continued activation, or regressive reactivation, can give rise to the delusional or near-delusional conviction that there is no life without a mother or a father who continues to have something of the godlike or diabolically magic power of the primal parent. We are all, I believe, subject to this delusion, but for some it becomes a predominant motivation of their existence.

IS THERE LIFE WITHOUT MOTHER?

This was one patient's *cri de coeur*, and it seems to me to express the feeling at the heart of an inescapable human dilemma that starts with the psychological and physiological separation trauma of birth. This primal distress continues despite the (never fully satisfactory) developmental achievement of a separate identity for the child. Every human being—man or woman—has to bear an individual version of this burden of incompleteness. For the fortunate (one needs luck as well as a strong ego) the weakness and dependence may not be apparent to others and, in the course of optimal development, may not appear to matter much to the self. But many either never achieve adequate psychological separation from parents or are, to varying degrees, subject to an intermittent compulsion, or at least intense longing, to regress and remerge. Such regressions to dependency are also reactions to trauma and loss in later life.

Freud felt that it was human beings' long period of dependence on the parents that made neurosis inevitable in everyone. This continuing dependence as the mind and body mature, together with our aggression-laden, inborn drives, gives rise to individually varying versions of the human dilemma of wanting to get rid of the parental person without whom we feel we cannot live. This inherent psychic burden and trap recedes with maturation and health, but it never disappears.

The double bind is strongest in those people who, because of traumatic circumstances, emotional and environmental deprivation, or deficient endowment, are unable to achieve a predominantly separate adult identity. There are many ways to remain psychologically a child or even an infant, with or without an adult façade. Even if a person has achieved a strong sense of separate identity, the vicissitudes of fate and the eventual inadequacies of physical and mental equipment can result in a regressive return (out of need) toward the earliest period of mental awareness in

Chapter 4

which the primal parent was felt to be an integral part of the self. My adult patient's cry was for his mother. It is the mother or the mothering person who usually initially inherits the primal parent's role in consciousness. People approaching death frequently call for their mother directly, but in displacement the cry for help can be directed to one of the mothering figure's supplementary successors. As I have stated, the first important one is usually the father, but both father and mother can, for religious believers or those who transiently want to become so when in great need, be replaced by God. The initial mental picture of the primal parental mothering figure as it emerges from symbiotic chaos—omniscient and omnipotent and possessing features of both sexes—is the psychological prototype of God, whether or not She or He or It exists. The first deities historically were apparently mother gods, and this makes good psychological sense. Between the initial chaos and merger and an eventual adequate separation from the primal parent is a stage of some sort of transient glimmerings of awareness of separateness. This protoego state, successor to the chaotic psychological condition of the period of early infancy, was imaginatively and dramatically characterized by Freud as (if it could be communicated) expressing the sentiment, "I am the breast; the breast is part of me" (Freud, 1941, p. 299).

CLINICAL ILLUSTRATION

One patient, an accomplished, intelligent, and educated man in his middle 30s, had achieved success and status in an important profession. In his work, he was regarded as a decisive person who could adaptively wield what looked like self-confidence or even an arrogance that seemed to justify the impression he made on others. But in his mind he "felt like a nobody." This was his complaint when he entered analysis, and it had been hard for him to face: "I should have come for treatment years ago." He went on to say that he had found it hard to keep up emotionally meaningful relationships with both women and men, despite having many admirers and acquaintances whom he called friends. What bothered him most was not having been able to sustain a long relationship with a woman. Initially he seemed more motivated by the vague but painful "awareness" that some deficiency might be noticed by others rather than by feeling any great distress about not being able to love. I felt he had retreated to a characteristic regressive narcissistic defense, to an automatic distancing of caring about others, and also, in many ways, about himself. There was something obscure and intellectualized in his descriptions of his emotions and his state of mind. He felt that his feelings were somehow inauthentic. He was good-looking and could be charming; his being able to act and even feel (with what seemed to be convincing honesty and disarming charm) *as if* he did not care gave him a kind of Byronic appeal that fascinated many people of both sexes.

But his insouciance was deceptive; it seemed to protect him only intermittently. In the analysis, he soon revealed how tormented he could become if he felt unloved or unvalued by his parents and those he cast in their roles. His torment was most intense in his relation to his mother. She had been alternatively overseductive and neglectful of him. He both hated and, more insistently, idealized and longed for her. He consciously shared his mother's devaluating opinion of his father, whom she had divorced when the patient was five or six. He was at first unaware of the strength of his emotional and passive sexual longings for a strong and loving father.

When he started analysis, he was in the habit of making a daily phone call to his mother from wherever he happened to be. He rationalized this long-established routine as aimed at keeping her happy. He traveled frequently, but dreaded any separation from her. It took many years for him to be able to work responsibly on the emotional dependence on mother and father as it became focused on me, but intense reactions that showed his vulnerability to separation were apparent from the very beginning.

He was able to live what looked like an exciting and varied social and sexual life. This life style too had an "as-if" quality; there had been no long-term sexual partners. He was wont to play with bisexuality and sadomasochism. He presented this to himself and to me as a kind of pleasurable sampling, but it turned out to screen, primarily from himself, a compulsion to be polyperverse, expressing the wish to be and to have everything. The overriding injunction from his conscience was to be faithful only to his overindulgent and seductive but capricious and intermittently rejecting mother.

There was an incident from childhood that burned in his

memory. His mother had been obsessed by a fear that his genitals were too small. He remembered repeated embarrassing references to this "defect" in family conversations. His mother frequently asked the family pediatrician about it in the boy's presence, and finally the doctor had laughed and told her to stop asking because "There was nothing to worry about." The assertion was not reassuring to the boy; it was the "nothing" that had rankled. He went on to tell me an associated phosphorescent memory. His mother had undressed him one night when he was five or six, the age at which his father had been banished. She had "looked hard" at his genitals, sighed deeply, and said, "You have *nothing* down there!" He could still feel the terrible combination of fear, rage, and humiliation that had overwhelmed him. His tears made her angry, and she left the room. This incident must have greatly increased the boy's separation anxiety. He began to cry in the session as he quoted her words. I have written elsewhere about the meanings of "nothing" (Shengold, 1991); Lewin (1948) has written that "nothing" can refer to the female genital. As a man, my patient was still preoccupied with the idea that his testicles were too small; no amount of reassurance by physicians or sexual partners was able to dispel this idea more than briefly. He did realize that others were being realistic, but the obsessive belief still persisted. (This is what I have called a "quasi-delusion" [see Shengold, 1995].)

Early in the treatment he revealed a specific hidden and inhibiting difficulty. In the course of his work, he occasionally needed to go to other parts of the country and the world. His anxiety was worse when travel required flying; he couldn't help feeling that his plane was bound to crash. He was able to leave, but not without struggle and great anxiety. It was even harder to leave his home city to go on vacation, which he felt he "ought to want" to do. He felt compelled to call his mother from airports and train stations when he was departing. He had only in recent years moved away to his own bachelor apartment from the grand family house of his mother. But he still frequently went "home" for his mother's meals and often slept overnight in his old bedroom. He almost always went there when he was really ill. In fact, he said with shame, he could not shake the ridiculous idea that, in case of any degree of illness, he could not possibly get well without being nursed by his mother—another "delusion of everyday life." He craved the magical promise of her presence rather than any actual nursing she might provide. Even if he was out of town, even if the illness was only a cold, he felt compelled to call and at least tell his mother about it.

I think it was after this confession that he first asked, with some humor, which I felt was an encouraging sign, "Is there life without mother?"—a question that was subsequently often repeated, eventually with great anguish. When anticipating a separation from his mother, he would obsess about becoming sick and often did become sick. Being away from mother would turn him into *nothing*. On the occasions dominated by these neurotic terrible expectations, he would wonder consciously if there was life without mother. The automatic, unconscious, negative answer to this question was obviously evoked by anxiety about the prospect of separation from her. He realized this intellectually long before he could accept it and own it emotionally.

For a long time the patient treated my vacations, cancellations, and even the weekend separations "as if" they did not exist, although it was obvious to me that he was deeply concerned about them. He began to report transient emotional reactions that he waved away by what almost seemed to be a magical mantra: "I don't accept that." Fairly late in the analysis he said to me after I had announced my plans for my summer holiday, "I've just realized that when you tell me that you are going away on vacation, I have been unable to believe that you really would do it. Isn't that amazing? Not believing was automatically there, and," he repeated, "I have just realized it." This was the beginning of his conscious, responsible awareness that what he had in passing usually called his disbelief—or his iterations of "I don't accept that"—was literally a nonacceptance of a past, present, or forthcoming reality. I had previously interpreted this many times in many ways to little effect. He had to feel it for himself and own it. I wish I understood more about how this acknowledgment was finally accomplished by him. But, after many repetitions of the interpretation, it was.

The triangular relationship with mother and, as his importance emerged late in the analysis, father featured the patient's conflicts over wishes to murder, rape, and passively submit sexually to both of them. He finally was able to work on these conflicts directly, and especially by way of transference onto me. By that time, despite a few significant regressive occasions, he had begun to establish that there could be life without mother; he could "accept" this idea and seemed to retain only the ordinary difficulties most of us have with it. He left the analysis with great trepidation about whether there would be life without his analyst, but from what I have since heard from and about him over a period of many years, I feel that he has maintained his gains. He has been able to make a good marriage and father children he could care deeply about.

In retrospect, I see that his deciding to start analysis was a crucially important first step—one he undertook on his own on the path toward a separate and more authentic identity. He was able only partially to achieve that goal and only after a very long struggle in treatment. Yet I feel he became a qualitatively different and more human person, with more meaningful (less as-if) relationships with wife and friends and, most fully, with his children. He has become able to feel and own his hatred toward both parents *alongside* his love for and need for love from them, and he can now love and care for himself and for others. His need to withdraw from others to whom to relate mainly or to whom to relate as his primal parent was reduced in the direction of the less intense and less frequent intermittent regression to narcissistic concerns that most people are subject to. (We are all made uncomfortable by being aware of how much of our mental functioning is narcissistic.) This shrinkage of narcissism allowed for periods of sustained caring that could even sometimes be arrived at with the use of his conscious will. I consider this to be within the shadowy range of "normal." And by being able to love others he could better love himself.

Simone Weil said, "The belief in the existence of other human beings as such is love" (quoted in Auden and Kronenberger, 1962, p. 90). That kind of love has made life without mother possible for him.

PART II

LITERARY LIVES

Chapter 5

JULES RENARD
Soul Murder in Life and Literature

> *At every moment Poil de Carotte returns to me. We live together, and I only hope I die before he does.*
>
> —Jules Renard, *Journal*

In this chapter I present a literary example that asks if life without mother is possible—a question that remained a lifelong burden for a soul murder victim, the great French writer Jules Renard, whose work has been comparatively neglected in the English-speaking world. Renard's (1894a) autobiographical novel, *Poil de Carotte*, tells of his tormented childhood and describes his father and mother (called in the book, M. and Mme. Lepic). In the novel, the mother is dishonest and sadistically malicious. Her favorite object of persecution and brainwashing is the youngest of her children, a redheaded boy nicknamed Poil de Carotte (Carrot-Top).

Like Poil de Carotte, Jules Renard was the last-born of four children. His father, François, became depressed after the death of his first child, a daughter. Later on, he told Jules he subsequently could not care as much about the other children. Renard writes (1887–1910) about a dialogue with his father: "His first daughter . . . 'I used to run up the stairs, to see her a moment sooner.' 'And me?' 'You? Oh, you came without my wishing it.' 'It doesn't hurt my feelings'" (p. 133).

Jules's mother, Anne-Rose, was apparently a cruel, hateful, and self-righteous woman. As Mme. Lepic in the novel, she is depicted by her son as exhibitionistically seductive, a sneak, a liar, a hypocrite, and a petty thief: "These are not the thefts of a grown-up person: they are the little thefts of a magpie" (p. 162).

The parents were bitterly at odds, partly because of their peculiarly contrary characters—her unacknowledged dishonesty and his righteous stubbornness—and partly because she professed to be a devout Catholic and he was intensely anticlerical; contrary passions about religion furnished external reasons for their incompatibilities. Shortly after Jules was born, his father stopped speaking to Jules's mother and apparently never spoke directly to her again for over 30 years. Blaming Jules for the father's silence may be part of the reason that she turned on the child as her principal *bête noir* and tormented him so.

Jules Renard hated his persecutory mother, was obsessed by her cruelty to him, and felt burdened for life by his miserable childhood. In the novel *Poil de Carotte*, Renard (1894a) illustrates how he was neglected:

> If a stranger leafs through the Lepic photograph album, he can't fail to be surprised. He sees sister Ernestine and big brother Felix in many aspects, standing, seated, dressed up or half-dressed, happy or scowling, amidst rich surroundings.
> —And Poil de Carotte?
> —I had photographs of him when he was very little, Mme. Lepic answers, but he was so beautiful that people took them, and I wasn't able to keep even one.
> The truth is that no one ever takes a snapshot of Poil de Carotte [pp. 174–175, my translation].

Poil de Carotte tells his father that he has had thoughts of, and made tentative and clumsy attempts at, suicide, but he is not taken seriously. Renard has Poil de Carotte say, in relation to feeling rejected by both parents, that he wishes he was lucky enough to have been born an orphan (*Tout le monde ne peut pas être orphelin*, p. 139).

Despite Renard's consciously predominant hatred toward his mother, it is obvious that he also continued throughout his life to long desperately for her to change and to love him. He wrote about his mother throughout his whole career as an author, at greatest length and depth in the *Journal* he kept for 23 years; he began the *Journal* in 1887, when he was 24 and continued until his early death in 1910. The mother of his childhood dominates the novel *Poil de Carotte* (Renard, 1894a); the one-act play of the same name about the family at the time he was 16 years old (Renard, 1900), and the last of the plays he finished, *La Bigote* [*The Bigoted Woman*] (Renard, 1909). Notwithstanding Renard's awareness of his rage and his use of his conscious will to react against his childhood of oppression, he never could shake off the family concentration camp aura of his childhood. This was true despite the talent and intelligence that enabled sublimatory discharge in his creativity and satisfaction in the success of his writings and despite his achievements in his roles as good husband and father. Toward the end of his life, Renard wrote in his *Journal*: "Poetry saved me from the contagious illness of nastiness" (Bouillier, 1990, p. 906, my translation). But this transcendence was achieved at the expense of great inner conflict with his need to denigrate himself. In 1888, when the 24-year-old was beginning to write and publish, he wrote of his future career:

> You will be nothing. In spite of all you do. You will be nothing. You understand the greatest poets, the most profound masters of prose, but, although one can pretend that to understand them is to be their equal, you will be as little comparable to them as what a tiny dwarf can be in relation to giants [p. 14; my translation].

Anne-Rose Colin was 27 and her husband, François Renard, was 40 when Jules was born in 1864. He was their third surviving child. His sister Amélie, given the same name as the daughter who had died at age two in 1858, was born in 1859. The birth of Jules's older brother, Maurice, followed in 1862. Toesca (1977), Renard's biographer, writes of "that acid atmosphere" ("*cette atmosphere acide,*" p. 14) of the family life in Jules's early years. By that time, the father would communicate with his wife only by writing to her on a slate. François would handle his rage and disgust at Anne-Rose by a kind of partial but effective emotional withdrawal. Despite his sadistic silence, he continued to sleep in the same room with her, on a cot across the room from the double

Chapter 5

bed that she sometimes shared with Jules when guests took over his room.

Mme. Renard apparently could be both a conscious and an unconscious liar, and it was hard to tell, perhaps even for her, which modality was operative on any given occasion. When Jules was two years old, the family moved to his father's home village, Chitry-les-Mines, where the adult Jules Renard continued to make his home—after his school years away, his early literary efforts in Paris, and military service—for most of the rest of his life. As an adult he would repeatedly go to and sometimes stay in Paris in connection with his plays and publications. We know most about the boy's childhood from *Poil de Carotte*. (According to the novel, the nickname Poil de Carotte had been given to him by Mme. Lepic herself [Renard, 1894a, p. 13].)

Here follow two short chapters from the novel (Renard, 1894b). They illustrate soul murder and obviate any need for definition of the term. They seem to me all the more powerful because of the sardonic, dry, and uncomplaining tone in which the torment is presented. The first is entitled, "The Nightmare":

> Poil de Carotte doesn't like overnight guests. They upset his routine, they take his bed and oblige him to sleep with his mother. And though in the daytime he has every fault, his main fault at night is snoring. Of course he snores on purpose.
>
> The big room, glacial even in August, has two beds in it. One is Monsieur Lepic's; Poil de Carotte will have to sleep in the other, on the wall side, next to his mother.
>
> Before dropping off, he coughs a few times discreetly under the sheet to clear his throat. But maybe he snores through his nose. He blows gently through his nostrils to make sure they are not stopped up. He practices not breathing too hard.
>
> But the moment he falls asleep, he starts snoring. It seems to be a passion with him.
>
> Immediately Madame Lepic digs two fingernails into the fattest portion of one of his buttocks. That is her chosen weapon.

[*Le pic* in French denotes a specific instrument that can be used as a weapon: the pick, or the pickaxe.]

> Poil de Carotte's scream wakes Monsieur Lepic, who inquires: "What's the matter?"
> "He's had a nightmare," says Madame Lepic.
> And softly, like an old nurse, she hums a lullaby. It sounds Indian.
> Bracing his forehead and knees against the wall as though to demolish it, pressing his palms against his buttocks to parry the pinch which is the inevitable response to the first note of his guttural vibrations, Poil de Carotte falls back asleep in the big bed, on the wall side, next to his mother [pp. 10–11].

Another chapter is called, "Begging Your Pardon." Jules was apparently not allowed by his mother to leave his room at night to use the bathroom without permission.

> It grieves me to say this, but at an age when other boys take communion clean in body and soul, Poil de Carotte still soils himself. One night, for fear of asking, he waited too long.
> He had hoped, by means of graduated wrigglings, to appease his distress. What optimism!
> Another night he dreamed that he was leaning comfortably against a secluded boundary stone, and still innocently asleep, did it in his sheets. He wakes up. . . .
> Madame Lepic is careful to keep her temper. Calmly, indulgently, maternally, she cleans up. And next morning Poil de Carotte even gets his breakfast in bed like a spoiled child.
> Yes, his soup is brought to him in bed, a carefully prepared soup in which Madame Lepic with a wooden spatula has dissolved a little of it, oh, very little.
> At his bedside big brother Félix and sister Ernestine watch Poil de Carotte slyly, ready to burst out laughing at the first sign. Spoonful by little spoonful, Madame Lepic feeds her child. She seems, out of the corner of her eye, to be saying to big brother Félix and sister Ernestine: Look sharp! This is too good to miss.
> Yes, Mama.
> They are already enjoying the grimaces to come. They

ought to have asked a few of the neighbors in. Finally, with a last look at the older children as though to ask them: Are you ready?—Madame Lepic slowly, very slowly, lifts up the last spoonful, plunges it into Poil de Carotte's wide-open mouth, rams it deep down his throat, and says with an air of mingled mockery and disgust:

"Ah, my little pig, you've eaten it, you've eaten it, your own from last night."

"I thought so," Poil de Carotte answers simply, without making the hoped-for face.

He's getting used to it, and once you get used to a thing, it ceases to be the least bit funny [pp. 12–13].

Renard's lifelong tie to his mother, full of hate as it is, is evident in his sad, wise, and bitter *Journal* (Bouillier, 1990), in which he (after the publication of *Poil de Carotte*) continues to call his parents Monsieur and Madame Lepic. When his books became popular, he—a blazing redhead—was often accosted as "Poil de Carotte" by people on the street.

François Renard was something of a homespun intellectual and philosopher; he believed in education and sent his intelligently precocious son Jules away at age 11 to a lycée in Nevers with his 13-year-old brother, Maurice. This separation from mother must have been, consciously, a welcome relief to the boy. As can be gleaned from the many confidential letters addressed to his father from his years away from home in Nevers and Paris, Jules loved his emotionally withdrawn father, but apparently very little depth of feeling was expressed between them when they were actually together. Renard wrote in his *Journal*, "My father and I did not love each other outwardly. We did not hang together by our branches: we loved each other by our roots" (p. 102). The relationship with his father seems to have ripened at a physical distance from the mother, whose spoiling presence dimmed the emotional exchange between father and son that appears in their letters. François was at least intermittently generous when Jules needed financial support in the early years of his adult life.

The published collection of Renard's correspondence starts with Jules's letters from Nevers to his father and sister at home. Full of profound observation of others, they are astonishing letters for a young teenager. They show his talents both for psychological mindedness and for good, direct, and honest writing. Toesca (1977) feels that the letters demonstrate a close relationship between father and son, and this assumption seems justified. In the *Journal* there is also strong evidence of an identification with his father, one that was furthered by their letters. Both in his writing and in his life as he turned 20, Jules showed a straightforwardness and a stoicism, a tendency to stubbornness, silence, and restraint, that he derived from his father. The boy was amazingly astute, fair, and specific about his critical observations of the adults that officiated at the school. His inclination to be a rebel and an outsider (like his father) was tempered by good sense and a balanced judgment that helped him to know how best to fulfil his needs tactfully.

But psychic conflict continued. Jules also identified with his mother. Poil de Carotte shows how tortured the boy was when his mother forced him to take on the hateful duty of killing the wounded partridges that his father would bring home in his hunting bag; his siblings called him "the executioner" (Renard, 1894a, p.17). In a later chapter, he sees a mole outside the house and follows an urge to kill it after playing with it, as a cat would with a mouse. He is horrified, and yet his rage at his victim increases when the mole, after he has thrown it up in the air and let it fall on a rock, seems to come to life after appearing to be dead. Despite himself, he has become a tormentor of animals.

Although he stresses his own masochism, his identification with his mother as a murderous sadist is expressed, albeit with conflict and guilt, in relation to the killing of animals. It was his assigned and hated job to finish off the birds his father had shot and brought home wounded. He also describes shooting an old and sick cat because he was told that baiting with cat meat is the best way to catch crawfish. And the reader learns, "Poil de Carotte is no beginner. He has killed wild birds, domestic animals, a dog, for his own pleasure or at the behest of others" (pp. 123–124).

Here is the short chapter from *Poil de Carotte* (Renard, 1894a) entitled "The Mole."

> Poil de Carotte finds a mole in his path, black as a chimney sweep. When he has played with it enough, he decides to kill it. He throws it into the air several times, adroitly, before he allows it to fall on a stone. At first everything goes well and briskly. Already the mole has broken its

Chapter 5

paws, split its head, and it seems not to be having a hard life. Then, stupified, Poil de Carotte perceives that it has stopped dying. In vain he throws it up higher than the roof of a house, up to the sky; things don't advance. My goodness, it isn't dead! he says. In fact, on a stone stained with blood, the mole is becoming stiff. Its belly, full of fat, trembles like a jelly, and because of that gives the illusion of life. My goodness! cries Poil de Carotte, who is deceived, it still isn't dead. He picks it up, swears at it, and changes his method. Turning red, with tears in his eyes, he spits on the mole and, holding it by one end, throws it directly with all his strength against the stone. But the shapeless belly still keeps moving. And then Poil de Carotte's frenzy lessens as the mole seems to him to die [pp. 33–34; my translation].

Jules consciously was on his father's side in the war between his parents, but of course part of him hated his father. This is a father's inevitable oedipal role for his son, a role magnified for Jules by his mother's exhibitionistic seductiveness and by her sadism; and also by his father's sadistic response to her with his silence. But, in his family concentration camp, perhaps Jules hated his father above all because François Renard, out of his own need for defensive isolation from his wife, characteristically neither interfered with his wife's ways nor sufficiently protected his child. Both in the novel and in reality, father did not rescue Poil de Carotte from the mother's persecution and seductiveness that Jules must have felt were too much a part of the family atmosphere for his father not to be aware of, despite Mme. Lepic's occasionally deceitful and hypocritical attempts at disguise. And sometimes the father would even, like Jules's older siblings, play the part of the amused or indifferent observer to the mother's uncontrollable depredations.

When Poil de Carotte becomes old enough to attend the lycée away from his home village for most of the year, he finally dares to disobey his mother's orders. She seems crushed by this behavior. It helps him greatly to sustain the defiance toward her—which had always been the stance of his older brother—when, afterwards, his father has the compassion to tell him that he too doesn't love the mother:

— Poil de Carotte: Today I demand justice for myself. Just tell me who isn't better off than I am. I have a mother. This mother of mine doesn't love me, and I don't love her.

And what about me? Do you suppose I love her? Says Monsieur Lepic with sudden impatience.

At these words Poil de Carotte lifts his eyes to his father. For a long while he scrutinizes his hard face, his thick beard, into which his mouth has withdrawn as though ashamed of having said too much, his creased forehead, his crow's-feet, and his drooping eyelids that make him seem to be walking in his sleep.

For a moment Poil de Carotte holds back from speaking. He is afraid that his secret joy and the hand he has seized and is almost forcibly holding will vanish.

Then he clenches his fist, shakes it at the village that is dropping off to sleep in the darkness, and cries out:

Wicked woman! See what you've done. I hate you.

Hush, says Monsieur Lepic. She's your mother after all.

Oh, replies Poil de Carotte, again his simple cautious self: I'm not talking this way because she's my mother [pp. 203–204].

The letters to his father when the boy was 16 show how much of an acute observer Jules had become. He was aware of the power situations at the school and of the different personalities, strengths as well as weaknesses, of the head of the school and of individual teachers. He describes these to his father with cool detail that shows his attempt at attaining objectivity. He is able to face his feelings—frequently those of an iconoclast who knows how to hold his tongue—with fairness, a balanced ambiguity, and even humor. These qualities of objectivity and honesty—alongside the mendacity of his childhood—are present in his adult writings and are evident in the chapters I have quoted from *Poil de Carotte*.

The development of this kind of vertical split in the mind, making for contradictory mental compartments of character and motivation, is present in all of us to some extent, but it is regularly present as a striking characteristic of those who have suffered soul murder (see Shengold, 1989, 1999). Renard shows the terrible ambivalence of the victim of soul murder toward the perpetrator.

Chapter 5

He here resembles another writer who suffered a similar childhood, Rudyard Kipling (see Shengold, 1989). Both men identified with the aggressor as well as with the victim. Kipling's sympathy with the underdog existed alongside an obvious hatred he expressed but denied; his official persona as a righteous militaristic chauvinist who looks down on "the lesser breeds outside the law" is repellent and has marred his reputation as an artist. In contrast, Renard reveals a scrupulous honesty in his *Journal*. He is responsibly aware both of his hatred of others and of his hatred of himself. Renard's idiosyncratic masochism is of the "honesty to a fault" variety. He knows that there is a split in his character—for example, he was an impassioned defender of Dreyfus and wrote scathingly of the anti-Dreyfusards; yet he also wrote, "We are all antisemites. Some among us have the courage or the coyness to not let it be seen" (Bouillier, 1990, p. 902; my translation.) [*Nous sommes tous antijuifs. Quelques-uns parmi nous ont le courage ou la coquetterie de ne pas le laisser voir.*]

Becoming an informed spectator of the smallest changes in his surroundings, especially, as a child, of minute changes in the emotions and actions of the people on whom he was dependent, was forged by Jules into an adaptive and prophylactic defensive attitude. It was focused on watching out for his mother's every move and shift in mood. Any change could bring on an assault. He had to be equally aware of the changes in himself to which she would react as provocations. He put this habit of observing others and himself to use in his writing, adding to his inborn and acquired talents and creativity. In this respect, Renard also much resembles Kipling, who felt that his literary powers of observation and description were attributable to his need as a child to constantly scan what was going on in and with his persecutors in what he called the "House of Desolation." He had been left by his parents, who returned to the family home in India, to be cared for by strangers in England for six years of misery that he never was able to forget or forgive (see Shengold, 1989).

At 17, Jules left the lycée at Nevers to continue his studies in Paris. He began to submit anonymous articles to newspapers and magazines. He wanted to be a poet, and his first publication to achieve some general interest was a poem he had written at 20 to his mistress, an actress ten years older than he. At that time, his sister Amélie was married, and he went back home for the wedding. By then, Jules had become close to Amélie, and, after his father, she was the main recipient of his letters and confidences.

SOUL MURDER

In the last chapter of Poil de Carotte, entitled "Poil de Carotte's Album," Renard (1894a, my translations) has a series of short entries that illustrate the effects of the abuse of children, soul murder (see Shengold, 1989, 1999):

1. How the child can develop the expectations of a no-win (or "doublebind") situation:
    — Madame Lepic: Poil de Carotte, answer when you are spoken to.
    — Poil de Carotte: Yeth, baba.
    — Madame Lepic: I think I've already told you that children should never speak when their mouths are full [pp. 176–177].
2. The inculcation of psychopathic behavior; here Poil de Carotte, in addition to being like his mother the liar, cites an adaptive use of lying:
    — Whatever they do to you, Poil de Carotte, kindly Godfather says to him amicably, you should not lie. It's a bad defect, and it does you no good because everyone knows you're lying.
    — Yes, replies Poil de Carotte, but it gains you time [p. 177].
3. An instance of masochism—a need to lose and to fail in order to suppress rage in oneself and others so as to try to hold on to a relationship:
    — The children measure their heights.
    — Big brother Felix is obviously a head taller than the others. But Poil de Carotte and sister Ernestine, even though she's a girl, are about the same height. And when sister Ernestine raises her heels and stands on her toes, Poil de Carotte, in order not to upset anyone, cheats and slouches slightly, to minimize the difference [p. 178].
4. Abused children compulsively hope or even sometimes almost delusionally insist—frequently while knowing better

Chapter 5

— that the next confrontation with the abuser will turn out differently.
— Believing that his mother is smiling at him, Poil de Carotte, flattered, smiles too.
— But Mme. Lepic, who was only vaguely smiling to herself, suddenly resumes her black wooden face with her black-currant eyes [p. 181].

5. The sadistic adult tormentor induces murderous impulses along with guilt and fear of loss in the child. Madame Lepic tells the boy:
— If your father were no longer here, you would have long ago struck me, plunged this knife in my heart, *and put me in the dirt* [p. 183; italics added].

The italicised expression in the original French (*"me mise sur la paille"* [*paille* = straw])—the idiom is translated by Manheim as "sent me to the poorhouse" (Renard, 1894b, p. 215)—can have definite sexual connotations analogous to the English "roll in the hay." The expression refers to walking and sleeping on straw rather than on a carpet or mattress. However, I believe it has "farmyard" connotations here (in the sense of Hamlet's provocative query to Ophelia that follows his asking her, "Lady, shall I lie in your lap?" (III, ii, 120): "Do you think I meant country matters?" (III, ii, 123]. In this sense, the seductive mother launches a prophecy, a self-fulfilling prophecy, that was to be effectively enacted and appear in Poil de Carotte's fantasies and dreams.

MATERNAL SEDUCTION AND SADOMASOCHISTIC INCESTUOUS IMPULSES

In his *Journal*, Renard wrote in 1901 after his father had died, that he had hated that his father was always talking about sex to him. He recollected:

> Oh how it bothered me when [M. Lepic] took me into his confidence concerning that pretty, dirty young girl. . . . [He once told me,] "Mme. Lepic had a certain freshness. I went to bed with her without love, but with pleasure." . . . [M. Lepic here] despises me because I don't seem to be preoccupied with women. His scabrous stories embarrass

me more than they do him. I turn away, not to laugh, but because I blush [Bouillier, 1990, p. 133].

In 1894, when Renard was 30, he wrote in his *Journal* about his mother's exhibitionism when he was a boy and a youth. He reveals his sexual response to her and his subsequent oedipal dreams with an astonishing frankness. He wrote this before he could have heard of Freud's theories about childhood sexuality and before Freud had even formulated the Oedipus complex. (Freud is not mentioned in Renard's *Journal*.)

> The secret Poil de Carotte. . . . Mme. Lepic was given to changing her chemise in front of me. In order to tie up the laces over her woman's breast, she would lift her arms and her neck. Again, as she warmed herself by the fire, she would tuck her dress up above her knees. I would be compelled to see her thigh; yawning, or with her head in her hands, she would rock on her chair. My mother, of whom I cannot speak without terror, used to set me on fire [Bouillier, 1990].

The fire is still alive in the married man years later.

> That fire has remained in my veins. In the daytime it sleeps, but at night it wakens, and I have frightful dreams. In the presence of M. Lepic who is reading his paper and doesn't even look our way, I take possession of my mother, who is offering herself to me, and I re-enter that womb from whence I came. My head disappears into her mouth. The pleasure is infernal. What a painful awakening there will be tomorrow, and how dejected I shall be all day! Immediately afterward we are enemies again. Now I am the stronger. With those same arms that were passionately embracing her, I throw her to the ground, I crush her; I stamp on her, I grind her face against the tiles of the kitchen floor.
> My father, inattentive, continues to read his paper.
> If I knew that tonight I should again have that dream I swear I would flee from the house instead of going to bed and to sleep. I would walk until dawn, and I would not drop from exhaustion, because fear would keep me on my feet, sweating and on the run.

Chapter 5

The ridiculous added to the tragic: my wife and children call me Poil de Carotte [pp. 85–86].

Jules thought of his mother as an actress, "a great actress to whom life gave nothing but poor parts" (p. 169), who was compulsively playing her poor part poorly. She often tried to express love and receive love—but this effort never would last long. Renard wrote of his mother's attitude to his wife:

> She would forget to set a place at table for her daughter-in-law, or give her a dirty fork. . . . No means of annoyance was too small. . . . Let's be fair. [She] had her changes of mood, and they were very touching. [She would say to my wife,] "My dear, my lovely, what can I do for you? I am as fond of you as I am of my own daughter. Here let me do the heavy work. Your hands are too white for that." Suddenly, her face would turn nasty: "Am I a maid of all work?" [pp. 24–25].

He wrote in his *Journal* when he was 32 years old:

> 'Oh God!' cried Mme. Lepic. 'What have I done to be so miserable! Oh, my poor Poil de Carotte, if I ever tormented you, please forgive me!' She wept like the gutter on the roof. Then suddenly, her face dry: 'If my poor leg did not give me so much pain I would run away from here. I would earn my living washing dishes in a rich house.' There is nothing harder to look at than the face of a mother you do not love and for whom you are sorry [p. 85].

A year later, when Jules was 33, his father became ill and shot himself in the heart with a rifle. Renard wrote that he was proud of his father because his father's suicide was motivated by his not wanting to live as an invalid. He documented his ambivalence in his journal; he was glad his father was dead but yearned for him and kept bursting into tears of sadness and longing. Passing his father's grave, he wrote, "Every instant I forget that he is there, that I am walking over him. No matter how far life may take me, death will bring me back to his side" (p. 200). It was also hard for Renard to conceive of life without father.

Earlier that year Jules had written, "Papa hates and despises [Mama]. Especially he despises her, and I do believe he is also a little afraid of her. As for her, she probably does not know. She is resentful because of her humiliation, [because] of his obstinate silence. . . . It is thirty years since he has said a word [to her]" (p. 96).

Renard's father had been the mayor of Chitry-les-Mines, the village in which Jules grew up. After his father's death, Jules succeeded him as Mayor. He stepped into his father's shoes. After his father's death, Jules kept away from his mother. This behavior repeated for her the shame she had felt in front of the neighbors about her husband's silences. Renard thought that this kind of shame motivated her more than any loving desire to see her children. But he did not seem to be aware that he had taken over his father's role in his mother's, and in his own unconscious, mind. Passing by her house when he knew she was alone, he would overhear her talking loudly to herself in order to make passers-by think she had visitors.

When his older brother, Maurice, suddenly died of a stroke or a heart attack in 1900, Jules's wife, who had been very badly treated by her mother-in-law but was a kind person—she was described by her husband and others as saintly[1]—persuaded him to visit his mother. Note that in this journal entry, following his brother's death, mother is not Mme. Lepic but Maman:

> Maman. My heart beats a little faster, out of uneasiness. She is in the passageway. She immediately begins to cry. The little maid doesn't know where to look. [Maman] kisses me at length. I give her one kiss. She takes me into papa's room and kisses me again, saying: "I'm so glad you came! Why don't you come now and then? Oh my God, I'm so miserable." I answer nothing and go into the garden. I am hardly outside before she falls at [my wife's] feet and thanks her for having brought me. She says: "I have only him left. Maurice never looked at me, but he came to see me." . . . It was more than a year since I had seen her.

---

1. Although Renard's wife, Marie, shocked after her husband's death at what appeared to be descriptions of Jules's infidelities (of which she had had no idea) found in his *Journal*, apparently burned some of it. (cf. Isabel Burton; see Lovell, 1998).

Chapter 5

> I find her not so much aged as fat and flabby. It is still the same face, with that something disquieting behind the features. Nobody laughs or cries as easily as she does. I say goodbye without turning my head. *At my age, I swear nobody affects me as much as she does* [p. 125; italics added].

He is here struggling with "Is there life without mother?" And, five years later, in 1905, he continued to hold on to his mother by identifying with her as the aggressor in his masochism, as can be seen in his writing in his journal of "the moments when, I know not why, I feel like punishing myself" (p. 179). (Earlier, he had written, "Unpleasant things make me very unhappy, and yet I prefer them to others" [p. 106].) He continued to write down the nasty things she said:

> [Maman] always says the wrong thing: to those who believe themselves ill that they look fine: to those who are worrying about their health: that they look poorly. I shall never get used to that woman; I shall never get accustomed to my mother [p. 183].

He saw her more often, but in her presence was almost as silent as his father had been.

In 1909, his mother was much weaker:

> Maman. Her illness, her stage-setting of the armchair. She gets into bed when she hears [my wife's] footsteps. Her moments of lucidity. That is when she does her best play acting. She trembles, rubs her hands, clacks her teeth . . . eyes slightly wild. . . . Three states, lucidity, enfeeblement, real suffering. In the lucid state, she is still entirely Mme. Lepic. She sends [someone] to tell us: "Don't leave! I feel I'm going!" In the manner in which she holds one's hands and presses them, there is almost an intent to hurt [p. 241].

Renard wrote that she had spoken of wanting to go and see the leaves floating in the well. She wanted to sit on the well curb. A month after this:

"Forgive me! Forgive me!" Maman says to me. She holds out her arms and draws me to her. She falls at the feet of [my wife and my sister]. To these "Forgive me! Forgive me!"s, all I can find as a reply is, "I'll come back tomorrow." Afterwards, she gives herself violent blows on the head with her fist [p. 242].

Shortly after, his mother died. She had apparently gone to sit on the well curb, probably suffered a seizure of some kind, fell backward into the well, and was drowned. Renard did not believe that she had thrown herself into the well, but he could not be sure. He wrote, "Whether she died by accident or committed suicide, what is the difference from the religious standpoint? In the one case, it is she who did wrong, in the other case, it is God. . . . What is left?" Here he was asking, is there life without mother? His answer: "Work" (p. 243).

"Maman" died in August of 1909. In October of that year Renard's last play, *The Bigoted Woman* (*La Bigote*) (1909), a two-act play whose title refers to a woman based on his mother, opened with great popular and considerable critical success. Mme. and M. Lepic (Renard again used these names) are central to the plot; there are both similarities to and differences from actual life and from what was described in *Poil de Carotte*. The Lepics are depicted late in their marriage; he is 50 and she is 42. The father refuses to speak to the mother. Mme. Lepic is still a hypocrite and a liar, but she is presented as less detestable than in the 1894 novel. (No abuse of children is depicted.) She is the outwardly devout Catholic "*bigote*" in the play. The father is perhaps rather heroically portrayed—but with his faults. The playwright is clearly on the side of his anticlerical father, whom he made state in *Poil de Carotte*, "*Je déteste, moi, le bavardinage, le désordre, le mensonge et les curés*" (quoted by Guichard, 1971, p. 825 ["I detest gossip, disorder, lying and priests"; my translation]). The Lepics have only two children in the play; the son, Félix (his motto: "*tout comme Papa*" [p. 840] "everything like Papa!") sides completely with the father, as did both Jules and his brother Maurice. (François Renard had insisted on arranging for a civil burial for himself and so did his son Maurice after him.) The daughter in the play, unlike the actual adult Amélie, is partly on her mother's side in the matter of religion.

Chapter 5

Poil de Carotte does not exist in *La Bigote* as a member of the family—as Guichard (1971), the play's editor, comments (p. 82). (There is a mention of "Poil de Carotte" when Félix says he is going to write him—as if he were a friend of the family—about the wedding of Amélie [Renard, 1909, p. 886].) However, Jules's presence as the author dominates the play. Some hostile critics denounced *La Bigote* as too much of a sermon or a lecture. The play depicts the battle between M. and Mme. Lepic in relation to religion and priests. In the play, the father feels that his marriage has been ruined by his wife's putting the curé's welfare and influence before those of her husband. She has been faithful to him but has used the curé to try to rob M. Lepic of his authority, and M. Lepic characterizes his marriage as a ménage-à-trois. He warns the man who wants to marry his daughter not to give in to Mme. Lepic's and the curé's wish that the couple be married in the church, as M. Lepic had been. The play also has M. Lepic echo to his prospective son-in-law advice Jules himself had given to his son, Fantec, the future doctor, in a letter of 1902. He tells his 13-year-old boy that when he gets married he should refuse to promise that his children will be raised in the Catholic religion. In the play, M. Lepic interferes with his wife's plans—as Jules's father had not actively tried to do on Jules's behalf when his son was a boy. It is not clear at the end that he will win, but the play is constructed so that the father morally triumphs over his wife and the priest. In writing *La Bigote*, Jules Renard could identify with his dead father and repudiate his recently dead mother.

But a month after the play was produced, Renard (1909) suddenly became ill with heart disease: "Crisis. Shortness of breath; disgust with everything. Death might come in an hour or in ten years. To think that I should prefer ten years!" (p. 244). He should, but does he? Later that month he wrote, "As soon as one has looked it in the face, death is gentle to understand. . . . Already, I am developing a taste for walking in cemeteries" (pp. 245–246). His heart condition worsened. He had arteriosclerosis, and his son Fantec (now a physician) discovered, on examining him, that his father had a dangerously enlarged heart.

Renard died in May of 1910, nine months after the death of his mother. He died in Paris but was buried beside his parents in Chitry. He was only 46 years old.

The last entry in his *Journal* (Renard, 1887–1910b) is in April of 1910:

> Last night I wanted to get up. Dead weight. A leg hangs outside. Then a trickle runs down my leg. I allow it to reach my heel before I make up my mind. It will dry in the sheets, the way it did when I was Poil de Carotte [p. 248].

The return to Poil de Carotte took place on the way to join Mme. Lepic in the grave. There was to be no life without mother. In his *Journal* entry of February 23, 1910, several months before the death he was at that time expecting momentarily, he wrote that ordinary men usually know little about themselves, about their hearts—they are as indifferent to that body part as they would be about a watch. He was thinking here both of the enlarged organ in his chest, ticking away like a watch, and of the machine-like unawareness of the nature of one's passions and of the meaning of death.

> *Un homme ordinaire ne se connaît pas. Il peut mourir sans rien savoir de son coeur. . . . L'homme est indifférent comme une montre.*

(Might Jules here have been connecting in conscious or unconscious fantasy his own heart disease with his father's having shot himself in the heart? The heart as guilty organ?) He adds:

> *Et puis, j'ai écrit La Bigote. Mme. Lepic attend. Mais pourquoi m'a-t-il laisser écrire La Bigote?* [Bouillier, 1990, p. 997].
>
> [And yet, I have written *La Bigote*. Mme. Lepic awaits. But why has *he* let me write *La Bigote*? (my translation; italics added].

But who is this mysterious, uncapitalized *he*? His dead father? God? His masculinized dead mother who awaits him and without whom there may be no life? It is an enigmatic statement, but surely Renard is ambivalently anticipating rejoining parents who "await."

Of course, the reasons for any death are complex and cannot simply be reduced to conscious and unconscious death wishes.

Chapter 5

Renard's cardiovascular system was, by the time he reached his early 40s, gravely compromised. The years of rage-filled feelings and fantasies, so much of the rage turned on himself, had undoubtedly contributed (in unconscious motivation, in masochistic action, and in motivating fantasy) to whatever potential organic deficiencies Renard had started out with. One cannot dismiss the possibility that the Poil de Carotte imago within his mind felt that survival was impossible without his parents—especially without his hated and longed-for mother. A need for punishment for the wish to destroy her as well as a wish to join her in a love-death[2] would have been powerfully present, at least in his unconscious mind. Here the psychopathology that was the subject of so much of Renard's life's work may have hastened the destruction of both life and creativity.

The hardest legacy of childhood abuse is the need to hold on to the tormentor (body and soul) by some personal mixture of identification, hatred and rebellion, and longing and submission, a mixture that leads to psychic conflict and pain. Some creative individuals, like Trollope and Renard, can master part of their conflict by externalizing it in their work and transcend or attenuate it transiently. But for all of us death can beckon as a return to the mother as primal parent, even for atheists or anticlerics like M. Lepic and his son Poil de Carotte, who in their prime despised the idea of an afterlife. It may be part of our fate as human beings that, in our unconscious minds at least, there continues to exist a struggle with the paradox that starts in early life as an accompaniment to our aggressive, murderous drive: rage pushes us to want to get rid of the indispensable parental other without whom we feel we cannot live. This contradictory burden flourishes both during an infant's preoedipal (two-person psychology) and a child's oedipal (three-person psychology) development, sustained by the onset and onslaught of murderous aggression. We are not all Poil de Carottes, but there is some Poil de Carotte in all of us. We can never lose, and in regressive need we can revive, the delusional conviction stemming from our early years of wakening psychic awareness that there is no life without mother.

---

2. A love-death implies merger. Tristan and Isolde, in their love duet, repeat to one another, "*Ewig!*" ("Forever!") and "*Nicht mehr Tristan!* . . . *Nicht mehr Isolde!*" ("No more Tristan!" . . . "No more Isolde!").

Here is the last passage of *Poil de Carotte* (Renard, 1894a). (This passage comes after the boy has told his father that he hates Maman. He wants to leave home and go to a boarding school. Father refuses to send him and has no rescue to offer him. But, as I have quoted, at least it comforts Poil that father says he hates her too.)

> Sister Ernestine is soon going to marry. And Mme. Lepic permits her to walk with her fiancé, under the surveillance of Poil de Carotte.
>
> —Go on ahead, she says to him, and skips away.
>
> Poil de Carotte goes on ahead. He tries to skip up front like a dog, and when he forgets and slows down, he hears, despite himself, the sound of furtive kisses.
>
> He coughs.
>
> This unnerves him, and suddenly, as he finds himself before the cross of the village, he throws his cap to the ground, crushing it underfoot and cries out:
>
> —No one will ever love me, me!
>
> At that instant, Mme. Lepic, who is not deaf, raises herself from behind the wall, a smile on her face, terrible.
>
> And Poil de Carotte, aghast, quickly adds:
>
> —Except for mama! [p. 184].

Mama is and has the last word.

Chapter 6

TROLLOPE
His Life and Creativity

Melchisedec was a really happy man. He was without father, without mother and without descent. He was an incarnate bachelor. He was a born orphan.

—Samuel Butler, *Notebook*

Many contemporary psychological writers on artists and creativity continue to assume that it is enough to explain creativity by connecting it with pathology, trauma, and deficiency. The implicated pathology is said to be the consequence of common enough early tragic or catastrophic events, like severe illness or the loss of parents. Alternatively, creativity is attributed to universal circumstances of the vulnerable human condition or ubiquitous general tendencies of the human mind that follow on the inevitability of aging and death.

Our vulnerability is aggravated by our long period of dependence on others in our early life. Infancy and early childhood are, for everyone—gifted and deficient alike—a time of initially inadequate physiological and psychological structure requiring maturation and maternal care. When life begins, the predominant experiences are of sucking and biting, satiation and pleasure alternating with frustration, overstimulation, and rage. As development proceeds, there grows an awareness of the presence and one's dependence on a nurturing and controlling parental other, accompanied by the anxiety and even terror of loss of that other. Initial

Chapter 6

fantasies center on early (preoedipal) conflicts involving cannibalism and murder. These are subsequently partially transformed into oedipal conflicts surrounding the parents and involving incest and murder. Both preoedipal and oedipal periods of development entail manifestations of inborn sexual and aggressive drives. (I am here stating magisterially what some would consider debatable Freudian theory. But psychic conflict is, I believe, central to life and not a moot issue.)

Some version of these common psychic burdens underlies every human manifestation—although each individual has his or her own idiosyncratic variety. But these pathological roots are too widespread to explain the presence and power of creativity or account for the differences between the creativity of a good post office employee and the creativity of a good novelist. I am thinking of Anthony Trollope, who was both—and creative as both. He became an energetic and ingenious public servant who worked successfully to reform the postal systems of England and Ireland and contributed to the invention and widespread installation in Great Britain of the public mailbox, or "pillar letter-box," as he called it.

> [It was my ambition] that pillar letter-boxes should be put up for [the public] of which accommodation in the streets and ways of England I was the originator, having, however, got authority for the erection of the first at St. Helier's in Jersey [Trollope, 1883, p. 282; see also Hall, 1991, pp. 127–128].

Trollope appears to have been a victim of what can only be regarded as neglect and traumatic emotional abuse in his childhood and adolescence. We have this on his own authority, supplemented by the testimony of others. Trauma and deficient parental care clearly motivated his creativity but did not provide its source. He was one of a family of writers, which suggests that inherited gifts were involved. Published family authors include his maternal grandfather, maternal uncle, father, sister Cecilia, brother Tom (Thomas Adolphus Trollope), and, most important, mother Fanny. The latter two also wrote prodigiously. Anthony led the family with 67 books, followed by Fanny's 41 and Tom's 35.

ANTHONY TROLLOPE

A contemporary reviewer of Trollope's (1883) *An Autobiography* said that the book showed "a happy, healthy nature, manifestly, in spite of a singularly depressing boyhood and a strangely unpromising young manhood" (quoted in Edwards, 1980, p. ix). Edwards notes that, in contrast to Charles Dickens, who also had a predominantly miserable boyhood and early adolescence but, like David Copperfield, a comparatively happy early childhood, Trollope in his novels "includes virtually no childhoods, happy or unhappy" (p. xi).[1]

Trollope begins his autobiography with a concentration on his early schooling; he tells the reader nothing about his infancy and very little about his earliest childhood experiences. These omissions are not unique in his writings, in which children are seldom given much importance; there are very few babies in Trollope's fiction. The autobiography was written in 1875–76, when Trollope was 60, and was published posthumously in 1883. The book portrays his life as divided into two parts: a miserably unhappy, inhibited, unpromising childhood and prolonged adolescence, contrasted with a predominately happy and creative maturity beginning in his late 20s. That was when he left England after working for years as a junior clerk in the postal service in London, having been transferred to Ireland, where he achieved advancement, self-confidence, marriage, and financial independence.

EARLY LIFE

Anthony Trollope was born in 1815, the fifth child (fourth son) of seven children born over a span of nine years to Thomas Anthony

---

1. There is an exception in a late novel, *John Caldigate* (Trollope, 1879b), which has a rare but short description of its hero's childhood. The eponymous hero's father, Daniel Caldigate, is called "a just, hard, unsympathetic man" (p. 1). Such a characterization could describe Anthony's father, but the fictional father does not sound as eccentric or paranoid as the real one. However, the novel's opening sentence could apply to the early troubled life of the author: "Perhaps it was more the fault of Daniel Caldigate the father than of his son John Caldigate that the two could not live together in comfort in the days of the young man's early youth" (p. 1).

and Frances (Fanny) Trollope. One girl died at birth; three other children died young, of tuberculosis. One sister, Cecilia, lived long enough to marry and have children; she succumbed to "consumption" at 32, and four of her five children died of the disease within a year of Cecilia's death. Of the siblings, only Anthony and his oldest brother Tom lived to old age. Anthony wrote:

> My boyhood was, I think, as unhappy as that of a young gentleman could well be, my misfortunes arising from a mixture of poverty and [gentleman status] on the part of my father, and from an utter want on my own part of that juvenile manhood which enables some boys to hold up their heads even among the distresses which such a position is sure to produce [Trollope, 1883, p. 2].

It is intriguing that Trollope held himself responsible for his unhappiness owing to a "want . . . of juvenile manhood." There seems to have been little overt effeminacy about him at any time of his life—his tendencies in that direction were probably unacceptable to his consciousness and were covered over by bluff masculinity. But Trollope certainly identified with his heroines, perhaps most enthusiastically with the unsubmissive or disobedient ones—especially with their plight as outcasts in relation to status and power in 19th-century England. I speculate that, in his boyhood, he may have had a great need to differentiate and distance himself from his failure of a father that made for a positive emphasis on masculinity. We simply know almost nothing for certain about his sexual feelings and very little about his sexual activity.

It is to be noted that Trollope spoke of himself as a "young gentleman."[2] Snow (1975) felt that, during young Anthony's 20 years of neglect and humiliation, he sometimes "seems to have had only one support. A frail support at any time, one would have

---

2. The importance of being a gentleman is emphasized in many of Trollope's novels—once specifically and significantly to justify the dignity of the learned but impoverished Reverend Josiah Crawley, the ambivalently drawn portrait of Trollope's half-mad and maddening, impossibly stubborn, masochistic, but in some ways admired father. Crawley, who appears in two major novels, can, as a gentleman, feel himself to be the equal of his clerical superiors and of aristocrats. Perhaps the positive, conscious linkage of the term with both father and mother (and Trollope's unconscious identification with both) explains the obsession.

thought. . . . He could tell himself that, after all, he was a gentleman" (pp. 11–12). Trollope seems to have been obsessed by the importance of being a gentleman. This canon is stated in many of his books and stories; it is mentioned at least three times in his autobiography. For Trollope, being a gentleman involved having good character, being trustworthy. Fanny Trollope (1832) in her book about America repeatedly condemned the bad manners and behavior of most of the Americans she met, especially the men, whom she saw as primarily motivated by, and interested in, making money. Toward the end of the book she laments the neglect of honesty as a prime mover: "Where every man is engaged in driving hard bargains with his fellows, where is the honored class to be found, into which gentleman-like feelings, principles, and practice are necessary as an introduction?" (p. 225).

TROLLOPE, DICKENS, AND PARENTS

Trollope recognized Charles Dickens's greatness, but he did not like his novels.[3] (In his 1855 novel, *The Warden*, he made fun of him as "Mr. Popular Sentiment.") He strongly disapproved of

---

3. There may have been more to this dislike than aesthetic distaste and professional envy of a successful novelist. A deeper envy could have stemmed from the close friendship of brother Tom with Dickens. Tom was a writer too; he had published a book before Anthony did—both brothers' first books were published with the aid of their mother; and Tom had articles published in Dickens's magazine, *Household Words*. But, perhaps most telling of all, Fanny, who openly preferred her older, less ambivalent and more reliable son Tom, was fond both of Dickens and of his work. She and Dickens exchanged letters expressing mutual admiration, and she even referred to his early, popular novels in her own books (see Neville-Sington, 1997, p. 318). Neville-Sington observes that both Fanny and Dickens mixed satire and social criticism in their novels, and "she was the only female novelist at the time [to share Dickens's] physical stamina and [the] facility with her pen required to keep two books going simultaneously" (p. 277.) Both writers had published popular books about their travels to America, and Dickens, who had had his predecessor's work well in mind, had sent a gracious reply to a congratulatory letter of Fanny's. There were many subsequent meetings between them both in England and in Florence, where Tom and Fanny lived and entertained English visitors for so many years. It would not have endeared Dickens to Anthony that his older brother Tom Trollope's second wife was the sister of Tom's friend Dickens's mistress, Ellen Ternan.

Dickens's implicit accusations against his parents as depicted in his novels. Trollope specifically condemned the revelations about them in the biography of Dickens by the latter's close friend John Forster (1874), completed shortly after Dickens's death. Forster, using material supplied by Dickens, revealed that the hero's childhood in *David Copperfield* and his exile as a boy to the bottling factory was largely autobiographical. Forster's book showed that Dickens's kind but irresponsible father's descent into Debtors' Prison was the cause of the promising boy's being removed from school, forced to live apart from his family, and abandoned to a fate of humiliation, deprivation, and slavery in a London factory. Meanwhile his older sister was allowed to continue her schooling. But it was his mother's indifference to his fate that Dickens found unforgivable. He depicts her in his fiction as silly and shallow. Forster's biography quotes Dickens's bitter condemnation of his mother's attitude after his father got out of Debtors' Prison and rescued his oldest son: "I never afterwards forgot, I never shall forget, I never can forget, that my mother was warm for having me sent back [to the blacking factory]" (p. 32). Trollope was probably frightened and certainly repelled by Dickens's dramatic denunciation of his parents. Dickens was revealing that even as a successful man he still felt the awful bitterness of life without a loving mother. The hostile and accusatory part of Trollope's intense ambivalence toward his mother was expressed in a much more muted way in his *Autobiography*. (We often hate in others what we cannot accept in ourselves.)

TROLLOPE'S FATHER

Trollope's father, Thomas Anthony Trollope, was felt as more expendable than his mother, as fathers generally are, and Anthony's ambivalence toward him is more deeply and directly expressed in the *Autobiography*. Anthony's boyhood was, like Dickens's, also marred by poverty that the son attributed to the character and actions of a father very different from Dickens's kindly and feckless one. Thomas Anthony Trollope was emotionally rigid, righteous, angry, and occasionally paranoid—no Mr. Micawber, he. But there were similarities. Both novelists' fathers had a masochistic need to be a loser, each showing a dreadful talent for cultivating poverty.

To allow himself to feel deeply and especially to show emotion meant terrible vulnerability for Trollope's father. As a young man courting his future wife, Thomas Anthony wrote Fanny a somewhat apologetic letter, telling her how difficult it was for him to express his feelings. He wrote that she had much to learn about his character and sentiments, about " [my] cold and phlegmatic . . . my lifeless manners, my stone-like disposition" (quoted in Neville-Sington, 1997, pp. 42–43). Both his writer sons, Tom and Anthony, certainly would have agreed with this characterization. Anthony's novels often portray mutual father–son hostility, which usually involves a grown-up son.

Anthony's parents' marriage had started out with great promise, and for several years the young couple seemed to be happy and prospering. But after the children began to arrive, Thomas Anthony began a self-defeating and self-lacerating series of financial and occupational moves that resulted in a downhill course of genteel poverty.[4] In his autobiography Trollope openly but guardedly blames his father for the family's financial distress.

A time came when there was not enough money. Trollope's father was a barrister, and apparently an able one, "but plagued with so bad a temper, that he drove the attorneys from him" (Trollope, 1883, p. 3).[5] He also purchased property that he could not afford to keep up. In 1816, a year after Anthony was born, Thomas Anthony, who had no experience in farming, took out a 20-year renewable lease on a farm at an exorbitant rate, on which, despite not owning the land, he proceeded to build a large and expensive country house. Sadleir (1945) called this foolish move the first instance of Thomas Anthony's giving "rein to the mania for rash experiment which was finally to ruin him" (p. 51). Anthony (1883) wrote: "That farm was the grave of all my father's hopes, ambition, and prosperity, the cause of my mother's sufferings, and

---

4. The family, early in Anthony's life, when they lived on Keppel Street in London, subsisted in genteel poverty. But still they were waited on at table by a servant in the Trollope livery. Want—magnified by the father's miserliness and brought on by his foolish expenditures—came later on; still, there were always servants. During these years after Anthony's birth, debt and disarray rather than real destitution prevailed.

5. Trollope's fiction is full of impatient, troublesome, and hostilely portrayed lawyers; there are some good ones too. For examples of both in one novel see *The Bertrams* (Trollope, 1859).

of those of her children, and perhaps the director of her destiny and ours" (p. 2).

Later on, some of the title-deeds to the London property he had purchased disappeared. Money the family had counted on was lost when the deed to Frances Trollope's marriage portion turned out never to have been signed by the witnesses (who were the trustees) and was therefore not legally valid—and Thomas Anthony was a lawyer! Trollope (1883) comments:

> Things went much against him; the farm was ruinous. . . . My father's clients deserted him. . . . He purchased various dark gloomy chambers in and about Chambery Lane, and his purchases always went wrong. Then, as a final crushing blow, an old childless widower uncle, whose heir he was to have been, remarried and had a family! [p.3].

Trollope does not mention that his father used the expectation of the inheritance to justify his often foolish expenses over many years, or that the uncle married and sired an heir of his own in his old age in part because of the ungrateful behavior and provocative quarrelsomeness of his curmudgeonly nephew. Thomas Anthony apparently could not abide being dependent or modify his characteristic irascibility, in spite, or probably because, of his confident expectations of being able to pay off all his accumulated debts when he inherited. Tom Trollope felt that his father could have kept the lonely uncle from remarriage, if only he had been able to humor the old man. Tom writes in old age:

> The Tory uncle was very far indeed from being an intellectual match for his Liberal nephew, and no doubt used to talk in his fine old hunting-field voice a great deal of nonsense which no consideration of either affection, respect, or prudence could induce my father to spare. I fear he used to jump on the hearty old squire very persistently. . . . It may be that had it been otherwise he might have sought affection and companionship elsewhere than from a young wife [T. A. Trollope, 1888, pp. 47–48].

The sense of grievance against the uncle lingered in the family, especially in the increasingly paranoid father. Glendinning (1992) points out that "the idea of obsessional grievance as an occupation for life was to pervade Anthony's novels" (p. 12). She adds that a generalization about this is stated in at least eight of them. Adolphus was the name of Thomas Anthony's disappointing uncle's son and heir and was also the middle name of Anthony's older brother, Tom, toward whom he felt profound ambivalence. Glendinning perceptively notes that there are four characters called Adolphus in Trollope's work, "and they are all either cads or morons" (p. 13).

Thomas Anthony, according to his son Tom, had a powerful body, as did the adult Anthony. But Thomas Anthony suffered, even before his marriage, from chronic severe headaches, probably migraine, which he treated with calomel (mercurous chloride), whose toxic properties were then not known. He characteristically took more than the usual dose. In those days of comparative ignorance of the dangerousness of many drugs—consider the many early 19th-century British writers who became opium addicts—calomel was freely used as a general medicine by the whole family, but only Thomas Anthony's use became addictive. Tom wrote:

> I believe that [calomel] had the effect of shattering his nervous system in a deplorable manner. He became increasingly irritable; *never with the effect of causing him to raise a hand against any one of us*, but with the effect of making intercourse with him so sure to issue in something unpleasant that, unconsciously, we sought to avoid his presence, and to consider as hours of enjoyment only those that could be passed away from him [T. A. Trollope, 1888, p. 41; italics added]. . . . It is difficult for one who has never had a similar experience to conceive the degree in which [my father's] irritability made the misery of all who were called upon habitually to come into contact with it. I do not think it would be an exaggeration to say that for many years no person came into my father's presence who did not forthwith desire to escape from it. Happiness, mirth, contentment, pleasant conversation seemed to fly before him as if a malevolent spirit emanated from him [p. 205].

Chapter 6

Chronic mercurial poisoning causes brain damage and emotional disturbances, and calomel taken addictively certainly made Thomas Anthony's symptoms progressively worse, although his conflicts and his character were established even before the toxicity. He became increasingly gloomy and quarrelsome, isolated and paranoid. Tom Trollope also wrote of his father, somewhat belying his statement that his father never "rais[ed] a hand": "Simple assent to his utterances of an argumentative nature did not satisfy him; he would be argued with. Yet argument produced irritability leading to scenes of painful violence" (p. 205). We do not know the details, but apparently the show, or at least the threat, of violence was chronically present for the Trollope children.

Thomas Anthony was preoccupied with writing an impossibly difficult book, never to be finished:

> an *Encyclopaedia Ecclesiastica,* as he called it—on which he labored to the moment of his death. It was his ambition to describe all ecclesiastical terms. He worked at his most ungrateful task with unflagging industry. When he died, three numbers out of eight had been published by subscription; and are now . . . buried in the midst of that huge pile of futile literature, the building up of which has broken so many hearts [Trollope, 1883, p. 14].

Anthony at 25, miserable as a clerk in the London post office, conceived an impossibly ambitious, massive writing project similar to his father's: a history of the literature of the Western world beginning with the Greeks. His detailed outline showed that the work "was to include fiction, poetry, science, mathematics, astronomy, history, philosophy, political economy, criticism, biography, the fine arts, periodical literature and 'miscellaneous'" (Glendinning, 1992, p. 111). It was, of course, abandoned. This project seems to have been an attempt to fulfill a desperate obsessional need to classify and order everything; it also was an expression of unconscious wishes to be like and perhaps even to outdo his father.

We know most about Anthony Trollope's unhappy childhood and youth from his autobiography, but even there he says very little about his crucial earliest years—the years, I speculate, marked by comparative emotional neglect (in contrast to later childhood and adolescence, when neglect was accompanied by loss and trauma).

In his *Autobiography*, Anthony concentrates on the inadequacies and ignominies of his incomplete and painful school experiences. The reader meanwhile is able to gather enough about what was wrong and lacking in the family to realize that home was where the emotional deficit centered, as did the financial one, which partially determined it.

Like Charles Dickens, and unlike most other major male, English, 19th century novelists, Trollope did not complete preparatory school, never went on to a university, and acquired most of his knowledge from his own reading. His teaching began at home; he was taught to read by his mother very early, and learning continued under the direction of his father, accompanied by the expectation of punishment.

> From my very babyhood, before [my] first days at Harrow, I had had to take my place alongside of him as he shaved at six o'clock in the morning, and say my early rules from the Latin Grammar, or repeat the Greek alphabet; and was obliged at these early lessons to hold my head inclined towards him, so that in the event of guilty fault, he might be able to pull my hair without stopping his razor or dropping his shaving-brush. No father was ever more anxious for the education of his children, though I think none ever knew less how to go about the work. Of amusement, as far as I can remember, he never recognised the need. . . . I cannot bethink me of aught that he ever did for my gratification, but for my welfare—for the welfare of us all—he was willing to make any sacrifice. . . . In those days he never punished me, . . . but in passion he knew not what he did, and he has knocked me down with the great folio Bible he always used [Trollope, 1883, pp. 14–15].

Tom Trollope (T. A. Trollope, 1888) similarly recorded having started studying Latin grammar when he was six years old. He had to study early every morning before breakfast and give an account of what he had learned to his father every evening. His father, when supervising his lessons, would sit

> with his arm over the back of the pupil's chair, so that his hand might be ready to inflict an instantaneous pull of the

hair for every blundered concord or false quantity; the result being to the scholar a nervous state of expectancy, not judiciously calculated to increase intellectual receptivity [p. 41].

Thomas Anthony couldn't abide the children's being idle. His son Tom wrote that "enjoyment or any employment of the hours save work [were] distasteful and offensive to him. Lessons for us boys were never over and done with" (T. A. Trollope, 1888, p. 41). The father insisted that the children continue to do lessons during school holidays. Any show of what the father considered idleness—and Tom wrote that any time away from book-work was so considered—brought condemnation, even if the assigned tasks for the day had been completed. Only when the children were alone or with their mother out of the father's presence could they relax and play. Thomas Anthony's increasingly harsh compulsiveness dominated the household, except when he was at work. And, as his law practice diminished and after his leasing of the farm, Thomas Anthony stayed at home for ever-longer periods of time. Fanny's presence made a difference, but she could not always modify or curb her husband's proclivities. And, when she was distracted in her frequent and favored role as a hostess or out of the home on her frequent social visits—or, later on in Anthony's early adolescence, away for years in America—the home atmosphere was much worse. I think that, in reality, for Anthony the father may have been more to blame than his mother, but it was his mother's not being able or even present to prevent and rescue him that hurt the most. Soul murder victims frequently blame the mother for the father's crimes or abuse for similar reasons.

ANTHONY AND HIS MOTHER

Anthony's relationship with his mother was never close. She had lost her own mother when she was five years old and had to rely on mothering herself for the most part; she may have had little memory or experience of being mothered. She had a more determined and outgoing character than did her three-year-older sister, and her father did not remarry until Fanny was 21. She grew up to be an enthusiastic doer and fixer like her father. After her marriage and the birth of her children, it was hard for her to resist the temptation of being a guest or a hostess at social occasions. But in many ways she was an attentive mother, especially to the older children. Then there came to be too many children and too many distractions. (Fanny's love of entertaining and visiting amounted almost to a compulsion, perhaps partly motivated after a while by a need to dilute the presence of her husband.) Most worrisome was the increasing scarcity of funds, as her husband became more and more withdrawn, difficult, and indigent.

Trollope's mother and the way she neglected him differed from Dickens's. Frances Trollope was a cheerful, clever, and talented woman who, in middle age, when faced with financial disaster and family illness, fought successfully to become a famous writer and the breadwinner for her family. Hall (1991) says of her as revealed in the courtship letters between her and Thomas Anthony, "She was, like so many women in her son's novels, recognizably wittier, quicker, more satiric than her man" (p. 8). Frances could be both a playful and a loving mother when she was at home with the children and not overwhelmed by her circumstances. This was easier with the children born before Anthony in the family's early, still prosperous years. Her firstborn and favorite son, Tom, described her as having the power of intense enjoyment and the even greater power of knowing how to make others happy. As an old man, Tom called her the happiest natured person he had ever known. She was a compulsive reader (so are most of the heroines of her novels), and she taught her children how to read English and the beginnings of speaking French and Italian. Tom Trollope (1888) wrote:

> Her plan for teaching the letters was as follows. She had a great number of bone counters with the alphabet in capitals and small letters on either side printed on them; then having invited a charming little girl, the daughter of a neighbor, she tossed the counters broadcast over the floor, instituting prizes for him or her, who should, in crawling races over the floor, soonest bring the letter demanded. Reading thus began to be an amusement to me at an unusually early age [p. 16].

We do not know if she still had the time to do this when Anthony was the right age for such lessons. Anthony was not considered as promising as his three older brothers, and at times of stress she seems almost to have forgotten him. "[Frances Trollope] loved Tom, whom even before Mr. Trollope died she made into a surrogate husband. She loved her other children when they were within sight, and otherwise *forgot them* almost entirely" (Snow, 1975, p. 18; italics added). (I think "could forget them" would be fairer.) Snow says that this fading of memory marked a "special kind of unfeelingness" that accounts for some observers characterizing her as "coarse." He may be right, but some of both Anthony and Fanny Trollope's biographers would disagree. The "facts" are not plain enough to clear away any individual biographer's generally positive or negative prejudices about mothers or specific ones about Fanny Trollope.

Anthony was, Raban (1987) comments, "the miserable runt of the family" (p. 75) for both parents. His backward glance at his mother in his *Autobiography* (Trollope, 1883) had, in contrast to Tom's remembrances, much bitterness and reproach in it, although toned down and disguised. He could directly describe his mother's liveliness, charm, and "joviality and industry" (p. 24), but his repressed rage leaked out in snide and deprecating remarks, hinting at hypocrisy and insincerity:

> She loved society, affecting a somewhat liberal *role*, and professing an emotional dislike to tyrants, which sprung from the wrongs of would-be regicides and the poverty of patriot exiles. An Italian marquis who had escaped with only a second shirt from the clutches of some archduke he had wished to exterminate . . . [was] always welcome to the modest hospitality of her house. In after years, when marquises of another cast had been gracious to her, she became a strong Tory and thought duchesses were sweet. But, with her, politics were always an affair of the heart, as, indeed, were all her convictions. Of reasoning from causes, I think that she knew nothing [pp. 23–24; italics added].

He praised her industry but showed little respect for her books. He wrote of her "considerable gifts. But she was *neither clear-sighted nor accurate*; and in her attempts to describe morals, manners, and even facts, was unable to avoid the pitfalls of exaggeration" (p. 33; italics added) Anthony here was repaying his mother for the disdainful attitude he felt she had toward his writing. (She had, in letters written from Italy after he had achieved success but before he wrote his autobiography, praised *his* industry without paying tribute to the quality of his work.)

Frances Trollope had to face her husband's character deterioration from eccentricity toward madness, his diminishing ability to earn money, and the gauntlet of her children's sickness and death. She was the more loving and lovable parent in a family setting that came to involve soul murder. Yet Fanny's comparative neglect of Anthony in his earliest years would have given him reason to hate her while yet loving her and longing for her love. We cannot know what he allowed himself to be conscious of in his ambivalent inner struggle, but the push toward hate and rage at Fanny would probably have been augmented because she was not able to control the deficiencies and depredations of her spouse. A child expects the mother to have the magical power to control everything. (Without being able to be certain of the details of Anthony's individual mixture of ambivalence toward his father or toward his mother, we have evidence that the father came to be clearly hated by the children who wrote about him.)

She was often away from home when he was a child. She loved to attend and give parties and picnics. (Anthony as a man despised picnics.) "Fanny was devoted to her family, but family life was not enough for her. She continued to thrive on the society of other people" (Neville-Sington, 1997, p. 52). Frances Trollope lived abroad apart from Anthony for years at a time, starting when he was an adolescent. After her husband died, when Anthony was 20 years old, Frances lived most of the rest of her life as a widow out of England; for the last 20 years of her life she lived in Italy with her oldest son, Tom.

For Anthony, probably hardest to forgive was his mother's complete unavailability in America from the time he was 12 1/2 and a half to 16 (1827–1831), a traumatic separation comparable to the young Dickens's exile from his family. "Is there life without Mother?" would have been a bitterly serious question for the miserable schoolboy.

In 1827, the Trollopes's marriage was under great strain and tension. This circumstance impelled Fanny to do something dramatic to get away from her increasingly bad-tempered husband without the disgrace of an overt separation. Soon after Anthony

Chapter 6

(aged 12) was sent away to board at Winchester School, his mother left for America. It is not known how much this move was supported by her husband. She was accompanied by her son Harry, her two daughters, and a painter, the Frenchman Auguste Hervieu, a relatively new acquaintance 15 years her junior (he was 33 years old, and Fanny was 48 when they met), whose relationship to her has never been quite clear. Hervieu had been engaged as drawing master for the children, and he soon became part of the household. Glendenning (1992) comments, "[Hervieu] remained and remains obscure. Before long, he was a member of the Trollope household, and remained so for over a decade, sometimes appearing to be Mrs. Trollope's chief solace and support and sometimes a demanding hanger-on" (p. 25). He was already a friend of the family before the trip to America. Fanny (F. Trollope, 1832) simply described him as "our friend Mr. H, who had accompanied Miss Wright to America, in the expectation of finding a good opening in the line of historical painting" (p. 91). He was the chief illustrator of Fanny's books until the middle of her career as author; he also illustrated Thomas Anthony's published *Encyclopaedia* volumes and Tom's first books. Then Hervieu, after 15 years of being almost a member of the family who owed him so much, was, at a time when Fanny decided she should leave London for the country or abroad, suddenly replaced as her illustrator by better known artists. He then disappeared from the collective family narratives. Tom and Anthony seemed rather glad to be rid of him.

The idea of going to America came from a slightly dotty friend of Frances Trollope's, the early feminist Frances Wright, who wanted the Trollope party to visit and help her run Nashoba, a "settlement" for freed blacks that she had founded in Tennessee. Hervieu and Harry were supposed to stay there and teach. Fanny Trollope was very taken with Frances Wright, an eccentric but charismatic enthusiast described by Tom (T. A. Trollope, 1888) as "a very remarkable personage ... handsome in large and almost masculine style of beauty, with a most commanding presence, a superb figure and a stature fully masculine" (p. 106). Fanny certainly seemed "swept away by [Wright's] personality" (Ransom, 1995, p. 37). Ransom quotes a letter of Fanny Trollope's to a friend:

> Never was there I am persuaded such a being as Fanny Wright ... Some of my friends declare that if worship may

be offered, it must be to her . . . and I for my part applaud and approve all they say. . . . Will it be possible to let this "angel" depart without vowing to follow her? I think not. *I feel greatly inclined to say where her country is, there shall be my country* [p. 37; italics added].

This identification with the Biblical Ruth (in relation to Naomi) implies an unconscious wish to be a widow. Fanny's infatuation with Frances and her decision to leave with her for America also may have been chiefly motivated by a wish to escape from her increasingly disturbed, destructive, and self-destructive husband. It was a time in England when a married woman had few legal rights, little power to separate from a husband who controlled money and property, and none to divorce. (The theme of women's plight under English law was often featured in the novels of both Fanny and Anthony.) In 1828 Fanny wrote a friend about her discontent with Thomas Anthony, who had just decided that he needed to lower his expenses by renting out the home that she loved so much. He was about to move the family miles away to Harrow Weald, where she would have been too far away from the busy social life with her friends and neighbors that she needed to make existence bearable. Ransom (1995) quotes from an earlier letter written by Fanny to another friend in 1827. The subject is Thomas Anthony: "He is a good, honorable man—but his temper is dreadful—every year increases his irritability—and also its lamentable effect upon the children" (p. 38). Ransom comments: "The scheme proposed by Frances Wright [would have allowed Fanny] to take herself and the children out of the range of Thomas Anthony's temper in a manner which would [have been] acceptable to society" (p. 38).

The move to Harrow Weald did not rescue Anthony from his persecution at school—we will hear more about this shortly—and his mother's abandonment of him accompanied by the other children probably made him bitterly aware that his welfare had not been considered by either parent. His life became even more painful later on when he was living completely alone in England with his father at Harrow Weald.

Frances Wright had given a delusory, idealized description of Nashoba, and when the party arrived there after the hard ocean and overland voyages it turned out to be a pestilential and desolate

Chapter 6

ruin—short of food, no fruits, no vegetables, only rain water to drink. Fanny and the three children, accompanied by Hervieu, left the "angel" behind and went on to Cincinnati. At this time Fanny's disillusionment with Nashoba and Frances Wright made her question the woman's sanity. Thomas Anthony, who initially had apparently needed to be talked into letting her go to America at all, then responded by encouraging her to start a commercial venture in Cincinnati that he hoped would restore the family fortune. He intended to send on money and goods and join her later. She did not return to England for more than three and a half years.

Things in America went from bad to worse. Harry became ill with what turned out to be tuberculosis. A year after the move to Cincinnati, Thomas Anthony and Tom made the journey to America, supposedly to set everything right. Tom describes how dirty and miserable they were on the trans-Atlantic voyage since his father had insisted that they take berths in steerage. Much of the remainder of the father's money was spent in Cincinnati on erecting a monstrous polyglot building—"Graeco-Moresco-Gothic-Chinese" (quoted in Sadleir, 1945, p. 79)—for a commercial bazaar. Both the structure and their plans were pretentious. Culture was to be supplied as well as goods. The building was to include a lecture hall, a museum, and a panorama of London painted by Hervieu. It was completed in 1828–29, but the project was never successful because they had neither enough of the right goods to sell—the items Thomas Anthony did send turned out to be worthless—nor enough money to buy them. The exotic edifice, known as "Trollope's folly," was a tourist attraction for decades until it was razed in 1881. This was but one of Thomas Anthony's ventures about which Anthony (Trollope, 1883) wrote: "The touch of his hand seemed to create failure. He embarked on one hopeless enterprise after another, spending on each all the money he could at the time command" (p. 31). After he returned alone from America, Thomas Anthony often forgot or refused to send money, and the party was obliged to live in poverty on the earnings of Hervieu as a portrait painter. Fanny had to threaten to write to her increasingly disturbed and irrational husband's family before he would send her enough money for their return passage to England.

THOMAS ADOLPHUS TROLLOPE

Anthony's oldest brother, Thomas Adolphus, was born when the parental marriage was comparatively happy, before the years of poverty, and may have had a very different infantile experience from that of the many siblings who followed. Fanny wrote a letter to her husband from her father's house during Tom's first year that shows her happiness with Tom and with her husband:

> Were I not *too wise* to be vain, I should certainly become so here—everybody exclaims that my darling is the loveliest creature they ever beheld, and most add (now pray endeavor to be as wise as I) that he is very like his father. I screw my features into all possible forms, that I may not look as delighted as I feel [quoted in Neville-Sington, 1997, p. 47].

Tom was his mother's favorite from his birth on; Harry, the next oldest, his father's, although he quarreled with him the most in later life; Anthony was no one's.

Fanny Trollope had many strong and admirable qualities. She is described as characteristically enthusiastic and optimistic, always smiling—"possessed of an optimism that bordered on the supernatural," says Pope-Hennessy (1971, p. 35). This probably did not make her comparative indifference to Anthony any easier for him to bear. Glendinning (1992) writes of Frances:

> She was, wrote Tom, "one of those people who carry sunshine with them." [When separated from her husband, Tom and Anthony,] it continued to be Tom to whom she wrote about her adventures, her hopes and her fears. [Tom] never had to doubt his central place in her life. That was the essential "sunshine" that Anthony missed [p. 37].

After Thomas Anthony's death, Fanny put Tom in the role of her companion and business manager; he was almost a kind of surrogate husband (Anthony was then 19). Tom wrote: "It was decided between us that I was to send in my resignation of [my teaching post] . . . and devote myself, for the present at least, to becoming her companion and squire" (T. A. Trollope, 1888, p. 246).

Chapter 6

Tom continued living with his mother as an adult bachelor for many years and, beginning in 1843, they shared a house in Florence for two decades. Tom married late, twice. He was 38 when he first married. Both wives were brought to live in his mother's household; this arrangement lasted until Fanny died at age 83 in 1863. There is evidence of the closeness between Tom and his mother in an 1849 letter that Fanny—she was then almost 70—wrote to Tom shortly after the death of her last daughter, Cecilia. Fanny had returned to England to nurse Cecilia; Tom had been away for several months with his first wife, Theodosia, visiting Theodosia's sick mother. Anthony was then married and living with his wife, Rose, in Ireland. Fanny herself was recovering from bronchitis:

> My health and spirits have been shaken by all the sorrow I have gone through. And I confess to you that I feel my separation from you to be almost too painful under my present circumstances. For very nearly forty years, my dear son, you and I have lived together in more perfect harmony than is often found, I believe, in any connection in life. And now, when I so very greatly need the comfort and support of your society, I am deprived of it. I should be very unwilling to put you and your dear wife to any serious inconvenience, but I feel that your coming to me for a few weeks now might be *very* beneficial to me [Neville-Sington, 1997, p. 338].

Tom taking exception to the cool (although not denunciatory) appraisal of their mother in Anthony's *Autobiography*, pointed out that Anthony had scarcely been with her from his school years on, while he, her closest companion, knew better. She left the bulk of her small legacy to Tom.

LIFE WITHOUT MOTHER AND MOTIVATION FOR WRITING

Trollope's friend and first biographer, Escott, wrote:

> "My mother," [Trollope] said to me in the year of his death, "was much from home or too busy to be bothered. My

father was not exactly the man to invite confidence. I tried to relieve myself by confiding my boyish sorrows to a diary *that I have kept since the age of twelve*, which I have just destroyed. And which, on referring to it for my autobiography some time since, I found full of a heart-sick, friendless little chap's exaggeration of his woes" [quoted in Terry, 1989, p. 26; italics added].

Was it, I wonder, the absence of his mother—he was 12 when his mother left for America—and the need for parenting, love and empathy that started off his writing in the form of the diary? Many a child of that age has begun a diary, even though the mother's presence at home could be taken for granted. Still, for Anthony, writing then and afterward would have involved at least an attempt, probably an unconscious one, to hold on to his mother by becoming like her. She had established herself as a writer in the family in the years before her journey to America, since she wrote prolifically for family theatricals (given in French as well as English) and for local celebratory occasions when Anthony was young. She tried to publish some of these writings, but the manuscripts were, prior to her successful debut in print in middle age with *The Domestic Manners of the Americans* [F. Trollope, 1832], always returned by the various publishers to whom they had been submitted. She perhaps had the then not uncommon habit of diary writing. It is quite possible that Anthony was aware of the diary she was writing *while* she was away in America, a diary whose quick transformation into the book made her an almost overnight success as an author. At any rate, Anthony would surely have read about the diary in his mother's book—a book that gave her the power to rescue the family from the disaster her husband had made. Awareness of this literary source of financial power would have heightened the intensity of Anthony's identification.

MURDEROUS RAGE AND ITS VICISSITUDES

It is my conviction, gained from my work with patients, that we are all assaulted in early life by a rage of such murderous intensity that it has to be, but is never completely, diffused and neutralized—and yet is unconsciously preserved—in the course of our becoming civilized adults. Unlike Dickens, Trollope needed to minimize his anger, especially toward his mother. Both men took disguised—and sometimes undisguised—revenge on their mothers in their fiction. Dickens was conscious of portraying his mother as the feckless and silly mother of Nicholas Nickleby. Trollope's (1873) picture of the opportunistic, selfish, and shallow woman writer and mother, Lady Carbury, in his novel, *The Way We Live Now*, may or may not have been connected with Frances Trollope in his consciousness, but there are resemblances. Anthony wrote ambivalently about his mother in *An Autobiography*; he did not reveal open rage.

He expressed more anger toward his father and his brother Tom. Anthony's masochistic provocativeness—documented, as we shall see, in *An Autobiography*—continued, with some attenuation, into adult life. It helped both to ward off and to discharge some of the murderous intensity of his hostility by converting it into potential guilt and the evocation of punishment. His compulsive orderliness, which I detail later, furnished much-needed defensive obfuscation, minimizing his responsibility for the mixture of deep guilt and rage he may have consciously felt as a child but did not reveal openly in his autobiography.

Another likely source of guilt when he was a boy was the death of so many siblings. In Trollope's (1883) *An Autobiography* there is no mention of his next-older brother, Arthur, a kind of invalid, who died at age 12 when Anthony was 8. Arthur certainly was memorable—he had been sent to Harrow at the same time as Anthony, who was then seven, but had to be withdrawn soon afterward and subsequently lived with Fanny's father, where he died. Brothers Tom and Henry formed a close pair, as did Anthony's sisters. Anthony was a loner and must have missed Arthur as a possible companion, as well as feeling guilty to be rid of him because of suppressed or repressed intense hostile competitive wishes, part of a sibling rivalry that was to be all too often punctuated by sibling death.

LIFE WITHOUT MOTHER

Anthony eventually was able to assert an increasingly effective and adaptive obsessive control over his guilt and rage, but we know too little about the price he paid for his defensive armor in the form of diminished spontaneity and an inhibited capacity for pleasure and love, especially during his adolescence. Recall that Ibsen (1896) defined soul murder as destroying the capacity for joy in another human being. Trollope was able in his fiction to execute a kind of retaliation against his parents, while paying grateful tributes to them, by his treatment of them there in fragmented and usually disguised fashion. In his writings he could sublimate and discharge his passions and exercise his control. Thus he was able to transcend his inner conflicts and achieve what appears to have been a relatively emotionally balanced view of life. The balance is especially evident in his novels and stories, in which his occasional (and often endearing) eccentricities are displayed in a predominant setting of sensible and realistic depiction and comprehension.

I feel that Anthony's chief narcissistic injury (like Dickens's) was what he felt as his mother's indifference to and abandonment of him in the awful family circumstances of poverty, separation, and illness.

> Because Anthony was younger by five years than Tom, his schooling was earlier subject to the father's bankruptcy and his share of the mother's undistracted affection considerably less. Entangled in the family distresses, his life as a small boy was harder and more cruelly solitary than that of either of his brothers. Nature and chance alike were against him. His clumsy stupidity provoked his father's most pitiless discipline.... Bundled from one place to another, continually the victim of his parents' money troubles, [he was] supported only by the hurried moments of affection which were all his over-busy, harassed mother could afford to him [Sadlier, 1945, p. 62].

Young Anthony felt deprived by both parents. As he grew older, he needed to be rescued from his increasingly disturbed father by the mother who was so often not there. He had had to suffer life without mother and had found it, and the emotions that accompanied it—felt and pushing to be felt in consciousness—unbearable.

Trollope can usefully be compared with Renard. There are obvious differences, both in actualities and in the aftereffects of

Chapter 6

the two men's troubled childhoods. Differences, of course, do not depend entirely on environmental events, yet these also count. Renard's mother—an open hater—certainly outdid Trollope's father in her rules as villain, seducer, and brainwasher; Trollope appears to have had a much better mother than Renard had a father. Above all, Trollope suffered much of his abuse at the hands of others beside his parents, whose most deleterious influence on him was that of neglect. In contrast, Renard was tormented, principally emotionally, as well as deprived, by his family, above all by his mother. There surely were similarities in the two writers' feelings in relation to their parents and themselves; they both show the defensive need to break with what had happened to them. But the dynamic effects of a disturbed and deprived childhood seem more muted and certainly less apparent in consciousness in Trollope than in Renard.

Chapter 7

SCHOOL DAYS AND AFTER
Disorder and Early Sorrow, and Recovery

The tygers of wrath are wiser than the horses of instruction.
—William Blake
"The Marriage of Heaven and Hell"

Like his brothers, Anthony first was sent to nearby Harrow School. He was there from ages seven to ten with the degraded status of day pupil. Day pupils were local children who did not sleep in; they were the objects of charity. Since they paid nothing, they were looked down on by the regular boarding pupils, who came from aristocratic or rich families. Tom wrote in his reminiscences, "How I hated it ... because I was a 'town-boy' ... a charity boy ... an object of scorn and contumely on the part of all the *paying* pupils" (T. A. Trollope, 1888, p. 53). The humiliation of this status for the Trollope boys was aggravated because their miserly father never bought them new clothes. Anthony had to attend school in old, patched, ill-fitting, and dirty hand-me-downs. The miles he had to trudge on the way to school made him so dirty that the headmaster once stopped him on the way and asked

> with all the clouds of Jove upon his brow and all the thunder in his voice whether it was possible that Harrow School was disgraced by so disreputably dirty a little boy as I! ... I do not doubt that I was dirty—but I think that he was cruel. He must have known me had he seen me as he was

85

Chapter 7

wont to see me, for he was in the habit of flogging me constantly. Perhaps he did not recognize me by my face. . . . [School was] a daily purgatory [Trollope, 1883, p. 4].

When he was 12 years old, after first spending two years away from home and living in at Sudbury School, Anthony was sent, also to board, at Winchester, which had been his father's school. At Harrow the school authorities were aware that Thomas Anthony planned ultimately to send his boys on to Winchester, and then on to New College Oxford, where both he and his father had gone. This knowledge perhaps contributed to the negative bias felt toward Anthony at Harrow. Brother Tom was already an advanced student at Winchester. It was the custom there to appoint an older student as a praefect-tutor to a younger one, and Tom was chosen to be Anthony's. The two brothers shared a room. In 1827, Fanny Trollope had written to Tom at Winchester, asking him to be a fraternal mentor and stressing how necessary it was for Anthony to do well at Winchester School—scholarships and prizes were financial necessities for the Trollope boys to proceed to Oxford. She was relying on Tom as a "praefect-brother [to see to this by] advice and remonstrance. I dare say you will often find him idle and plaguing enough," she wrote, although she also characterized Anthony as "a good-hearted fellow" (Terry, 1987, p. 16). In spite and perhaps because of this plea, the position of power over Anthony apparently brought out Tom's identification with his father as sadistic educator, a role much reinforced by the school beating policy. (Tom had also been subject to severe beatings by the masters and tutors at Winchester.) Tom may have supplied kindly advice, but his "remonstrance" took the form of teaching with the use of physical abuse. Anthony (Trollope, 1883) writes that he and Tom became close friends as adults, but

> in those school-days he was, of all my foes, the worst . . . "Hang a little boy for stealing apples, he used to say, and other little boys will not steal apples." . . . As a part of his daily exercise, he thrashed me with a big stick. That such thrashings should have been possible . . . as a continual part of one's daily life, seems to me to argue a very ill condition of school discipline [p. 8].

(Anthony, perhaps out of depression or spite, never gave himself a chance of winning a scholarship.)

Many years later, in 1852, by which time both brothers were married (Anthony already had two sons and Tom was about to become a father), Anthony wrote to his brother:

> The pleasures of paternity have been considerably abridged since the good old Roman privilege of slaying their offspring at pleasure has been taken from fathers. But the results of flagellation, though less keen, are more enduring. One can kill but once: *but one can flog daily*, and always quote Scripture to prove that it is a duty [quoted in Hall, 1983, pp. 31–32: italics added].

In the letter, Anthony calls this "joking," which seems an attempt to attenuate the fratricidal fury that surfaces in the clear reference to Tom's daily Winchester beatings (cf. Glendinning, 1992, p. 200). There is also in Anthony's letter a deeper, harder-to-own reproach toward, as well as an identification with, the "Roman" infanticidal father who inspired the rage of both brothers.

Punishment, early linked in Anthony's mind with the shadow of his father's razor, was a regular part of his school experiences; he says of his teachers:

> It was by their ferules that I always knew them, and they me. I feel convinced in my mind that I have been flogged oftener than any human being alive. It was just possible to obtain five scourgings in one day at Winchester, and I have often boasted that I obtained them all. Looking back over half a century, I am not quite sure whether the boast is true—but if I did not, nobody ever did [Trollope, 1883, p. 18].

Trollope describes how cruel the boys at Winchester were when his father did not pay his fees "and the school tradesmen who administered to the wants of the boys were told not to extend their credit to me. . . . My schoolfellows of course knew that it was so, and I became a Pariah. . . . I had no friend to whom I could pour out my sorrows" (p. 9). But Trollope takes on a good deal of guilt for his being an outcast: "I was big, and awkward,

Chapter 7

and ugly, and, I have no doubt, skulked about in a most unattractive manner" (p. 9). He writes of feeling agony and thinking of suicide (jumping off the school tower).

For much of Anthony's four years at Winchester the other members of the family were out of the country. In 1828, when Thomas Anthony took Tom out of Winchester and both went to America to join Frances and the other children, Anthony was left completely alone, his tuition unpaid, with no spending money and no provision made for his holidays. He felt even more humiliation now than he had at Harrow since his fellow pupils were aware of the circumstances of his poverty and his deserted state. He writes that he was not allowed to join in the school's games and that he felt the other students as well as the teachers were against him.

Sadleir (1947) quotes from a former schoolmate, Sir William Gregory (husband of Yeats's great friend, Lady Gregory), who wrote in his 1894 autobiography:

> Anthony Trollope . . . sat next to me. He was a big boy, older than the rest of the form, and without exception the most slovenly and dirty boy I ever met. He was not only slovenly in person and in dress, but his work was equally dirty. His exercises were a mass of blots and smudges. These peculiarities created a great prejudice against him, and the poor fellow was generally avoided. . . . I had plenty of opportunity of judging Anthony, and I am bound to say, though my heart smites me sorely for my unkindness, that I did not like him. I avoided him, for he was rude and uncouth, but I thought him an honest, brave fellow. He was no sneak. His faults were external . . . but [they] were of that character for which schoolboys would never make allowances, and so poor Trollope was tabooed, and had not, so far as I am aware, a single friend. . . . He gave no sign of promise whatsoever, was always in the lowest part of the form, and was regarded by masters and by boys as an incorrigible dunce [p. 67].

Anthony returned to Harrow for his final three years of schooling—"ill-dressed and dirty," as a charity day boy again in an aristocratic school. (Gregory's description is of Trollope's later stay there.) He had been taken out of Winchester when his father,

School Days and After

having left the rest of the family in America in destitution, returned to England with Tom. Thomas Anthony felt he had to bring Anthony home when he was forced to attend to unpaid school bills from Winchester that he had, wittingly or unwittingly, ignored. By then Thomas Anthony was almost mad. It was at this time that he refused to respond to his wife's urgent pleas from America for financial support; he justified his denial of her need by rationalizing his parsimony with paranoid suspicions.

Tom subsequently went on to Oxford, and Harry, who was supposed to have run the business in Cincinnati but returned to England alone because he had become so ill, went to Cambridge. Thomas Anthony wanted them to go to college but resisted paying for their education. He was unwilling and perhaps ultimately unable to spend any money on his boys. Anthony was left alone at home with his deranged father; they now lived in a broken-down farmhouse at Harrow Weald. The roof leaked; some of the wall timber was rotten; the furniture was inadequate. Anthony again had to walk the three miles to Harrow school and back twice a day; there was no way to keep from always being dirty. He wrote, "Perhaps the eighteen months which I passed [at Harrow Weald] in this condition, walking to and fro [twelve miles] on those miserably dirty lanes, was the worst period of my life" (Trollope, 1883, p. 11). Hatred and parentocidal fantasy must have been blended with the dirt; no wonder Trollope became compulsively clean and orderly. When a man, as his novels show, he hated dirtiness, especially in women. His clothes were sometimes ill assorted and rumpled, but never dirty. This behavior was a compromise, an example of Anthony's taking on in later life a trait of his mother's. Fanny was described by her daughter-in-law and others as being indifferent to how she dressed.

Trollope wrote of the terrible time at Harrow Weald:

> Here were the same lanes four times a day, in wet and dry, in heat and summer, with all the accompanying mud and dust.... I might have been known among the boys at a hundred yards' distance by my boots and trousers—and conscious at all times that I was so known [pp. 15–16].

But it was probably living absolutely alone with his father as the chief target of his neglect and verbal abuse that seems to have been the hardest burden of all in Anthony's conscious awareness. Quarreling, mutual dislike, and even enmity between fathers and sons abound in Trollope's novels (see Hall, 1991, pp. 33–34). But blaming his mother for leaving him with his father would have given rise to a hatred of her that was, I feel, even harder to bear in consciousness. Hating her would have meant arousing the psychic danger of losing her, which, in turn, would have intensified the boy's need for his hostile and feared father. I speculate that this heightened need involved a deepening of an identification with his father as aggressor, turning the hostility toward his father inward on himself. This would have escalated Anthony's masochism and left the boy feeling an emotional contradiction and turmoil, trapped with his half-mad father as the only parent.

Trollope (1883) says he learned little from any teacher:

> When I left Harrow I was all but nineteen, and I had at first gone there at seven. During the whole of those twelve years no attempt had been made to teach me anything but Latin and Greek, and very little attempt to teach me those languages. I do not remember any lessons either in writing or arithmetic. . . . I do assert that I have no recollection of other tuition except that in the dead languages. . . . There were twelve years of tuition in which I do not remember that I ever knew a lesson! [pp. 17–18].

Some biographers and ex-fellow students believe that Anthony exaggerated his lack of achievement and perhaps even his miseries when he wrote of his school years in late middle age. For example, he says he won no prizes, but research turned up one presented for an English essay (see Snow, 1975, p. 31). Perhaps what he recalled was not strictly historical truth, but this was the way his mind had registered his past. He tells the reader of his autobiography that he is consciously trying to be truthful. The floggings appear not to have been exaggerated. In *An Autobiography* in general, there is obviously much distortion and dramatization, but it does reflect the emotional tone of what and how he remembered, which is probably more important than the "facts" of the past. He certainly learned his Latin; he uses Latin quotations and mottoes as freely as, or perhaps even more than, most British Victorian writers. But it is probably true that, as it had been for his mother, most of his learning came from his own impassioned and solitary reading.

MASOCHISM

The neglect and cruelties at home and the mortifications and beatings at school pushed Trollope toward masochism by inducing him unconsciously to equate being beaten with being loved in his vulnerable situation of emotional deprivation (see Freud, 1919). Being beaten afforded at least some attention to the child who felt so unloved and neglected. Also, and perhaps more important, turning aggression inward against the self was a way of retreating from, as well as being punished for, his murderous, aggressive impulses. All this was strenuously resisted in Anthony's consciousness in later life. Trollope's masochism took the predominant (and relatively active) form of provoking authority and simultaneously allowed for the expression of some of his sadism. Obsessional control dominated him as an adult, but there was also a compulsion to re-create actively something of the ignominious disorder forced on him in his boyhood.

The humiliation at school was worse than the beatings. Probably the main reason he resisted learning so much was his spiteful bitterness at being shunned by his masters and his fellow pupils. He was a loner, convinced that he was unwanted. From the *Autobiography*, one feels that, little as the boy could control the conditions that made for the dirt and the disorder, there was masochism in his reaction of passivity and withdrawal and that he found a spiteful pleasure in his anal offensiveness. All this is very like what we have seen documented by Poil de Carotte.

MOTHER'S RETURN

Anthony was almost 17 when his mother finally returned from America, in 1831. Frances Trollope was then 52 years old. Making use of previously written notes, she promptly wrote and published her first and most famous book, *The Domestic Manners of the Americans* (F. Trollope, 1832). It was an immediate success and sold well enough to allow her to rescue her family temporarily

Chapter 7

from the financial disaster that her husband had placed it in. She published her first novel that same year. For the next 25 years, Fanny Trollope was obliged to keep up a continuous stream of books, mostly novels and travel books (a mixture that Anthony was to imitate) in order to support her family. Anthony comments: "She continued writing up to 1856, when she was seventy-six years old—and had at that time produced 114 volumes" (Trollope, 1883, p. 32). That means that she produced an average of four or five "volumes" (it was a time of three-volume novels) a year!

During many of those first years of depending on her pen for a living, Frances Trollope had to do her writing late at night, after her daily work, which for years involved looking after her difficult ailing husband and sick children. For a period of over a year, Fanny had to nurse two children (Henry and Emily) dying of tuberculosis as well as her moribund husband in what became a terrible family gauntlet of illnesses and then deaths. There was not much time to think about Anthony. Again, he must have felt comparatively motherless. Anthony's novels are full of motherless women, as are his mother's; there is no doubt empathy as well as hostile identification with her in this, since Fanny's mother died when she was so young.

After her return from America, Fanny Trollope's earnings kept things going well financially for a year or so. Apparently Thomas Anthony never told Fanny the full extent of his growing debts, and during that time she was spending her money with her customary lack of caution. General financial depression, especially affecting agriculture, prevailed in 1833; the owner of the land the family lived on went to law to collect the rent Thomas Anthony could not pay. Bankruptcy suddenly became necessary. The Trollopes' belongings were to be sold for debt, and the father fled secretly from England to escape debtors' prison. Anthony, no longer at Harrow, was put in charge of sneaking him on board ship to Belgium. The rest of the family followed. Then, after some months with the others at Bruges, Anthony returned to London, at age 19, to take up the junior clerkship in the postal service, a job he obtained through family friends.

He left behind the tragedy of his very sick father and two dying siblings. The older ones, Tom and Cecilia, had already gone back to England. Trollope (1883) writes:

A sadder household never was held together. They were all dying—except my mother, who would sit up night after night nursing the dying ones and writing novels the while, so that there might be a decent roof for them to die under. . . . [I was] becoming alive to the evidence of the strain which my mother was enduring. But I could do nothing but go and leave them [p. 34].

ALONE IN LONDON

Anthony lived in London in lodgings, most of the time entirely alone. His mother did not summon him to attend the funerals in Bruges of his brother Henry and then of his father although she asked Tom and Cecilia, who also were in England, to come. The contrast must have been painful to Anthony. (It was perhaps justified by Fanny's fear that he might endanger his much-needed position in the Post Office.) After her husband's death, Fanny moved back to London for a while, but soon left again, with Tom and Cecilia, for a long visit to the Continent to write another travel book.

Anthony was unhappy and alone again, working rather miserably at his menial job in the general post office. His starting salary, on which he had to support himself, was £90 a year, which was not quite enough to get by on. For two of the seven years of his London clerkship his mother was nearby or he lived with her, and he could borrow from her. But he was reluctant to do it and felt that he had no other reliable source of ready money. There were hungry days when he simply did not have enough money to eat more than the breakfast that was part of his prepaid room and board. He made a few friends; walking expeditions outside London with them were his happiest times. He had almost no social life and was awkward with women; nothing is known of his sexual experiences. He hints at dissipation—"the temptations of loose life . . . [that] prevailed with me" (Trollope, 1883, p. 51); this might mean frequenting prostitutes, but it is not clear what, if anything, his sexual activities amounted to. He got into minor trouble with moneylenders and with a girl who claimed he had promised to marry her (both situations appear more than once in his fiction). He recalled his life during these years in London as

Chapter 7

miserable and remembered having asked himself, "Could there be any escape from such dirt?" (p. 52). The language is significant; his identity could still be that of the wretched schoolboy forced to trudge the filthy roads of his youth. At age 60, he described this period poignantly:

> [I]n truth I was wretched—sometimes almost unto death, and have often cursed the hour in which I was born. There had clung to me a feeling that I had been looked upon always as an evil, an encumbrance, a useless thing, as a creature of whom those connected with him had to be ashamed. And I feel certain that in my young days I was so regarded [p. 60].

During this time Anthony conceived of becoming a writer but did not act on the idea. Nor did his mother support his plan. Yet, the determination to become a writer continued despite her discouraging advice. Fanny was worried that Anthony might desert his work at the post office. She wrote him:

> Make good the dropped aitches of your education before you take upon yourself to teach or amuse others in print. Remember the time for reading is now. . . . *We Trollopes are far too much given to pen and ink as it is. Without your turning scribbler when you might do something better.* Harrow and Winchester will stand you in good stead at the Post Office: *make [the Post Office] the instrument that will open the oyster of the world* [quoted by Ransom, 1995, pp. 135–136; italics added].

Ransom comments: "Excellent advice, and similar to the counsel she had given Tom seven years before; but for Anthony, who was searching desperately for a way of escape from his humdrum post office job, it must have seemed as though she had no faith in his abilities" (p. 136). This statement is kindly, but it seems to me that it *was* an expression of little faith in him; he must have been especially riled at the letter's reference to the hated Harrow and Winchester, which would have set off memories of misery at school when Fanny was away in America.

TURNING POINTS

Trollope describes himself, in the early days as a clerk in London, as slipshod in his functioning—provoking, and disliked by, his superiors, not quite able to support himself, and barely holding on to his government job. Later, in Ireland, where a raise in salary and decreased living expenses meant that he no longer needed to borrow from his mother, he became an efficient, trusted, and creative public servant, working indefatigably and effecting creative reforms and efficiencies. His hard work earned him a promotion and an eventual transfer back to England. In Ireland, he became a trusted, although sometimes difficult, civil servant of superior rank. He was sent all over the world to inspect, correct, and negotiate about postal regulations and installations.

The interlude in Ireland is significant. After seven years at the London post office, Anthony contrived his own escape. He applied for and was granted a transfer to Ireland to work as a surveyor's clerk, a sort of traveling inspector of the mail system. His London superiors were glad to be rid of him; the official under whom he had worked in London sent on a letter calling him "worthless." His surveyor/master in Ireland dismissed this designation "with the statement, 'I shall judge you on your own merits.' From that time to the day on which I left the service, I never heard a word of censure, nor had many months passed before I found that my services were valued. Before the year was over I had acquired the character of a thoroughly good public servant" (Trollope, 1883, p. 63). It must have been wonderful to have someone in authority trust him.

> I acknowledge the weakness of a great desire to be loved—of a strong wish to be popular with my associates. No child, no boy, no lad, no young man, had ever been less so. And I had been so poor and so little able to bear poverty. But from the day on which I set my foot in Ireland all these evils went away from me. Since that time who has had a happier life than mine? [p. 60].

Trollope abandoned his high position in the postal administration after 33 years, at the age of 53, only when he felt that he had been overlooked for further promotion. By that time (1867)

Chapter 7

his books were earning him a good income. It was in England that he became partly responsible for the institution of public mailboxes.

Glendinning (1992) believes that the turning point in Anthony's spirits, the influx of self-confidence that helped him get to Ireland, followed a recovery from a severe and mysterious illness during his sixth year as a junior clerk in London. When he was 25 years old, after visiting his mother in Paris, where she was living with Tom, Anthony developed a life-threatening sickness that persisted for months. It apparently was not tuberculosis; it was called asthma, but it is not clear exactly what it was, possibly one of those psychosomatic illnesses that can arise when things are emotionally just too much to bear—when there is too much wretchedness. If so, his sickness was perhaps an unconscious bid for Fanny's attention, a competitive reaction to Tom's having left his teaching job to begin his long stint as his mother's companion. Anthony lost a great deal of weight and was not expected to live. Fanny Trollope, so inured to tending the dying, returned to London to nurse Anthony, who recovered his health under her care. This may have been the first time since his infancy that Anthony's needs were given priority by his mother; it must have been a fulfillment of a desperately desired and long-frustrated wish. I think it may indeed have marked a turning point. Perhaps the decision after his recovery—taken, Trollope says, "boldly" (p. 58)—to confront his hostile superior in the Post Office and apply for the transfer to Ireland was already a consequence of psychic change. His active turn toward improvement, almost a rebirth, was launched.

This developmental step was like a child's suddenly becoming able to get up and walk. Anthony's job in Ireland required much travel—walking and, especially, riding. The great amount of time, "an average of forty miles a day" (p. 90), spent on the job in the active and controlling role of riding horseback—rather than being passively confined in an office—must have helped him feel less dependent, less the reluctant and shunned trudger through mired roads of his past. Paradoxically, as an adult, Trollope loved to walk for miles and miles. Of course, by this time he was doing it on his own initiative. He claimed that his creative activity took place often when he was walking or riding. I have elsewhere (Shengold, 1963, 1989) stressed the importance for psychic development of the acquisition of the power of locomotion—the ability to walk away from mother—for the attainment of a sense of separate identity. In this regard, I find it meaningful that Mullen and Munson (1996) note, "Almost all Trollope's travels saw him involved in arguments with porters" (p. 273). Porters were potential interferers with Trollope's locomotion.[1] Porters—like waiters, maids, and other servants and servers—have unconscious parental connotations because they assist with basic bodily functions and thus can arouse conflicted and ambivalent (and potentially even paranoid) reactions in those susceptible to conflicts about dependency. Dispensable and usually degraded parental substitutes, they frequently serve as displaced objects of the child's or former child's often suppressed or unconscious rage over having been mistreated. Pope-Hennessy (1971) comments on the middle-aged Trollope's complaints about the behavior of people in North America whose job was to serve him:

> The women in shops he found to be the worst of all: "An American woman who is bound by her position to serve—who is paid in some shape to supply your wants, whether to sell you a bit of soap or bring you a towel in your bedroom at an hotel—is, I think, of all human creatures the most insolent" [p. 234].

The social observation may have been accurate, but the malignant bias behind it was, I feel, unconsciously aimed at his mother. At the same time it reveals his identification with her complaints about the insolence of American servants in her book, *Domestic Manners of the Americans* (F. Trollope, 1832).

It was a psychological as well as a financial bonus that his new post in Ireland included a generous and liberating travel allowance that greatly augmented his income. He could at last easily support himself. He never afterward had realistic worries about money.

---

1. Trollope traveled all over the world, to every populated continent, both in the course of his duties for the Postal Service and after he retired, when he was sent to the United States to negotiate a new postal treaty. His job in Ireland enabled him to move about ("locomote") freely, but even in his hobbled youth he had allowed some of the associated spontaneous, active, peripatetic impulses to come through—he loved to dance. As a man, despite his bulk and ungainliness, he was a good and enthusiastic dancer. This was a trait of his mother's; Fanny had been very fond of dancing as a young woman (see Neville-Sington, 1997).

But his obsessive concerns about it continued, together with what Hall (1991) speaks of as his characteristic, "almost quixotic honesty" (p. 75).

In his new job, Trollope increasingly became an active executive force, an inspector of the failings of others. His superiors permitted him to get the job done as he thought best. He became more confident and successful; his wages increased, and his work was appreciated. He bought a horse and hired a groom who became a lifelong servant. Riding his own horse enhanced his mastery of locomotion with its unconscious developmental potential. Trollope, despite his large size and ungainliness, grew proficient enough on horseback to take up fox hunting. This sport became a passion, and hunting scenes appear perhaps a little too frequently in his novels. In *An Autobiography*, Trollope (1883) wrote of the pleasure he had in writing them. I think that taking the active role of the hunter, as well as allowing himself to enjoy the social contacts involved in hunting, marked some newly acquired flexibility of his conscience, some liberating ability to act as the aggressor and shift from masochism and passivity toward sadism. Here I am speaking from a Freudian perspective; one can put it more simply: Anthony could now be in active control. Frances Trollope was fond of horseback riding and even of going hunting when Anthony was young; it was the riding, and not the shooting, that she enjoyed. So identification with his mother as well as separation from her could have been involved—not necessarily in his consciousness—in the grown-up Anthony's riding and hunting passion, one of the many aspects for him of life with or without or as mother.

Trollope could easily allow himself to express anger and rage in his parental role of administrator. Snow (1975) describes Trollope's working persona in Ireland:

> Postmasters dreaded the sight of him. He had developed or grown into an official manner which was curiously unsympathetic and which became a characteristic of his career. In fact, it was the face that acquaintances met in his casual human relations. The manner was peremptory, aggressive, interrogatory, hectoring. It was the same with his superiors but more of an affront to subordinates [p. 59].

The once-timid although occasionally cheeky postal clerk had become transformed. He could, with the best of official motives, be one of the wielders of aggressive power, even a tyrant like his father, although a successful and sometimes appropriate one.

WRITING AND MOTHER

Although he had written privately in his journal from ages 15 to 25, Trollope began in Ireland to write novels and think of publication. This advance was evidence of the release of inhibition of creativity that comes with a more positive feeling of identity. The first two novels had an Irish setting. Although his father had written his *Encyclopaedia*, his sister Cecilia had a book in manuscript, and Tom had already published, Anthony's main model was his mother. By now she was a popular author of novels and travel books, as he was also to become many years later. (He wrote five travel books between 1858 and 1868.) Fanny helped him by getting a publisher to accept his first novel. But she did not want to read it. In his autobiography (Trollope, 1883) he comments, with cool bitterness:

> My first manuscript I gave up to my mother, agreeing with her that it would be as well that she should not look at it before she gave it to a publisher. I knew that she did not give me credit for the sort of cleverness necessary for such work. . . . My mother, my sister, my brother-in-law, and I think, my brother . . . had not expected me to come out as one of the family authors [p. 74].

His first three novels were not financially successful, although he received some encouraging reviews. He was quite discouraged after the third one was published in 1850. He was not to adopt his daily writing ritual (see later) until after he published his fourth book, *The Warden*, begun in 1853 and published in 1855. *The Warden* was the first of his novels to earn money—nineteen pounds, twenty-three shillings, and nine pence in the first two years. (Trollope kept exact accounts of what each of his works earned.) It was also the first book of his that he placed with a publisher without benefit of his mother's influence. *The Warden*

Chapter 7

began selling well when *Barchester Towers,* a kind of sequel with the same main characters, became a success, after its publication in 1857. Sometime between the writing of these two books, he began with the regular routine he was to follow for most of the rest of his life of having himself awakened every weekday morning so that he began writing at 5:30 A.M. and continued until 8:30 A.M. He then would go on to his full day of work at the post office. He kept this schedule until he retired 10 years later. He also habitually used his traveling time on trains and ships to do his self-assigned daily amount of writing.

Chapter 8

TROLLOPE'S WRITING METHOD

Labor omnia vincit improbus.

—Virgil, *Georgics*

Anthony started writing on an almost daily basis while he was employed at the postal service. He kept his full-time job there, with increasing responsibility, until 1867, when he was 53. He worked hard as an editor of a literary magazine for some years afterwards; ran unsuccessfully for Parliament; and continued writing books, reviews, articles, and stories up to the time of his physical incapacity some months before his death at age 67. In his desk was found his autobiography, a completed unpublished novel, and an unfinished one. In his lifetime he published prodigiously, more than his mother: travel books, stories, biographies and 47 novels, most in more than one volume. It has been claimed that he wrote and published more words than any other English novelist. During the first (financially unsuccessful) years of writing (1847–1857) he produced five novels. After 1857, Trollope wrote from one to four books every year—most years it was three—until his death in 1882.

There are, of course, many kinds of writers, varying as greatly in writing habits and methods as they do in their personal characteristics. Vladimir Nabokov, endowed with a prodigious memory, would fashion, revise, and polish his novels in his head over a period of months and write them out only when all had been completed. Schiller stated that he wrote best when there was the smell of rotting apples in the drawers of his writing desk. Kipling claimed he could write well only when overtaken by what seemed an outside force, which he called his "Daemon." Freud in a letter of 1896, described himself as dependent on a "modicum of misery [that I find] necessary for intensive work" (Masson, 1985, p. 181). Gubrich-Simitis (1998) comments on this statement: "This subtle unhappiness remained the spur to Freud's creativity throughout his life" (p. 18). Some writers work slowly, some rapidly, some impulsively, some compulsively. Anthony Trollope seemed to regard his writing as a prosaic and practical way of earning money and fame. He boasted of performing it as if it were a mechanical task and was fond of shocking people by telling them he regarded himself as working like a shoemaker. He often made it sound as if this were free choice. He may not have been aware of being dominated by needs of a transparently obsessive–compulsive character (about which more later). Trollope (1883) wrote of his routine:

> There are those who would be ashamed to subject themselves to such a taskmaster, and who think that the man who works with his imagination should allow himself to wait till inspiration moves him. When I have heard such doctrine preached, I have hardly been able to repress my scorn. To me it would have not been more absurd if the shoemaker were to wait for inspiration, or the tallow-chandler for the divine moment of melting [pp. 120–121].

Trollope often needed to distance emotions, which could lead him to disown what he wanted to claim and cling to. He titled his autobiography *An Autobiography*—not *My Autobiography* or even simply *Autobiography*.

As a young man, Trollope witnessed his mother, chiefly motivated by the need for money, driven to an almost daily churning out of book after book. The role of prolific writer as wage-earner is another of the many instances of Trollope's taking over attributes of his mother. Frances Trollope wrote because necessity demanded it, but there is no description of her using anything of the compulsive routine that later dominated Anthony's writing. She was, however, often forced to start her writing work at 4:00 or 5:00 in the morning and finished "her work before the world had begun to be aroused" (Trollope, 1883, p. 25) Anthony turned out to write daily starting at similar very early hours, even after he stopped working at the Post Office. When he was 44 years old, he wrote of himself:

> It was my practice to be at my table every morning at 5:30 A.M.; and it was also my practice to allow myself no mercy. An old groom, whose business it was to call me, and to whom I paid 5 pounds a year extra for the duty, allowed himself no mercy. During all those years at Waltham Cross [1859–1871] he never was once late with the coffee which it was his duty to bring me. I do not know that I ought not to feel that I owe more to him than to any one else for the success I have had. By beginning at that hour I could complete my literary work before I dressed for breakfast [p. 271].

Trollope sounds more grateful to his groom than to his mother, whose habits of writing early in the morning every day he was imitating.

Trollope could make his fixed method sound like clockwork, literally:

> It is still my custom, though of late I have become a little lenient to myself to write with my watch before me, and to require from myself 250 words every quarter of an hour. I have found that the 250 words have been forthcoming as regularly as my watch went [p. 272].

Perhaps the process was not quite as methodical as he depicted it. Certainly he took pride in his work and put passion into it, as few shoemakers would. But when writing generalizations about the process of writing, he described it coolly enough—in contrast to how emotionally involved he could be when thinking and daydreaming about his characters.

> I had arranged a system of task-work for myself, which I would strongly recommend to those who feel as I have felt, that labor, when not made absolutely obligatory by the circumstances of the hour, should never be allowed to become spasmodic. There was no day on which it was my positive duty to write for the publishers, as it was my duty to work for the Post Office. I was free to be idle if I pleased.

Chapter 8

> But as I had made up my mind to undertake this second profession, I found it to be expedient to *bind myself by certain self-imposed laws*. When I have commenced a new book, I have *always* prepared a diary, divided into weeks, and carried on for the period which I have allowed myself for the completion of the work. *In this I have entered, day by day, the number of pages I have written, so that if at any time I have slipped into idleness for a day or two, the record of that idleness has been there, staring me in the face, and demanding of me increased labour, so that the deficiency might be supplied.* According to the circumstances of the time—whether my other business might be then heavy or light, or whether the book which I was writing was or was not wanted with speed—*I have allotted myself so many pages a week. The average number has been about 40.* It has been placed as low as 20, and has risen to 112

We may note the exactitude! The passage continues in the same vein:

> *And as a page is an ambiguous term, my page has been made to contain 250 words; and as words, if not watched, will have a tendency to straggle, I have had every word counted as I went.* In the bargains I have made with publishers I have—not, of course, with their knowledge, but in my own mind—undertaken always to supply them with so many words, and *I have never put a book out of hand short of the number by a single word.* I may also say that the excess has been very small. *I have prided myself on completing my work exactly within the proposed dimensions. But I have prided myself especially on completing it within the proposed time—and I have always done so.* There has ever been the record before me, and a week passed with an insufficient number of pages has been a blister to my eye, and a month so disgraced would have been a sorrow to my heart.... *Nothing surely is so potent as a law that may not be disobeyed. It has the force of the water-drop that hollows the stone....* I *have not once, through all my literary career, felt myself even in danger of being late with my task* [pp. 118–120, italics added].

I have italicized some of the phrases and details that highlight the obsessive–compulsive cast of mind that dominated Trollope's method of writing. The potency of the water-drop metaphor, with its cleansing, regular, slow, dependable, almost inevitable, and timeless connotations is to be noted. It also connotes penetration, in relation to the stone—and torture. Aggressive penetration would be the subject of inner struggle, of wish as well as avoidance, for Trollope.

Part of his writing style was an insistence on penetrating the flow of his fiction with general observations and personal comments. They also appear in his mother's novels. Sometimes these comments by the author can be irritating if they are not appreciated as playful by the reader. For example, in *The Bertrams*, Trollope (1859) says of one of his heroines, "Adela Gauntlet was—No; for once I will venture to have a heroine without describing her. Let each reader make what he will of her; fancy her of any outward shape and color that he please, and endow her with any amount of divine beauty" (p. 41). My response to this is, "No thanks, I'd rather not." Trollope was fond of indulging in occasional remarks in some of the novels which would predict future turns of his plot, an intrusive habit to which Henry James (1883) strongly objected. But all these "penetrations" are an active taking control that may have reassured an author so intent on control.

Further obsessional details are furnished by Lady Juliet Pollock, a writer and friend and neighbor to whom Trollope confided his writing method in 1866:

> His manner of writing a novel was thoroughly methodical. Before commencing it he would settle its length, and assign so many days to writing it, at so many words a day. Every morning the appointed portion for the day would be duly put on paper, and the day marked out, in a section of the calendar prepared for the purpose, *as the days are by schoolboys to show how nearly their holidays are approaching*. Without fail or mistake the novel was always finished in this way upon the exact date previously fixed for its completion. Trollope's writing for the press was very distinct and regular, and entirely free from alterations or additions, etc. It seems to have flowed from his *pen like clear water from a tap*. When he went, I think for the first

Chapter 8

time, to Australia, he asked me to correct the proofs of one of his shorter tales—*The Golden Lion of Granpere*—but there was really nothing for me to do [quoted in Terry, 1987, pp. 90–91; italics added].

Lady Pollock's metaphors are, perhaps unconsciously, quite empathic. She has caught the connection with the degraded schoolboy's need for order, and the relief from the water-drop urgency in the image of the flow of water from a controlled but not exigent tap.

One more example—Trollope (1883) describes writing his short novel, *Lady Anna*, while sailing to Australia:

> Every word of this was written at sea during the two months required for our voyage, and was done day by day—with the intermission of one day's illness—for eight weeks, at the rate of 66 pages of manuscript in each week, every page of manuscript containing 250 words. Every word was counted. . . . I have sometimes been ridiculed for the methodical details of my business. But by these contrivances I have been preserved from many troubles; and I have saved others with whom I have worked—editors, publishers, and printers—from much trouble also [pp. 346–347].

Trollope shows the conflict (drive and defense) when he writes that he is a rapid writer who has made errors:

> But the writer for the press is rarely called upon—a writer of books should never be called upon—to send his manuscript *hot from his hand* to the printer. It has been my practice to read everything four times at least—thrice in manuscript and once in print [p. 178; italics added for the unconscious masturbatory reference].

Trollope seems too modest in the estimate of his own powers when he says of his method: "I have never fancied myself to be a man of genius, but had I been so I think I might [still] well have subjected myself to these trammels" (p. 120).

Glendinning (1992) points out that the publishers, especially those who contracted for a three-volume novel, first to be printed (serially) in parts in magazines as well as the all-powerful lending library chains that dominated sales in Trollope's time, had stipulated requirements that favored these methodical ways. Trollope's ways and devices were adaptive; but no other Victorian author is known to have responded with quite the determined and enthusiastic regularity of Trollope, who (paradoxically) put passion into obeying his emotion-constricting "laws" and into his depiction of his characters and their fates.

ANONYMITY

There was at least one uncharacteristic change in Trollope's ways in the 1860s, during the middle of his writing career. He had been criticized for writing too much and too quickly. He responded, as if to a challenge to see whether his novels would sell on their own, by deciding to try to publish anonymously several one-volume novels with a Continental rather than an English setting. It could not have been easy for him to put aside the remunerative value of his reputation. But perhaps there was here the considerable attraction of fulfilling a wish from his miserable childhood: to be able to make a new start. He may also have wanted to break with his compulsive regularity. He read about Bohemia and Germany and, using his visits abroad for more background material, persuaded a (for him) new publisher, John Blackwood, to accept two short novels, *Nina Balatka*, set in Prague (Trollope, 1866b), and *Linda Tressel*, set in Hamburg (Trollope, 1868). Neither novel sold well or attracted much favorable notice. The anonymity yielded to a few critics perceptive enough to recognize Trollope's style; Henry James, who reviewed *Nina Balatka*, recognized the author at once. Blackwood was understandably reluctant for financial reasons to continue with a projected third anonymous novel, and Trollope gave up the experiment. He did later write short stories with foreign settings under his own name; in 1877 he wrote a lengthy story that he set in Austria, "Why Frau Frohmann Raised Her Prices," which has its own biographical significance; I return to it in a subsequent chapter.

DISORDER AND PROVOCATION

It is not uncommon that compulsive characters feel constrained to be disorderly as well as orderly. I have noted how the need for order would certainly have been intensified by the complete lack of control of Trollope's circumstances when he was a child and by the failure of his parents to provide him with predictable ways of living and safe places to be in. Poverty, exile, and death haunted the family. There were also the boy's reactions to the repulsive dirtiness he could never avoid in his miles of walking back and forth from Harrow in dust and mud over so many years.

All these could also have evoked the contrary and provocative wish for disorder, both out of spite toward the "bad" parents (and their internalized mental representations—the bad parental part of his conscience) and from a compulsion to repeat the traumatic past. The neurotic need to repeat would have been motivated by an attempt to hold on (in unconscious fantasy, I speculate) to the promise of the much-needed mental images of good (beloved and loving) parents, in the vain but insistent hope that everything would turn out good and loving. These sadomasochistic reactive mental conflicts—hating and yet spitefully cultivating dirt, disorder, and rage—are typical of victims of child abuse and deprivation, of soul murder.

The contrary wish for disorder was manifestly present in Trollope's interpersonal relations as a young man: he was actively and compulsively provocative in his unhappy early working days when he was regularly "late with my task." This behavior is in great contrast to the older Trollope's never being late with his writing deadlines. Before he began to supplement his income by writing, there were the early years in London at the general Post Office:

> I must certainly acknowledge that the first seven years of my official life were neither creditable to myself nor useful to the public service. These seven years were passed in London, and during this period of my life it was my duty to be present every morning at the office punctually at 10 a.m. I think I commenced my quarrels with the authorities there by having in my possession a watch which was always ten minutes late. I know that I very soon achieved a character for irregularity, and came to be regarded as a black sheep by men around me who were not themselves, I think, very good public servants [Trollope, 1883, pp. 43–44].

Trollope's Writing Method

Some stubborn provocativeness continued even after he had achieved advancement, had become "known to be a thoroughly efficient public servant" (p. 133), and had been sent on official inspection and consultation missions to Scotland, Egypt, and the West Indies. He says of his work at the post office: "I was fond of the department, and when matters came to be considered, I generally had an opinion of my own. I have no doubt that I often made myself very disagreeable. I know that I sometimes tried to do so. But I could hold my own because I knew my business and was useful" (p. 134). Here Trollope was describing his official functioning in the late 1850s, when he was being sent all over Britain and abroad on responsible special assignments—inspecting, negotiating, troubleshooting. In 1859 his good work was rewarded by an appointment as Surveyor to the Eastern District of England, a permanent transfer from Ireland; he had had only temporary assignments to England before this. He was well respected and of course was not always difficult. He was also doing well with the sale of his books; 1859 was the first year he earned more from his writing than from his salary.

In *An Autobiography* (Trollope, 1883), he makes clear that there was a kind of sadistic delight in his provocativeness. He could enjoy hating and quarreling. He is writing chiefly of his feuds with his superior, Sir Rowland Hill, whom, only slightly disguised as Sir Gregory Hardlines, he made the object of ridicule in his novel *The Three Clerks* (Trollope, 1858). It was brave of him to do this; he was still working for the post office when he wrote the book, but he was no longer serving under Rowland Hill.

> How I loved, when I was contradicted—as I was very often and no doubt properly—to do instantly as I was bid, and then to prove that what I was doing was fatuous, dishonest, expensive and impracticable! And then there were the feuds,—*such delicious feuds*! [pp. 282–283; italics added].

Provoking quarrels in which he could feel the active winner was a reliving, with the reversal of his role and the outcome, of the terrible "worst" time of his boyhood at Harrow Weald alone with his father.

He wrote poignantly of his post office career:

I think that I became popular among those with whom I associated. I have long been aware of a certain weakness in my own character, which I may call a *craving for love*. I have ever had a wish to be liked by those around me—a wish that during the first half of my life was never gratified. In my school-days no small part of my misery came from the envy with which I regarded the popularity of popular boys.... Among the clerks in the Post Office I held my own fairly after the first two or three years; but even then I regarded myself as something of a Pariah" [Trollope, 1883, p. 159; italics added].

He had, of course, described himself "as a Pariah" as a schoolboy earlier in his autobiography.

POSTSCRIPT: BENJAMIN FRANKLIN'S *THE AUTOBIOGRAPHY*

"Let thy child's first lesson be obedience, and the second will be what thou wilt."
—Benjamin Franklin

I have been examining the compulsivity that dominated Trollope's method of working. I have cast about for ways of understanding how the orderliness, diligence, and exactitude (even to the extreme of counting words) may have functioned usefully for him—chiefly as a counter to, and an attempt to, control the dirt and disorder that had assaulted him as a child and a youth. But, as follows from my earlier chapter on creativity, Trollope's use of his method should not be reduced to defense against psychopathology. As a kind of antidote to the tenor of my remarks so far, I want to make a comparison with the writing habits of another versatile creative figure, Benjamin Franklin. He too supplies an example of compulsivity combined with creativity. I think this comparison grants some perspective into the unknown: the issue of how inborn capacity, not determined by circumstance, needs to be taken into account.

Benjamin Franklin lived a long and creative life. He was born in 1706 in Boston, and his life spanned most of the 18th century (as Trollope's did most of the 19th). He was the 15th child and the youngest son (therefore, named Benjamin after his prototype in *Genesis*) of his father's 17 children (by two wives). His own mother had 10 children. Little is known about her, and she is scarcely mentioned in his autobiography. Franklin (1771) simply writes that she had "an excellent constitution" and then skips to her death (at 85) and quotes from the tombstone for his parents he erected on which he had had inscribed, "She [was] a discreet and virtuous Woman" (pp. 1315–1316).

Benjamin was sent to grammar school at age eight and had less than one year of formal schooling; he was self-taught after that. He was a compulsive reader. "From a child I was fond of Reading, and all the little Money that came into my Hands was ever laid out in Books" (p. 1317). As a young man he taught himself Latin, Italian, French, and Spanish. When Benjamin was 10 years old, his father—a successful tradesman, a chandler—took him out of school in order to teach his youngest son the family trade. Benjamin did not like that trade, and his father, kindly and considerately, tried to help him find apprenticeship in another. Finally, because Benjamin was so fond of books, his father apprenticed him after a few years to Benjamin's 21-year-old brother, James, who had set himself up in Boston as a printer. Benjamin was then 12 years old, and he reluctantly signed indentures to serve as apprentice to his brother until he was 21. He worked long, hard days as his brother's printer's devil. He also wrote, and his brother printed, ballads based on the news of the day, and then sold them on the street. He also began to do some experiments and fashion some minor inventions. Later James Franklin started a newspaper and Benjamin, submitting his essays under an assumed name, began to write for it without his brother's knowledge. In the little spare time that was left to him of his working day, he continued his education by voracious reading. He wanted to teach himself to write well and to enlarge his vocabulary; to do this he developed his own "method." Franklin spent much of his spare money to buy books. He much admired a volume he bought of Addison and Steele's *Spectator*, from which

> I took some of the papers, and making short hints of the sentiment in each sentence, laid them by a few days, and then, without looking at the book, tried to complete the papers again by expressing each hinted sentiment at length, and as fully as it had been expressed before, in any suitable

Chapter 8

words that should come to hand. Then I compared my *Spectator* with the original, discovered some of my faults and corrected them. But I found I wanted a stock of words, or a readiness in recollecting and using them, which I thought I should have acquired if I had gone on making verses; since the continual occasion for words of the same import, but of different length, to suit the measure, or of different sound for the rhyme, would have *laid me under a constant necessity* of searching for variety, and also have tended to fix that variety in my mind, and *make me master* of it. Therefore I took some of the tales and turned them into verse; and, after a time, when I had pretty well forgotten the prose, turned them back again. *I also sometimes jumbled my collection of hints into confusion, and after some weeks endeavored to reduce them into the best order,* before I began to form the full sentences and complete the paper. This was to teach me *method* in the arrangement of thoughts [Franklin, 1771, pp. 1319–1320; italics added].

Franklin's compulsivity, as well as his ingenuity, are evident here. His very style shows his obsessive–compulsive frame of mind, that is so egregiously and occasionally charmingly displayed in his *Poor Richard's Almanack* (Franklin, 1732). Franklin did not make up most of the maxims. He took most of them from books he had read but often rephrased them in his own words. Here is a selection that features money, control, and order:

Industry pays Debts, Despair increases them [p. 10]. Early to bed and early to rise, makes a man healthy, wealthy, and wise [p. 16]. Forewarned, forearmed [p. 16]. Proportion your Charity to the Strength of your Estate, or God will Proportion your Estate to the Weakness of your Charity [p. 21]. Neither trust, nor contend, nor lay wagers, nor lend; and you'll have peace to your Life's end [p. 27]. Beware of little Expenses: a small Leak will sink a great Ship [p. 38]. He that pays for work before it's done, has but a pennyworth for two pence [p. 42]. Get what you can, and what you get hold; 'tis the Stone that will turn all your Lead into Gold [p. 52].

Franklin's way of proceeding shows both similarities to and differences from Trollope's obsessive–compulsive method of writing. Both men had (probably inherited) great natural talents. Both were capable of working hard and long. Both were ambivalent about their compulsive needs. Both were capable of humor. Franklin rebelled against the obedience he preached and often practiced. He is perhaps the greatest of the American Revolutionaries. He left his apprenticeship to his brother and, at 17, ran away from Boston to Philadelphia before his assigned time was up, much to the disapproval of his father. He worked there at first as a journeyman printer. In Philadelphia, out of the shadow of his father and older siblings, his great gifts were recognized and appreciated, and he began his successful and varied career as printer, writer, inventor, scientist, and diplomat.

A need for control similar to Trollope's is shown in a later part of Franklin's autobiography. He is writing about a time after his marriage in 1730:

> It was about this time I conceived the bold and arduous project of arriving at moral perfection. I wished to live without committing any fault at any time.... For this purpose I therefore contrived the following methods.... I included under thirteen names of virtues *all that at that time occurred to me as necessary or desirable*, and annexed to each a short precept, which fully expressed the extent I gave to its meaning:
> 1. Temperance. Eat not to dullness; drink not to elevation.
> 2. Silence. Speak not but what may benefit others or yourself; avoid trifling conversation.
> 3. Order. Let all your things have their places; let each part of your business have its time.
> 4. Resolution. Resolve to perform what you ought; perform without fail what you resolve.
> 5. Frugality. Make no expense but to do good to others or yourself; i.e., waste nothing.
> 6. Industry. Lose no time; be always employed in something useful; cut off all unnecessary actions.
> 7. Sincerity. Use no hurtful deceit; think innocently and justly, and, if you speak, speak accordingly.

Chapter 8

 8. Justice. Wrong none by doing injuries, or omitting the benefits that are your duty.
 9. Moderation. Avoid extremes; forbear resenting injuries so much as you think they deserve.
10. Cleanliness. Tolerate no uncleanliness in body, clothes, or habitation.
11. Tranquillity. Be not disturbed at trifles, or at accidents common or unavoidable.
12. Chastity. Rarely *use venery* but for health or offspring, never to dullness, weakness, or the injury of your own or another's peace or reputation. [Italics added to indicate some righteous self-serving and priggishness.]
13. Humility. Imitate Jesus and Socrates [Franklin, 1771, pp. 1383–1385].

He continues:

> I made a little book, in which I allotted a page for each of the virtues. I ruled each page with red ink, so as to have seven columns, one for each day of the week, marking each column with a letter for the day. I crossed these columns with thirteen red lines, marking the beginning of each line with the first letter of one of the virtues, on which line, and in its proper column, I might mark, by a little black spot, every fault I found upon examination to have been committed respecting that virtue upon that day. I determined to give a week's strict attention to each of the virtues successively. . . . Proceeding thus [from first to last] I could go through a course complete in thirteen weeks, and four courses in a year [pp. 1386–1387]. . . . The precept of order requiring that every part of my business should have its allotted time, one page in my little book contained the following scheme of employment for the twenty-four hours of a natural day [p. 1389].

A diagram containing the scheme with space and instructions for each hour follows.

The tone here is very much like Trollope's. Of course, Franklin did not reach moral perfection. (As for virtue number 13, on Humility: "Imitate Jesus and Socrates," I wish I could feel that

Franklin was fully conscious of the humor and irony here, but I cannot.) But perhaps the compulsion involved in his use of the little book, which he kept on with for years, and the eventual, perhaps temporary, diminution of the black spots of his faults gave him a kind of consolatory permission for the occasional disorder, fault and sin that seemed to have been part of the behavior of this complex, worldly and, despite his presentation of simplicity, contradictory man.

Chapter 9

DAYDREAMING IN THE SERVICE OF CREATIVITY AND OF SEXUALITY

At the age of fifteen, I had commenced the dangerous habit of keeping a journal, and this I maintained for ten years. The volumes remained in my possession, unregarded—till 1870, when I examined them, and, with many blushes, destroyed them. They convicted me of folly, ignorance, indiscretion, idleness, extravagance, and conceit. But they had habituated me to the rapid use of pen and ink, and taught me how to express myself with facility.

—Anthony Trollope
An Autobiography

Alongside and in contrast to his dry obsessional methods and compulsive actions, Anthony Trollope was an inveterate daydreamer, a habit begun on his long, dirt-gathering walks to school as a child that encouraged "extravagance and conceit." But, on further reflection, there was a similar intensity behind both modes of operation. Daydreaming appears to have had for him the obligatory, even addictive, quality that later adhered to his professional writing, the ending of one book being followed the very next day by the beginning of another. Conscious fantasizing was another way of creating a world full of order and success and of satisfying his "craving for love"—as well as expressing hate and revenge. Trollope (1883) wrote that the habit of daydreaming "had been the occupation of my life for six or seven years before I went to

Chapter 9

the Post Office" (p. 43). Glendenning (1992) points out that the "occupation" started about the time that Fanny Trollope went away to America. I agree with her feeling that daydreaming then became his "refuge and comfort" (p. 41). It unconsciously evoked the presence of, and replaced with his own imagination, the absent nourishing and protective mother, who, however unreliable, had first taught him the value of imagination and play.

Freud (1908) linked creativity to daydreaming. Trollope (1883) attributes to this habit his motivation and even in part his facility for novel-writing. He calls daydreaming "castle-building" (p. 43).

In "The Panjandrum," one of his *Editor's Tales*, a collection of stories written when he was editor of the *St. Paul's Magazine*, Trollope (1870) in his fictional role as editor-narrator tells of writing a story at the end of the 1830s—a time when Trollope was in his teens—based on a sentence of a young girl overheard in a walk in a park, "Oh Anne, I do so wonder what he's like." The narrator then begins to daydream, in which he turns the girl into his own sister who is about to get married; this daydream leads to his producing a plot for his story. The narrator of "The Panjandrum" is one of a group of five young would-be writers who intend to found a magazine, under the leadership of an older married woman. He is expecting to become the editor of the proposed but ultimately never-to-be-launched magazine, to be called "The Panjandrum." The narrator, who at first felt unable to think of a subject for a short story, describes the creative functioning of the daydreaming that followed his overhearing the young girl. He tells how, unexpectedly, "unforced imagination came to play upon the matter" (p. 162) to form his plot, and adds:

> These wondrous *castles in the air* never get themselves well built when the mind, with premeditated skill and labor, sets itself to work to build them. It is when they come uncalled for that they stand erect and strong[1] before the mind's eye with every mullioned window perfect, the rounded walls all there, the embrasures curt, the fosse dug, and the drawbridge down [p. 163; italics added].

---

1. An erection of the mind—see my quote from Flaubert on p. 120.

The phrase I have italicized is the same that Trollope uses to designate daydreaming in his *An Autobiography*.

I have noted that in that later book Trollope (1883) criticizes daydreaming as "a dangerous mental practice" (p. 43); whatever the dangers, he felt he had put it to good use during his lifetime. It was a habit derived from the need to turn to his own resources when deserted and rejected by family, teachers, and schoolmates—introversion as a way to some narcissistic (in the sense of taking care of himself) and perhaps even sexual satisfaction.

> As a boy, even as a child, I was thrown much upon myself. I have explained, when speaking of my school-days, how it came to pass that other boys would not play with me. I was therefore alone, and had to form my plays within myself. Play of some kind was necessary to me then, as it has always been [p. 42].

Miller (1987) interprets this passage from *An Autobiography* as the author's defining "his habit of daydreaming as substitute play, solitary play or play with himself, with an implicit sexual connotation also present in [his] phrase [characterizing it as a] 'dangerous mental practice'" (p. 83). In his autobiography, Trollope had also called his writing in a journal for 10 years, starting at age 15, a "dangerous habit" (p. 42). The semihumorous, repetitive use of the word dangerous by Anthony in association with writing as well as with "castle-building" suggests resonance with some unconscious masturbatory meaning here—action coupled with fantasy, involving perhaps the forbidden simultaneous use of his hands and of his mind.

I agree with Miller that there is also evidence of sublimated conflictive sexuality in Trollope's description of his sometimes daring to break his "rules" in the flush of excitement provided by his characters. In contrast to the measured ("water-drop") doses of time, lines, and words, Trollope (1883) writes that there were occasions—I venture to think of these as "occasions" of mental ejaculation—

> when my work has been quickest done—and it has sometimes been done very quickly—the rapidity has been *achieved by hot pressure*, not in the conception, but in the

telling of the story. Instead of writing eight pages a day, I have written sixteen; instead of working five days a week, I have worked seven. . . . And I am sure that the work so done has had in it the best truth and the highest spirit that I have been able to produce. At such times I have been able to imbue myself thoroughly with the characters I have had in *hand.* I have wandered alone among the rocks and woods, crying at their grief, laughing at their absurdities, and thoroughly enjoying their joy. *I have been impregnated with my own creations till it has been my only excitement to sit with the pen in my hand, and drive my team before me at as quick a pace as I could make them travel* [pp. 175–176; italics added].[2]

The quoted passage would certainly illustrate the breaking through of the "hot pressure" of drives that can transiently overcome the artist's individual and characteristic defensive "rules" and "laws." The sexual imagery—again with stress on fantasy, solitude, and references to the hand—suggests unconscious masturbatory equivalence, evoking for me Flaubert's descriptive remark about literary creativity; he noted that erections of the mind, like those of the body, do not always come at will. (I have been unable to find the source of this, which I think is somewhere in Flaubert's marvelous but voluminous letters.)

Trollope (1883) continues: "Study was not my bent, and I could not please myself by being all idle. Thus it came to pass that I was always going about with some castle in the air firmly built within my mind. Nor were these efforts at architecture spasmodic, or subject to constant change from day to day" (p. 42). So controls were still in place.

Miller's (1987) observation underlines Trollope's caution: "Both in his account of his daydreams and in his account of the process

---

2. The metaphor of being in control of a team of horses might remind those who have read Freud's (1909) case of "Little Hans" that the small boy's fear of horses was due to his sexually charged fantasies (sadomasochistic and involving his parents) in which Freud felt the boy was equating the horse primarily with his father. It does not necessarily follow that Anthony had such fantasies, but if he did he dealt with them (as an adult) chiefly by active mastery as an enthusiastic rider of horses and hunter of foxes—like his mother— rather than by developing phobic symptoms about animals.

later on in writing, Trollope emphasized the way his acts of imagination were rule-bound, made to submit to laws of internal consistency, continuity, probability and moderation" (p. 82). Trollope (1883) writes: "For weeks, for months, [even] from year to year, I would carry on the same tale, binding myself down to certain laws, to certain proportions, and proprieties, and unities" (p. 42). The daydreaming was characteristically monitored by the child's, and later the man's, compulsive need for control: anything too strange, violent, or glorious was kept out. Anthony's conscience allowed a moderated gratification of narcissistic and libidinal wishes.

> Nothing impossible was ever introduced—nor even anything which, from outward circumstances, would seem to be violently improbable. I myself was of course my own hero. Such is the nature of castle-building. But I never became a king, or a duke—much less when my height and personal appearance were fixed could *I become an Antinuous,* or six feet high. . . . But I was a very clever person, and beautiful young women used to be fond of me. And I strove to be kind of heart, and open of hand, and noble in thought . . . and altogether I was a very much better fellow than I have ever succeeded in being since. This had been the occupation of my life for six or seven years before I went to the Post Office, and was by no means abandoned when I commenced my work. There can, I imagine, hardly be *a more dangerous mental practice*; but I have often doubted whether, had it not been my practice, I should ever have written a novel. I learned in this way to maintain an interest in a fictitious story, to dwell on a work created by my own imagination, and to *live in a world altogether outside the world of my own material life.* In after years I have done the same—with this difference, that *I have discarded the hero of my early dreams, and have been able to lay my own identity aside* [pp. 42–43; italics added].

HOMOSEXUALITY AND BISEXUALITY

Trollope began publishing at a time when in England and America wide precirculation of novels in the magazines in serial form and

Chapter 9

the flourishing of lending libraries made reading fiction (especially reading aloud in the evening in the family setting) as popular among the middle classes as television is today. But these practices led to the prudish censorship of anything even faintly sexual. Nothing could be permitted, as Dickens put it (in the mouth of Mr. Podsnap, from *Our Mutual Friend*), that would bring a blush to the cheek of a young person; this was unlike English fiction from Elizabethan times to the early 19th century. Trollope was a man of his time, and he usually had to give in to the Podsnappery of his publishers, despite his seeming (judged from some of his novels) but perhaps reluctant willingness to give sex its due as a powerful motivational force. Sex is there in his novels, sometimes obliquely or symbolically referred to. And sexual sin is almost always punished; he wrote about dissipation, prostitution—without using the word—and adultery. He did not write directly about homosexuality.

Trollope wrote in his disquisition on "castle-building" that he could not aspire to be an Antinous; I take this to be a negation that, in the context, may reveal a suppressed wish. Antinous was the beautiful Bithynian youth, the beloved catamite of the middle-aged Emperor Hadrian, who had many statues made of him after the young lover's early death. Referring to him suggests a passive homosexual wish on Trollope's part, expressed by way of negation and surely unconscious.

There is one instance of a youth's infatuation with a somewhat older man in Trollope's (1860) novel, *Castle Richmond*, that seems also to involve homosexual attachment; here too the author was probably not aware of the implication. The 23-year-old man and the 16-year-old youth embrace, but there is no overt sexual contact. Trollope could have unconsciously seen himself in the role of either of these characters; he certainly had needed a father figure or a loving older brother when he was 16. Hall (1991). in his biography of Trollope, without mentioning homosexuality, points out the adult Trollope's similarity in personality to the older man, the impetuous Owen Fitzgerald (pp. 109–110) with his impatience, compulsive and often selfish honesty, and passion for fox hunting. But there is no physical resemblance, except perhaps to the young Trollope as transfigured in his daydreams. Owen is described as spectacularly beautiful: "His tall figure . . . was perfect in its symmetry of strength. His bright chestnut hair clustered round his forehead, and his eye shone like that of a hawk. . . . Owen Fitzgerald's lips were as full and lusty as Apollo's" (Trollope, 1860, p. 238). Here is a young Greek God: an Apollo, if not an Antinous; but like Antinous, one who could be the love of an older man like Hadrian. There is, in the same novel, a corresponding, and a fox-hunting, older man, Sam O'Grady, who resembles the then 45-year-old author/fox-hunter. O'Grady makes a striking appearance in a few paragraphs that suggests the author was conscious of portraying himself. He is described as "impetuous . . . *a stout heavy man* . . . some fifty years of age [riding a large horse]. This was Sam O'Grady, the master of the Duhallow hounds, the god of Owen's idolatry" [pp. 248–249; italics added]. So Owen is both the worshipful younger boy and the worshipped older man. Antinous after his death was to become the god of Hadrian's idolatry.

In the same novel, Trollope (1860) also makes an observation that shows the devaluative side of his ambivalence toward the passivity and submissiveness of women: "The obedience of women to men—to those men to whom they are legally bound—is, I think, the most remarkable trait in human nature. Nothing equals it but the instinctive loyalty of a dog" (p. 379). This novel contains a description of the heroine's, Lady Clara's, feelings toward Owen Fitzgerald, whom she ultimately does not choose to marry: "His was a spirit before which hers would bend and feel itself subdued. With him she could realize all that she had dreamed of woman's love; and that dream which is so sweet to some women—of women's subjugation" (pp. 162–163). Unconscious resonance with such passive sexual yearnings—what Freud would call the negative oedipal side of Anthony's hatred for his father—could well have motivated similar identifications with some of his heroines, many of them full of conflicting ambivalence about submission—notably his beloved "pet," Lily Dale (see chapter 10).

Glendinning (1992) cites a passage from *The Duke's Children* (Trollope, 1880) that she feels is indicative of Trollope's tender affection for his sons, especially the older one, Harry. One of Trollope's favorite characters—he writes of loving him "so much" (Trollope, 1883, p. 360)—Plantagenet Palliser, now Duke of Omnium, is talking with his son in the library of the Beargarden Club. "Then the father looked around the room furtively, and seeing that the door was shut, and that they were assuredly alone, he put out his hand and gently stroked the young man's hair. It was almost a caress, as though he would have said to himself, 'Were he my daughter, I would kiss him'" (Glendinning, 1992, pp. 395–396). Glendinning adds, "This . . . cannot have been comfortable reading for Harry" (p. 396).

The many men and women in Trollope's fiction with marked tendencies usually associated with the opposite sex imply, I think, a deeper than average intensity of the inevitable human and inherently disturbing quality of unconscious bisexuality (cf. Glendinning, 1992, p. 200). We cannot know if, how, or how much of this homosexual feeling Trollope allowed himself to apprehend (either in himself or in others), but there is no evidence that it was in his responsible conscious awareness. (As I point out repeatedly in this book, Trollope's identificatory tie to the mother who neglected him was central to his adult adjustment; I am suggesting that part of this identification, and often a healthy and adaptive part, was an intermittent unconscious life *as* mother.)

ANGER AND CONFLICTING FANTASIES

Not all Trollope's daydreams were benevolent, loving, or about making love. Sadism and revenge also surfaced: "Like Johnny Eames in *The Small House at Allington*, he sometimes built 'pernicious castles in the air . . black castles, with cruel dungeons, into which hardly a ray of light would find its way'" (Glendinning, 1992, p. 105). There were also narcissistic daydreams. Trollope, after leaving the postal service, tried to get elected to Parliament. (This had, parenthetically, been an aspiration in his boyhood.) The attempt failed—he came in third in a field of three. But he wrote the Palliser series of parliamentary novels, in which, as Glendinning astutely remarks, "The adventurous career of Phineas Finn was Anthony's climactic, definitive castle in the air" (p. 385). At least it was definitive insofar as fulfilling the boyhood wish for success and power as represented by being in Parliament. The omnipotent author could make and break not only Members of Parliament, but Cabinet Members and Prime Ministers.

Miller (1987) points to the resemblance between Trollope's linking his creativity to daydreaming and Freud's (1908) generalizations about an artist's ability to fulfill his wishes, including narcissistic, sexual, and hostile wishes, in the transformed creative fantasy of his art. Freud also noted that an artist's creative transformations of reveries into art—that is, if the art is successful—could enable him to achieve fame, wealth, and the admiration and love of others in reality. But both Freud and Trollope were describing the impetus for creative imagination and not the source of its power. The daydreams also had another adaptive and practical role for Trollope: they provided a vehicle for working out details of plot and character before he would sit down and write his 250 words per quarter hour.

In *An Autobiography* and elsewhere, Trollope was wont to ascribe his ability to write to the two somewhat contradictory methods I have detailed in this and the last chapter. These ways involve clashing emphases concerning the importance of the use of imagination and inspiration. He insisted repeatedly, in conversation and in his books, that writing was only a craft that depended on sitting down and doing the work methodically and routinely.

The application to duty was characteristic of the work (writing and otherwise) of both parents. Fanny's compulsive potentials were a response to need, used willfully and adaptively to accomplish the financial support of her family in the face of so much unexpected poverty and family illness. Thomas Anthony's version was a stubborn, hostile, and plodding aspect of his compulsive character. That character may have had a healthier and more dependable quality before it became increasingly rigid, self-defeating, and paranoid with the toxic deterioration that followed calomel addiction. Anthony's compulsive methodology followed more the paternal than the maternal model—although he may have exaggerated it in his descriptions; there was a flexibility and certainly much more humor in Anthony's compulsive tendencies than in his father's darker and more destructive ones. What was paranoid in the father is more like eccentricity in the son. Trollope could compromise. In a letter written in 1866 to one of his publishers about serialization of a prospective novel, he alludes in a kind of oxymoron to his "mechanical genius:

> It would not be practicable to divide 20 numbers into 30 equal parts, unless the work be specially done with this intent. I commonly divide a number of 32 pages . . . into 4 chapters each. If you wish the work to be so arranged as to run either to 20 or to 30 numbers, I must work each

of the 20 numbers by 6 chapters, taking care that the chapters run so equally, two and two as to make each four into one equal part or each 6 into one equal part. There will be some trouble in this, but having a mechanical mind I think I can do it.... You will also understand that if your mind be made up either to 30 or to 20, you need not put my mechanical genius to work [quoted in Hall, 1991, pp. 291–292].

(It seems to me that here Trollope's rage for order makes what he writes almost incoherent, but probably the publisher knew what he meant. Note that he links his compulsive bent to "genius.")

Fanny tended to be overindulgent with her children; Thomas Anthony was harsh and always interfered with their play or leisure by ordering them to do lessons or chores. Anthony (Trollope, 1883) wrote:

During the last ten years of [my father's] life, he spent nearly the half of his time in bed, suffering agony from sick headaches. But he was never idle unless when suffering.... He allowed himself no distraction, and did not think that it was necessary to a child [pp. 13–14].

The emotionality, flexibility, humor, spontaneity, and easy flow of inspiration that are expressed in Anthony's creative daydreaming seem much more connected to his mother.[3] His daydreams may have had a forbidden feminine and maternal quality, in contrast to what he felt as a more masculine paternal compulsivity. I assume that some underlying and ongoing conflict observed and fantasized between his parents—especially before and after Fanny's long sojourn in America—was internalized and continued on as his own opposing tendencies in the mind of the son, both in his character and in his creativity. The related underlying conflicts about bisexuality and the Oedipus complex (being and having the

---

3. During his courtship of Fanny, Thomas Anthony wrote her one of his self-castigating letters, apologizing for his rigid character and inability to express feelings in his manners and in his words. "Are you still to be informed in what detestation I hold all ardent professions & in what admiration actions that want not the aid of declamation but boldly speak for themselves?" (quoted in Neville-Sington, 1997, p. 430).

mother, being and having the father—and wanting to be rid of both) would then have adhered to and determined Anthony's awkward unease about the "dangerous" but necessary spontaneity of fantasy and inspiration. This danger needed to be kept in control by what threatened to be equally dangerous powerful and destructive compulsions. The play and conflict of his conscious and unconscious fantasies then partly determined Anthony's method of and motivation for his creativity. They do not explain how they were transformed into the talent for good and great writing. Despite his disclaimer, Trollope was a genius; Henry James, who at first did not admire him, changed his mind later on and accorded him that creative rank.

Trollope is a realist in his fiction. Nathaniel Hawthorne paid the following tribute in an 1860 letter to a friend:

> [Trollope's novels] precisely suit my taste, solid and substantial . . . and just as real as if some giant had hewn a great lump out of the earth, and put it under a glass case, with all its inhabitants going about their daily business, and not suspecting that they were being made a show of [quoted by Pope-Hennessy, 1971, pp. 22–23].

It is reported that Trollope always carried a copy of this letter in his wallet. Pope-Hennessy says that the friend to whom Hawthorne sent the letter was Kate Field, the young American writer to whom Anthony Trollope felt a romantic attachment in his middle age. (She appears later in this narrative.) If the copy of Hawthorne's letter was her gift to him, which is probable, that made for an additional reason to keep it with him constantly.

POSTSCRIPT: TROLLOPE AND MANN

There are similarities, and of course many differences, between the writing methods of Trollope and Thomas Mann. Both men show a mixture of dependence on imagination and compulsivity in their work; both formed identifications with being a writer that centered on their mothers. Thomas Mann and his four-year-older brother, Heinrich, (like Anthony and Tom) became important writers. The Manns' father was a straight-laced business man who

Chapter 9

disapproved of writing as a profession. The imagination came from their mother. She was a beautiful and exotic woman whose father had been a German business man in Brazil (where his daughter was born) and her mother a Brazilian woman of mixed blood, part white and part Creole. Julia da Silva Bruhns Mann, like Fanny Trollope, was an avid reader and intellectual who read to her children regularly. Mrs. Mann was enthusiastic about her sons' becoming writers.

Prater (1995) describes Thomas as a child acting out scenes from myths derived from Homer and Virgil that his mother had read to her children. He exercised his imagination as a small child: "waking one morning, he would decide to be an eighteen-year-old prince named Karl, and the day could be spent 'proud and happy in the secret of my dignity'—no lessons, walks or being read to need interrupt the game for a moment, and the character could be changed at will from day to day" (p. 5). The young Thomas went on to write plays he could act out with his sisters and others in the family. Prater describes an obsessional method of composition that Mann began when he first started writing for publication as a teenager. He methodically took notes and kept a daily journal and diary for most of the rest of his life. The inclusion of notes for what he wanted to write

> marked the beginning of the craftsmanship approach which would turn the writing-desk of his maturity into a workshop of book-making, rather than the scene of inspiration, his material carefully assembled and items struck through as they were used. "The devil lies in the details," he said towards the end of his life, in the excerpts and notes to be made, a preparation "taking hours and days . . . the actual writing is more a question of discipline" [p. 16].

That could have been said by Trollope.

Chapter 10

IDENTITY AND FICTION
Father and Son

During the last ten years of [my father's] life, he spent nearly the half of his time in bed, suffering agony from sick headaches. But he was never idle unless when suffering.
—Anthony Trollope, *An Autobiography*

Despite Trollope's claim that as a writer he laid aside his own identity in a world different from that of his own, his many characters inevitably contained, in varying proportions, projected parts of his own personality as well as transferred aspects of his parents, siblings, and others emotionally meaningful to him. There is of course a sense in which every character in a work of fiction is a projection of some semblance of the writer's self, parent, or important other, as every character in a dream is for the dreamer. This not always enlighteningly meaningful cliché is, and has been described as, relevant for two characters who turn up in one of Trollope's best novels, *The Last Chronicle of Barsetshire* (Trollope, 1867). Reverend Josiah Crawley had appeared first in *Framley Parsonage* (Trollope, 1861); Johnny Eames had previously been in *The Small House at Allington* (Trollope, 1864). (Such was Trollope's compulsive productivity that he published 13 other books in the six years between the first and last of these three novels.)

The character of "the hobbledehoy," (more of this later) John Eames, is probably the closest to a conscious and comprehensive self-portrait in Trollope's fiction. He is a daydreamer, like his author. There are other obvious partial self-portraits: for example, Dr. Wortle in *Dr. Wortle's School* (Trollope, 1881), Charley Tudor, another "hobbledehoy," in *The Three Clerks* (Trollope, 1858). Hall (1983a) characterizes a single flirtatious letter of 16 August 1838 to a Miss Dancers as "the only surviving evidence of Trollope's 'hobbledehoyhood' while a junior clerk in the General Post Office" (p. 5). (It certainly could have been written by Johnny Eames in *The Small House at Allington*.)

The impoverished, masochistic, stubbornly upright, and determined Reverend Josiah Crawley as he is portrayed in *The Last Chronicle of Barsetshire* (Trollope, 1867), is probably Trollope's finest work of psychological characterization. Josiah Crawley is as close to a full depiction of his father as Trollope produced in his fiction. It is full of ambivalence, a perhaps somewhat idealized, although still bitter recognizable portrait; whether Trollope consciously recognized it as such has been questioned.

These two characters illustrate how Trollope's putting himself and important people in his life into his fiction was a continuation and extension of his lifelong habit of daydreaming, which is relevant to the incentive for his writing and the way his fantasy life furnished some of its content. Again, we can learn something about how and why he wrote what he did without solving the mystery of how he did it so well.

John (called Johnny) Eames, the unsuccessful lover of one of Trollope's favorite heroines, Lily Dale, is, like his author, a "gentleman" reared in poverty whose rather feckless father has died. His "gentleman" father, like Trollope's, had impoverished himself and his family by foolishly and unsuccessfully attempting to become a farmer. Hall (1991) points out that "[s]ome of the paragraphs in *The Small House at Allington* on Eames are almost word for word those used later in *An Autobiography*" (p. 57).

Eames is first presented as a lowly and lonely government clerk in his early 20s, as Anthony himself had been. Like his author, he ends up a responsible government official. Johnny, like young Anthony, is fond of reading, especially Shakespeare and Byron;[1]

---

1. Trollope grew to dislike Byron, whom he found overly emotional. Perhaps this was a reaction to Anthony's mother's favoritism toward the poet. In *An Autobiography* Trollope (1883) wrote of his mother, "But she raved also [about] him of whom all such ladies were raving then, and rejoiced in the popularity and wept over the persecution of Lord Byron" (p. 22).

he also considers leaving the civil service to turn to literature. Young Johnny is repeatedly described as a "hobbledehoy" in terms that are applicable to his creator's description of himself as a youth and young man in *An Autobiography*, in which Trollope [1883] writes of himself in the family setting at Bruges, "I was an idle, desolate hanger-on, that most hopeless of human beings, a hobbledehoy of nineteen" (p. 28).

Here is how Trollope (1863) defines "hobbledehoyhood" when describing Eames's leaving home (at about the same age his author had done) in order "to begin his life in the big room of a public office in London":

> They do not come forth to the world as Apollos, nor shine at all, keeping what light they may have for inward purposes. Such young men are often awkward, ungainly, and not yet formed in their gait; they struggle with their limbs, and are shy; words do not come to them with ease, when words are required, among any but their accustomed associates. Social meetings are periods of penance to them, and any appearance in public will unnerve them. They go much about alone, and blush when women speak to them. In truth, they are not as yet men, whatever the number may be of their years; and, as they are no longer boys, the world has found for them the ungraceful name of hobbledehoy [p. 46].

But the shyness and ungainliness vanish in Johnny's daydreams, in which he can become

> the most eloquent of beings, and especially eloquent among beautiful women. He enjoys all the triumphs of a Don Juan, without any of Don Juan's heartlessness, and is able to conquer in all encounters, through the force of his wit and the sweetness of his voice. But this eloquence is heard only

---

Neville-Sington (1997) remarks that all Fanny's heroes are, unlike her large-framed husband, "predictably slight of frame, with big expressive eyes and rich brown curls" (p. 30)—like Byron. Byron was also one of the curly-headed, handsome (Antinous-like, but it is doubtful that Trollope would have been aware of the poet's bisexuality) darlings, who are always being bested by plain (and sometimes balding) "manly" rivals in Trollope's fiction.

by his own inner ears, and these triumphs are the triumphs of his imagination [pp. 44–45].

There is no mistaking the autobiographical tenor of part of the description of Eames in *The Small House at Allington* (Trollope, 1864): "The true hobbledehoy is much alone, not being greatly given to social intercourse even with other hobbledehoys.... He wanders about in solitude, taking long walks, in which he dreams of those successes which are so far removed from his powers of achievement" (pp. 45–46).

Anthony draws an unforgettable portrait of his father in *The Last Chronicle of Barset* (Trollope, 1867) in the person of an impoverished gentleman clergyman, the masochistic and misanthropic Rev. Josiah Crawley, who consciously and unconsciously courts disaster at the expense of his loving family. It is predominantly a sympathetic, painful portrait with a tragic *Lear*-like dimension, in contrast to the more hostile but still ambivalent portrayal of Crawley in the earlier novel, *Framley Parsonage* (Trollope, 1861). There, he is called "a strict, stern, unpleasant man, and one who feared God and his own conscience" (p. 120). Anthony may have hated his father, but he also wanted to love and be loved by him. In the later book, the author obviously takes pleasure, and gives similar pleasure to his reader, in Reverend Crawley's pride and self-possession when he is up to resisting his enemies. This is especially so in the wonderful scene in which he confronts the bishop and bests the bishop's marvelously monstrous wife, Mrs. Proudie, the comic antiheroine of the Barsetshire novels.

In *An Autobiography* Trollope (1883) writes of the further delineation of Josiah Crawley in *The Last Chronicle of Barset*:

> I regard this as the best novel I have written.... I claim to have portrayed the mind of the unfortunate man with great accuracy and great delicacy. The pride, the humility, the manliness, the weakness, the conscientious rectitude and bitter prejudices of Mr. Crawley were, I feel, *true to nature* and were well described [p. 274; italics added].

Trollope's rather general list does not specifically mention his character's disturbed mental state, which so resembled his father's and was therefore true to life as well as to nature, although he depicts

Identity and Fiction

it clearly in the novel. He portrays in detail the character's stubborn provocativeness; lurking rage and quick temper; alternation of envy of others and satisfaction with his own accomplishments; insistence on courting punishment and failure and on avoiding easy solutions; disregard of the needs of his family, whom he also loves—these were all characteristics of his father. Mr. Crawley teaches his daughters Greek, as Thomas Anthony had taught Anthony. Mullen and Munson (1996) list other similarities between Crawley and Thomas Anthony: "financial ill-luck, pride in their knowledge of the classics, insistence on their rank as 'gentlemen' and a staggering inability to get on with others and even with their own family" (p. 109). Trollope (1867) writes of Mr. Crawley in *The Last Chronicle of Barset* in ways that make him sound as depressed and paranoid as Thomas Anthony: "He was morose, sometimes almost to insanity. . . . There was something radically wrong with him, which had put him into antagonism with all the world, and which produced these never-dying grievances" (p. 4). Josiah Crawley is clearly shown to be sometimes uncertain whether or not he is insane. The mixture of anger, envy, and pride that, alongside provoking (or administering his own) punishment for these sins, so besets Crawley is surely taken from Thomas Anthony. Trollope does not directly accuse his father of envy of his children.

There are many examples of disturbed old men who resemble Thomas Anthony in Trollope's novels. There is a picture of someone like Trollope's father in the character of the unfortunate and ultimately depressed attorney George Bertram in the novel, *The Bertrams* (Trollope, 1859), in which the narrator remarks that in 19th century England, "there is little sympathy for the man who falls by the wayside." Mullen and Munson (1996) comment:

> For an example of such a man Trollope only had to recall his father, who like George Bertram achieved great success at Winchester and Oxford but who, after being disappointed as Bertram is by not inheriting an uncle's fortune, sank into a morose and purposeless existence [p. 41].

The depiction of the very different Louis Trevelyan, the disturbed, masochistic and paranoid central figure of Trollope's 1869 novel *He Knew He Was Right* (the title conveys the character's delusional righteousness) is based largely on other facets of Thomas

Anthony's pathology. Madness and near-madness, especially in men, are frequently important in Trollope's fiction. Mr. Crawley combines more likenesses than any other of the characters, and his portrait is the most apposite and psychologically astute. One cannot be certain how consciously aware Trollope allowed himself to be of the chief source of this "true to nature" portrayal, yet I cannot help feeling convinced he must have known what he was doing. If so, perhaps the treatment of Crawley in what his creator felt was his best novel represents a conscious attempt to forgive his father.

Mullen and Munson (1996) point out that in *The Last Chronicle* "some of the best analysis of Crawley's near-madness comes from his wife, Mary. Her assessment of her husband bears several parallels with Fanny Trollope's private letters about her husband" (p. 275). They also cite George Eliot's report that Trollope was angry with Dickens for the latter's portrait of his own father as Mr. Micawber in *David Copperfield*; but, as I have noted, we are often angry with people who allow themselves to fulfil our own forbidden wishes. I assume there was inner conflict about making use of his father that would go along with these shades of contradictory feelings and actions. Glendinning (1992) writes, "The ghost of Anthony's father . . . was laid to rest by Anthony's unsentimental understanding of Mr. Crawley" (p. 380). I am not sure this is entirely true. I think Trollope continued to wrestle mightily although unconsciously with the question of whether there was life without father as well as life without mother; but Glendinning's remark shows her awareness of the ghost-laying function of Trollope's creativity. It surely helped Anthony (even if he was driven from within to do so) to be able to depict Thomas Anthony in fictional form and thereby discharge some of his exigent ambivalence, but I doubt that this accomplished a successful exorcism. That there was a strong positive side of Trollope's conflicted feelings about his father (and projected on Mr. Crawley) is attested to in *An Autobiography*:

> The worst curse to him of all was a temper so irritable that even those whom he loved the best could not endure it. We were all estranged from him, and yet I believe that he would have given his heart's blood for any of us. His life as I knew it was one long tragedy [Trollope, 1883, pp. 31–32].

Chapter 11

IDENTITY AND FICTION
The Nuances of Resentment

Frau Frohmann . . . believed in the principles of despotism and paternal government—but always on the understanding that she was to be the despot.

—Anthony Trollope
"Why Frau Frohmann Raised Her Prices"

In this chapter, I present two pieces of Trollope's fiction, a novel written when the author was 44 years old, when his mother was still alive and living with his older brother, and a later short story written when Fanny was dead. In the novel there are several bad father figures; the influence of mothers is present mainly by virtue of their absence, although it also features a rather self righteous mother who has no insight into how selfish she is in relation to her son. The later story depicts a selfish, tyrannical mother whose whim of iron inhibits her daughter's marriage and aims at destroying her son's power to separate from her. In both these works of fiction, Trollope can be expressing something of his bitter resentment toward his parents, and also—in the novel at least—something of his need and longing for a mother's love.

THE BERTRAMS

One of Anthony Trollope's (1859) early novels, *The Bertrams*, is relevant to the psychological impact of dependency on parents. I do not consider it one of his best, but it was a favorite of Tolstoy's, who liked Trollope's novels; he had a dozen or so of them in his library.

The plot centers on the lives, marriages, and careers of three young men, George Bertram, his cousin Arthur Wilkinson, and their slightly older fellow pupil at Oxford, Henry Harcourt. All three, before the novel begins, had been pupils at Winchester, one of Trollope's schools. One of the novel's main themes is the (sibling) rivalry of the three protagonists. The year of the book's publication, 1859, is the year Darwin's *Origin of Species* appeared (see Harvey, 1991). Competition and struggle, power and preeminence in society are central motifs of the novel. *The Bertrams* is a rather gloomy book full of masochism and failures—in careers and in love. "*Vae Victis*!" (Woe to the Defeated!) is the title of the novel's first chapter, in which the author decries the decline of religious and moral values in mid-Victorian times; money and success have become the triumphant guiding standards. Trollope can be as realistic about the power of money as Dickens or Balzac; it is masterfully depicted in one of his best novels, *The Way We Live Now* (Trollope, 1875). Yet *The Bertrams* is not unrelievedly gloomy. The novel has considerable humor and contains some comic characters.

The Bertrams shows no unselfish parenting. The few surviving parents (or parent-substitutes) are, each in his or her own way, incapable of empathic contact or dependable, true caring about their children. George Bertram's father, an army officer in the diplomatic service who is always away from home, uses his adult son as a fulfiller of his needs, chiefly as a source of money. The father's brother, George's more tragic, paranoid, rich, and capricious uncle (also named George), has become a kind of substitute father to his nephew. The uncle is, despite his financial success in business, predominantly cold-hearted, selfish, and intermittently miserly. He can admire no career or standards except his own. However, he is more generous than his brother and pays for his nephew's schooling, even though he knows that George's feckless father will never even mention, much less consider, repayment. Whenever the uncle feels slighted, he maliciously, and not quite sincerely, reminds his nephew that repayment is expected. George's resultant resentment estranges him further from his seeming benefactor. The uncle finally does not leave his fortune to George, who

Identity and Fiction: The Nuances of Resentment

will not play up to him (as Uncle Adolphus had, for similar reasons, not left his money to Thomas Anthony Trollope).

The cousin Arthur Wilkinson's self-centered mother cheerfully and righteously deprives her son of the full salary due to him when he, as a young clergyman, takes over his dead father's ecclesiastical holding. His unprotesting acceptance of his mother's naïve feeling of entitlement leaves him without enough income to get married to his beloved fiancée. Henry Harcourt, about whose background we learn little, is an orphan who hasn't much money and has to make his own way in life.

Trollope's characters are never as one dimensional as Dickens's. The initially poor but self-confident Henry Harcourt successfully schemes to take George's fiancée from him and becomes increasingly dishonest; but he is no monster. Nor are most of Trollope's villains, who usually have some good characteristics. In this novel Trollope is, as is so frequent in his fiction, psychologically astute and subtle. He depicts convincingly the complex clash of younger George Bertram's pride with that of Caroline Waddington, the fiancée he loses; he portrays Caroline's discontented ambivalence, her fear of and longing for passion. Trollope's chief "hero," the younger George Bertram, is brilliant, successful, and full of promise in college—at graduation he is a victor, winning double first honors and a fellowship—but a failure as a lawyer, like Trollope's father. He at first wants to be a clergyman; he feels he has found a vocation in a kind of epiphany experienced on the Mount of Olives when he goes to Palestine. This calling is abandoned when he decides to become a lawyer in order to earn enough to please his fiancée, Caroline. She admires his intellect and character but does not want to be poor. George stops courting success, in law and also as an author, when he feels that the exigent and emotionally cool Caroline does not love him enough to put aside her wish for a rich and successful husband. Caroline marries the less intelligent but more ambitious Harcourt, who has meanwhile prospered as a lawyer and is making his way toward the Cabinet as an influential Member of Parliament.

At the start of the novel, George's mother is long dead; Caroline plays the role of the lost, deserting mother for George Bertram that Fanny Trollope so strongly played for Anthony. Caroline herself is without mother or father and has not been acknowledged as the granddaughter of the senior George Bertram. She and the younger George turn out to be cousins, so their mutual attraction has a quasi-incestuous aura.

The absence or defectiveness of mothers affects the three young men whose lives, careers, and interactions form the center of this novel. Arthur Wilkinson's passivity toward his selfish mother causes him to postpone his wedding for years and live in depressive and masochistic abstinence, although he (the *"victis"*—loser of the first chapter) is the only one of the three ultimately able to achieve a happy marriage. George Bertram loses his ambition, his religious vocation, and the women he feels he loves or can love; after Caroline's marriage, he longs in vain for Adela, Arthur's beloved. His life ends in failure and apathy. The initially successful Henry Harcourt (about whose parents, evidently poor if still living, we learn nothing) ends as a suicide, after having lost his political power and been made miserable by his marriage to the beautiful but cold Caroline. The orphaned Caroline regrets her renunciation of George, cannot or will not love her husband, and is unhappy before and after she separates from Henry.

Five years after Henry's suicide, Caroline and George do marry. Their marriage is announced on the last page of the novel and is followed by a short but chilling description of their apathetic life together. The account ends: "Their house is childless, and very, very quiet; but they are not unhappy" (p. 580). What the ironic author makes very clear is that they are not happy. There follows:

> Reader, can you call to mind what was the plan of life which Caroline Waddington had formed in the boldness of her young heart? Can you remember the aspirations of [the young] George Bertram, as he sat upon the Mount of Olives, watching the stones of the temple over against him? [p. 580].

It is a bitter ending, both for the motherless child, George Bertram, and for the deserting young woman who can be seen partly as playing the role of the deserting Fanny as a young woman. The sad and unsettling novel with an ending that expresses so much emotional barrenness captures something of what it is to lose a mother and in that sense can serve as an object lesson to illustrate the potential pathogenic power of the question, "Is there life without mother?"

FRAU FROHMANN

In 1877, 14 years after his mother had died, Trollope wrote a rather lengthy story—seven chapters appeared in three installments in the magazine *Good Words*—called "Why Frau Frohmann Raised Her Prices." It features one of Trollope's many depictions of a dominating mother who inhibits the separation, maturation, and marriage of her children. Although her character is different from Fanny's, Frau Frohmann shows enough similarities and connections to suggest that Trollope may have used this story to express something of his resentment of his mother.

Frau Frohmann is a widow carrying on her long-dead husband's calling as innkeeper. She is "about 50" (p. 7)—Fanny Trollope's age when she left Anthony to go to America. The Frau is a well-meaning but righteous tyrant of her well-run and popular establishment, a thriving inn in the Austrian Tyrol named The Peacock,[1] situated in a valley called the Brunnenthal, which means "valley of the well or spring" (water symbolism plays a large part in the story). The good Frau is a conservative clinger to old ways; Trollope designates her political preferences by using the English political term "Tory" (p. 1) to describe the Austrian lady.

The story is good-humored and amusing, with a generally happy ending, but there is more than a suggestion of soul murder in it. I believe there is a passing, symbolic reference to the story's ominous implications in the description of the setting of the Peacock Inn. The author comments about the property, "you can hardly find a prettier spot" (p. 7), but paradise is followed by hell, located "below":

> Below the Peacock, where the mill is placed, the valley is closely confined, as the somber pine-forests rise abruptly on each side; and here, or very little lower, is that gloomy and ghostlike pass through the rocks, which is called the Höllenthor; *a name which I will not translate.* But it is a narrow ravine, very dark in dark weather, and at night as black as pitch. Among the superstitious people of the valley

---

1. In Greek mythology, the peacock was a bird sacred to the Goddess Hera, wife of Zeus. Hera was one of the great mother goddesses, and her feeling about her errant husband and males in general, as portrayed in myths and literature, were generally quite malign.

the spot is regarded with the awe which belonged to it in past ages [p. 7, italics added].

The landscape suggests (and can symbolize) the female genitals. The dark significance of the dark place is underlined by Trollope's gratuitous mention that he is not translating "Höllenthor," which means Gate of Hell, evoking Dante's "Abandon hope, all ye who enter here." The female genital (paradise to lovers of women) would become dangerous and castrating when symbolized by the entrance to Hell. Glendinning (1992, p. 435) speculates that the Austrian village of Brunnenthal that contains the Peacock is based on the village in Germany in which Anthony and Rose Trollope spent many vacations, which was named "Höllenthal" (Valley of Hell); this name would have similarly dark symbolic meanings. We do not know if Trollope had read Blake's (1804) "Milton," but, if so, the place name "Gate of Hell" could have made the mill for him one of the "dark Satanic mills" from that poem (p. 110)—a metaphor that in Trollope's time was still haunting England. The mother as witch lurks in this story.

Trollope characterizes Frau Frohmann as "a woman who loved power, but who loved to use it for the benefit of those around her—or at any rate to think that she so used it" (p. 1). The words, here and elsewhere in the story, portray a woman with masculine qualities in whom one can discern aspects of both Trollope's parents.

Frau Frohmann's character on the surface does not at all resemble Fanny Trollope's. The Frau is Austrian, lower middle class, intelligent but uneducated, and suspicious of those who might know more than she does; she cares too much about what people will say about her. With all the differences, the tie to Austria, the position of a widow who has to support her family, and the psychology of a "Tory" are links with Anthony's mother. Fanny loved Vienna, visited often, and wrote a travel book about it describing how popular she had become there. Despite the politically liberal ideas and friends of her early married life, she was very fond of the paternalistic and conservative Austrian restorer of the old order, Prince Metternich. The fondness was mutual. Fanny was perhaps a closet-Tory—or at least a Tory in Austria, like Frau Frohmann. Anthony, in *An Autobiography* (Trollope, 1883), wrote that his mother, after her first years of widowhood "became a strong Tory" (p. 22).

Identity and Fiction: The Nuances of Resentment

Unlike Fanny Trollope's disposition, there is little joy in Frau Frohmann's. Ironically, her name literally means joyful human being (*Froh* = joyful plus *Mann* = man or human being). She has some of the traits of Anthony's father: obstinacy, hatred and distrust of change, a tendency to silence and melancholy when thwarted. She does not want to listen to others. Like Fanny Trollope, she is strong willed, determined, and ambitious. The Frau is compulsively honest; she wants to be generous and enjoys giving good food and service to her guests. Since she hates change so intensely, she does not want to raise her prices, even though her prospective son-in-law, Fritz, points out to her that if she doesn't she cannot make a profit. To hear this makes her miserable—that she would be acting contrary to the *raison d'être* of trade is unbearable for her. She tries to compromise by forcing those from whom she buys food and to whom she pays wages to accept less. When this strategy does not work, she cannot accept the failure. Her need to remain in active control is threatened. A psychoanalytic reading supports what Trollope depicts. Having to change prices threatens Frau Frohmann's control of money—a symbolic threat to the control of the anal sphincter (money equaling feces, according to Freud) that underlies toilet training conflicts between the child and the mothering figure. These can be easily revived for obsessive–compulsive persons like the Frau. For such people, there is a psychological situation of great danger involved in even a small loss of the power to control, which can evoke potentially terrifying expectations of regressing toward losing all control over the internal (body and mind) and the external worlds.

What becomes increasingly apparent is how stubbornly Frau Frohmann needs to be right and needs to insist on the denial of unwelcome truths, even to the detriment of her own welfare and sense of well-being. (In this she is like the paranoid and masochistic Louis Trevelyan in Trollope's (1869b) novel *He Knew He Was Right*, a character who resembles Trollope's father.)

Frau Frohmann's need to dominate has potentially devastating effects on her two unmarried children. She loves them in her way, but she cannot be empathic with them or put their needs above her own. Her son Peter is about 30 years old. Her daughter Amalia (called Malchen) is five years younger and has long been engaged to a young lawyer who is one of Frau Frohmann's counselors—he is an advocate of changes whose advice she usually

Chapter 11

does not follow. His marriage to her daughter has been postponed for two years because she refuses to decide how much money she will give him as a *Mitgift*, a kind of preliminary dowry that was the local custom and without which he will not proceed with the wedding. (Here again the struggle involves control of money in the context of resisting change and separation.)

> Frau Frohmann's son and daughter are, respectively, the outdoors right hand [and the] indoors right hand [of the mother] with no real authority. But they are only hands. The brain, the intelligence, the mind, the will by which the Peacock is conducted and managed, come from Frau Frohmann herself. To this day she can hardly endure a suggestion either from Peter her son or from her daughter Amalia [p. 3].

The thriving inn and the farm that surrounds it dominate the Brunnenthal valley and village by their prestige and the financial support of the poorer and dependent neighbors from whom Frau Frohmann purchases eggs, chickens, meat, and fruit. The good Frau enjoys the position of a kind of provincial Queen Victoria. Her fall from this perch of almost royal ascendency, when her neighbors will not go along with her insistence on paying them less, leaves her puzzled and distressed. She is consciously concerned not primarily with the loss of money—she has saved more than enough during the years of the Inn's prosperous functioning—but with the loss of power, repute, and, above all, control:

> Things had gone pleasantly with her. Nothing is so enfeebling as failure; but she, hitherto, had never failed. Now a new sensation had fallen upon her, by which at certain periods she was almost prostrated. The woman was so brave that at her worst moments she would betake herself to solitude, and shed her tears where no one could see her. Then she would come out and carry herself that none should guess how she suffered [p. 39].

When her son Peter reproaches her and advises her to accede to her neighbors' needs and demands, he says,

Identity and Fiction: The Nuances of Resentment

"I don't see that you do any good by ruining yourself," [and she] turned at him very fiercely. "I suppose I may do what I like with my own?' she replied." [And the author/narrator echoes,] "Yes; she could do what she liked with her own" [p. 38].

Frau Frohmann had been (up to the time of the opening of the story) a successful narcissist. Such people can be most difficult in relation to others because they have little insight and consequently little motivation to change. Failure threatened to shatter the powerful but brittle defensive armor that had served the Frau so well. Her long history of success had left her vulnerable to the unfamiliar experience of failure.

Frau Frohmann strongly resists the separation and maturation of her two children—*her own* two "right hands." Amalia is a strong-minded, bright, and attractive woman of 25 or 26, an advanced age in those times to be comfortable with an indefinitely prolonged engagement. She is angry with her loving but hardly ardent suitor, Fritz, who delays out of a mixture of financial cautiousness, stubbornness, and fear of Frau Frohmann. Despite his ideas of liberalism and being open to change, he has some characteristics similar to those of his "Tory" prospective mother-in-law. Amalia fears she will lose him. When the Frau's emotional difficulties start and the Inn does begin to lose money, Malchen is further alarmed at her mother's continuing and even increased resistance to giving or even setting the amount of the *Mitgift*. Amalia says to her:

"Well, mother of course it is not pleasant to be as [Fritz and I] are now. Fritz is a good young man, and there is nothing about him that I have a right to complain of. But of course, like all the rest of 'em, he expects some money when he takes a wife. Couldn't you tell him what you mean to give?"
"Not at present, Malchen."
"And why not now? It has been going on two years."
"Nina Cobard at Schwatz was ten years before her people would let it come off" [pp. 32-33].

Frau Frohmann finally but reluctantly changes her mind, raises her prices, and agrees to pay more to her neighbors. This move

Chapter 11

is marked by her troubled acceptance of the advice of her old butcher and of a rich and respected Englishman, Mr. Cartwright, a favorite frequenter of the Inn. (Anthony and his wife, Rose, were fond of vacationing at inns in Germany and Austria.) Cartwright, surely a version of the author,[2] furnishes Frau Frohmann with an explanation of what has been happening for years in European finance following the increase in the gold supply and the resultant general inflation of prices and costs. The Frau accepts but does not really understand what he is saying; what she responds to is the Englishman's endorsement of her old friend the butcher's metaphoric advice that she should "swim with the stream." That homely image she can understand, and her reluctant acceptance of it allows for the flow of change, even though "she did not like swimming with the stream" (p. 45). Also, a chance remark by the local chaplain enables her to link her defiance to this change in strategy. In any event, she recovers from the blow to her narcissism. She may have to see herself as only one swimmer among many, but she is gratified by the resultant

---

2. Cartwright is a name based on craftsmanship, almost as if Trollope were tempted to hide his identification with this character by using a name describing a man who worked with his hands, like Mr. Cobbler or Mr. Baker. (He at least put aside the temptation of calling himself Mr. Shoemaker.) Trollope may have been making fun of himself here; he, as I have stated, repeatedly and provocatively compared, in his talk and in his writings, the work of writers to that of shoemakers—and also to chandlers and bakers. There is another Cartwright connected with his mother. One of her hated neighbors, when the Trollopes were living at "Julian's Hill" in Harrow after her return from America, was the Reverend William Cunningham. Cunningham gained a considerable notoriety and an increase in Fanny's contempt by refusing to put up a plaque in his church in Harrow to commemorate Lord Byron's illegitimate daughter, Allegra, who was buried in the churchyard. Fanny had a running verbal feud with Cunningham. Three years after moving from Harrow, she modeled the central figure of her novel *The Vicar of Wrexhill* (F. Trollope, 1837) on Rev. Cunningham and named the character Reverend Cartwright. He is a hypocritical, dishonest and lubricious villain (see Neville-Sington, 1997, pp. 69–71). Both Neville-Sington and Ransom (p. 119) point out the strong resemblance between the characterizations of Fanny's Reverend Cartwright and Anthony's hypocritical, unscrupulous, and unforgettable Reverend Obadiah Slope in his novel *Barchester Towers* (Trollope, 1857). Here again, in his making use of the name "Cartwright," there are unconscious and conflicting forces in Anthony's mind to be found in relation to his mother.

Identity and Fiction: The Nuances of Resentment

restoration of her prestige and popularity, allowing her, to stretch the watery metaphor, again to become a big fish in a little pond. A restored current of benevolence even enables her to relax her control, give the *Mitgift*, allow for the marriage of Amalia to Fritz, and let Amalia move out of the Peacock.

But separation and marriage are not to be allowed for Peter, a man of "nearly 30" (p. 3)—Trollope's age when he married his wife, Rose. The thought of Peter's possible marriage and some stranger becoming a future mistress of the Peacock provides the final determinant for Frau Frohmann's decision to raise her prices. She had always planned to retire in the distant future to her birthplace, the village of Schwatz, the home of her childhood. Her distresses had caused her to feel she must either

> yield [to the advice], or go. Schwatz! Oh yes; it would be very well to have a quiet place ready chosen for retirement when retirement should be necessary. But what would retirement mean? Would it not be to her simply a beginning of dying? A man, or a woman, should retire when no longer able to do the work of the world. But who in the world could keep the Brunnenthal Peacock as well as she? ... The [priest] had indiscreetly suggested to her that as [Amalia] was about to marry and be taken away into the town, it would be a good thing that Peter should take a wife, so that there might be a future mistress of the establishment in residence. The idea caused her to arm herself with renewed self-assertion. So they were already preparing for her departure to Schwatz. They had already made up their minds that she must succumb to these difficulties and go! The idea had come simply from [her chaplain], without consultation with any one, but to the Frau it seemed as though the whole valley were already preparing for her departure. No, she would not go! [pp. 54–55].

This bit of paranoia is followed by a sensible decision:

"But if not, then she must raise her prices" (p. 55).

So poor Peter has no prospect for a wife or an independent life as master of the Peacock at the relatively happy end of the story. The Frau is ultimately "quite satisfied that she had done the right thing in raising her prices; but still feeling that she had

Chapter 11

many a struggle to make before she could understand the matter" (p. 65).

Peter's remaining his mother's right hand is reminiscent of Frances Trollope's relation to both her surviving sons. Tom was her chosen and willing companion following her husband's death. He did not marry until he was 39 years old, and both his wives lived in his mother's house, the Villa Trollope, in Italy until Fanny died (at 83). Peter is a kind of *lumpen*-hobbledehoy"—like Anthony, but with less light to hide under his bushel. Peter is described as

> attached altogether to the conservative interest [like his mother.] But he, though he was honest, diligent, and dutiful to his mother, was lumpy, uncouth, and slow both of speech and action. He understood the cutting of timber and the making of hay—something perhaps of the care of horses and of the nourishment of pigs; but in money matters he was not efficient [p. 11].

This does not at first glance sound like Anthony at "nearly 30," but the description does resemble (*mutatis mutandis*) how Anthony showed himself and was regarded by others in his schoolboy and early hobbledehoy years. Anthony became engaged without his mother's knowledge or permission to a girl he met in Ireland, the place where he truly found himself able to live a full life without mother, but, as with all of us, of course not entirely. There remained as the subject of his continuing intrapsychic conflict the identification and the relationship with his mother that was such a large part of his identity.

Both *The Bertrams* and "Frau Frohmann" have to do with the question of whether life can exist without mother.

Chapter **12**

WHAT WAS TROLLOPE LIKE?

Do I contradict myself?
Very well then I contradict myself.
(I am large; I contain multitudes)
—Walt Whitman, "Leaves of Grass"

Several critics have noted that we do not know what Anthony Trollope was really like—he was a man of façades and disguises. Of course, this is true of everyone to some extent. Every life reveals some as-if functioning, obfuscation, and disguise. Frequently these exist, as they did with Trollope, in some variety of the basic defensive forms of dynamic, transiently regressive narcissistic withdrawal from the mature self, as well as from the rest of the world, and of emotion-distancing, obsessive-compulsive functioning. Again, the intensities, proportions, and mixtures of these universally held ways of diluting emotional intensities and authenticity vary from individual to individual. Allen Ginsberg is said to have remarked "Every once in a while you become aware that you're alive." Defensive emotional deadening is usually most needed by those who, like Renard and Trollope, were traumatized and neglected in childhood—or those who (unlike the two great writers) were born with deficiencies that caused them to be incapable of feeling enough about others to provide or even receive loving care.

The mind and the personality of a person are too dynamic and complex to enable us to have more than a general grasp of some predictable trends, with some, but never enough, knowledge of specifics. Even close and prolonged acquaintance will turn up surprises; certainty is risky. We are all to a great extent enigmas to ourselves, and it is even harder to pluck out the heart of the mystery of what another human being is really like. Some people present more difficulty than others do in this regard, even if we are close to them in life—and even if they are trying to reveal themselves in the deep scrutiny of their unconscious minds that is the aim of psychoanalysis. Knowing about others without personal contact is even more difficult, although writers reveal more about themselves, consciously as well as unconsciously, in their work than do those who do not create such records. The artifacts and documents great artists and writers leave behind and the opinions and memories of their acquaintances tend to become subject to intense critical examination by students and biographers. Yet both the observations of witnesses and the collection and synthesis of so-called facts by biographers working at a second-hand distance are filtered through distortions inevitably motivated by their own conscious and unconscious prejudices. The results usually cannot be effectively checked by the artist/subject who, even if alive and consulted, would still have his own biases. Autobiographies conceal and distort as well as reveal.

Yet biographies can give the reader at least the impression of grasping something definite about the character of the subject. Certain of Trollope's qualities are obvious: for example, his predominantly good and responsible character as a gentleman. Perhaps the most important of these qualities is shown in the primacy of honesty in his fiction and in his life. "For Trollope, honesty was the greatest and most important virtue both for individuals and for nations. One of the vital tasks for fiction was to teach honesty, 'in these times when the desire to be honest is pressed so hard' [from T.'s *Autobiography*, p. 220]" (Mullen and Munson, 1996, p. 221). It follows that "dishonesty—in sexual as in commercial and public life—is the quintessential Trollopian sin" (Glendinning, 1992, p. 221). Perhaps the latter statement is especially important to a formerly abused or neglected child: with authority that is dishonest, one can never know where one stands. Dishonesty, as a threat to psychic and bodily control, motivated both Trollope's hatred of it and his compulsive honesty. (His writings show that Trollope, like Freud, felt that women were less honest than men. Perhaps this belief stemmed from Trollope's conflicts about distrust of and dependence on his mother, which were deeper than those about his father.)

Another character trait was the sense of humor that emerged when he did not feel threatened or enraged. This gift was manifest in his life and flourished in his fiction. Mullen and Munson (1996) observe that there is a private joke in "almost every Trollope work of fiction" (p. 410). Another consistent and obvious positive quality was his great energy and stamina. He could work and play hard day after day with relatively little sleep. Voracious reading, especially of his large collection of old English plays, which he copiously and compulsively annotated, often lengthened his waking hours. Many observers commented on his blustery façade, his generosity to needy friends and acquaintances alongside crotchety objections to public charities. He was full of contradictory and eccentric habits, opinions, and beliefs.

In general, however, I share the frequently expressed opinion that biographies of Trollope, including his own, and the partial self-portraits in his characters and in the ubiquitous narrator in his novels do not provide a satisfying feeling that one knows what the man was like. This may be an impossible goal; but one can get a much more fully dimensioned, dynamic impression, no matter how deficient, of what Jules Renard or even Dickens was like from reading them and about them, than from reading accounts of Trollope. All three novelists show contradictions between their inner lives and public personae, between their actions and what comes through in their fiction. But the glimpses that come through in relation to Trollope—full of verisimilitude as well as of contradiction—seem much harder to integrate. (For example, how does one fit Trollope's ability to be an enthusiastic friend and contented member of more than one London club with his intermittently powerful misanthropic and distrustful propensities?) I think Trollope's defensive psychic shield was more effective and less translucent than that of most writers.

Jonathan Raban (1987), one of Trollope's most trenchant critics despite the relatively few pages he has devoted to him, makes much of Trollope's bent for disguise, calling him

> the yeti of the English novel; a creature of rumor, footprints, blurred portraits, most of which are faked. He has left his biographers stumped: both [biographers] Michael

Chapter 12

Sadleir and James Pope-Hennessy succeeded in producing books which appeared to be about no one in particular at all.... Trollope himself is responsible for much of this. He was a pathological ironist who, both in his life and in his work, loved to disappear behind an endless succession of elaborately raised smokescreens. In the *Autobiography*, he tried to pass himself off as a no-nonsense literary grocer. Elsewhere he pretended to be a waggish old buffer, or a philistine hunting man, or a whey-faced public servant. Like many people haunted by a terror of their own unpopularity, Trollope liked to sneer at himself before anyone else got the chance to.... The most revealing sentence in the *Autobiography* is a chance remark: "In our lives we are always weaving novels, and we manage to keep the different tales distinct" [pp. 73–74].

This is lively, wonderful writing, but I think Raban goes too far. He suggests that Trollope consciously planned his defensive disguise and fortifies this notion with Trollope's "chance remark." Much of the role-playing, I would judge, was genuinely felt and at least transiently given credence by Trollope. It was part of Trollope's nature to live "as if" he were what E. M. Forster called a "flat" (one-dimensional, Dickensian) character in a novel. Perhaps it would be better to say a series of "flat" characters; and I feel that, probably alternating with his conscious wish for, and even pleasure in, the assumption of eccentric disguises, Trollope often believed in them himself. His behavior was characteristically blunt and straightforward; honesty was passionately important to him, and he despised hypocrisy—all along with protective façades consciously assumed.

Trollope is full of conflicting and contrary views that make for mental splits—islands of antithetical functioning. He is described by contemporaries as a kind of bellicose bull in social situations, charging into a party bellowing in deafening tones; bluff, boisterous, brusque, buffalo-like are some of other alliterative adjectives used by observers. In his official life, when he held high office in the Post Office in England, he is described as habitually "bursting in on any round table discussion and trying to yell everyone else down" (Pope-Hennessy, 1971, p. 224). Yet many witnesses felt that his obstreperous manner—social or official, assumed or

What Was Trollope Like?

spontaneous—served to disguise and deny his intense shyness.

Raban (1987) writes, "Trollope's letters are duller, far duller, than those of any major writer, of any century, in any language" (p. 81), and little of his emotional life is expressed in them in contrast to those of most poets and novelists. I find it hard to leave out any of Raban's comments. He stresses Trollope's need to hide and disguise:

> Trollope's parents made no secret of thinking him a stupid boy; his intelligence, like almost everything in his life, had to be his own secret. Even now, it remains a well kept one. His childhood was spectacularly awful: despised, neglected, bullied, carelessly shifted about from school to school, he learned of necessity how to play all his feelings very close to his chest. His later success in the Post Office, and in the Garrick Club too, were really triumphs of impersonation. Exactly the same exhaustive artifice which created the novels transformed the miserable runt of the family into a brisk, sociable, conventional pillar of middle-class society [p. 75].

An observer tells of Trollope's stopping in front of a mirror before entering the room, apparently deliberately to disorder his hair (see Terry, 1989, p. 98). I would speculatively interpret this act as a combination of a (probably unconscious) need to repeat as an active agent something of the disorder thrust on him in his awful childhood and a provocative and hostile challenge to authorities in the present. Trollope may have had an unconscious impulse to reproduce the early childhood daily experience of being tested while standing beside his father, who was plying his razor. If so, Anthony would here have been playing the roles both of the father and of the boy having his hair pulled "in the event of guilty fault." Trollope was proud of the full beard he wore most of his adult life; it did allow him to avoid daily shaving and associated reminiscenses and differentiated him from his clean-shaven father. Anthony also may have had mixed feelings about his own eventually considerable baldness. His father had a distinguished receding hairline. It is not uncommon for bald men to win out over hirsute rivals in Trollope's fiction.

There is a rare instance of Trollope's showing that he was

Chapter 12

capable of conscious pretending. In a letter to a young relative of 5 December 1881, he wrote:

> *Barchester Towers* was written before you were born. Of course I forget every word of it! But I don't. There is not a passage in it I do not remember. I always have to *pretend* to forget when people talk to me about my own old books. It looks modest—and to do the other thing looks the reverse. But the writer never forgets. And when after 30 years he is told by someone that he has been pathetic, or witty, or even funny, he always feels like lending a five-pound note to that fellow [Hall, 1983b, p. 933; italics added].

This excerpt also shows the conflict underlying Trollope's intermittently characteristic modesty—not always conscious—which was interspersed with outbreaks of arrogance. Such dynamic shifts in feeling (sometimes dramatically contradictory mixtures of the fixed and the changeable) are not only to be found in victims of soul murder; in less exaggerated form, they are part of the human condition.

TROLLOPE'S MARRIAGE

When he was almost 30, Anthony married an English girl, Rose Heseltine, whom he had met when she was on vacation in Ireland where he had been working for a year. Their engagement lasted several years, and for a good part of that time Trollope did not mention it to his mother. (The two women seemed to take to one another after they met.) Anthony married Rose in 1844, and she came to live with him in Ireland after their wedding. Rose became a good, maternal Victorian wife to her husband but we know few details about the marriage. Because it was so necessary for Anthony to travel to fulfill his almost daily duties, he and Rose were more apart than together for a good portion of the time they lived in Ireland. Even after his transfer to England from Ireland, Trollope was away from Rose for as long as six months at a time or more when he traveled to other continents for the Post Office or to write travel books.

Many have noted that Trollope's *An Autobiography* both reveals and hides. We learn much about his travails and antipathies but very little about his loving feelings. There are general statements about loving and caring, but they lack depth and specificity. (See the exception concerning Kate Field later in this chapter.) He writes in *An Autobiography* that he is determined to say little about his wife, and, indeed, we learn almost nothing from it of his marriage or of his relationships with his two sons, and not too much more from his letters.

Some of this need for emotional distance in the face of deep feeling was evidenced after Trollope put his autobiography in a drawer, to be published after his death. Trollope left with it a letter to his older son, Harry. In the letter Trollope told Harry he was leaving the manuscript to him as a gift and added, "Now [I can] say how dearly I have loved you." Hall (1991) recounts how, when Trollope showed Harry the manuscript in the drawer, "he was unable to resist telling [him] that he ought to ask 1,800 pounds for the book" (p. 411]. It was easier for him to talk of money than of love.

One can say only that Trollope appears from letters and quoted remarks to have been a fond and faithful husband (he writes in *An Autobiography* (Trollope, 1883), "I have betrayed no woman," p. 366) and a good but somewhat disappointed father. Most commentators feel that his marriage was happy—in spite of Trollope's occasional statements suggesting that his early overwhelming love for Rose faded. Perhaps her attractiveness did too; it is not evident in her few extant photographs, all taken when she was middle-aged. His short and cryptic declaration in *An Autobiography* is that his marriage was "like the marriage of other people and of no special interest to any one except my wife and me" (Trollope, 1883, p. 71). Contradictory speculations abound (for example, was Rose Trollope jealous or tolerant of her husband's inveterate but apparently harmless "flirting" with younger women?). Impressions of marital discontent arise mostly in connection with hints in his letters and, by implication, in the novels and short stories, which are, like most fiction, full of marital conflict and troubles. Two major novels, *He Knew He Was Right* (1869b) and *Phineas Finn* (1869a) contain long, painful descriptions of destructively impossible marriages of the Trevelyans and the Kennedy's, respectively. Trollope's writings contain many discouraging generalizations about marital discontent. Henry James (1883) points out that in the typical Trollope novel, there is "always primarily a love story, and a love story constructed on an inveterate system. There is a young lady who has two lovers, or a young man who has two sweethearts; we are treated to the innumerable forms in which this predicament may present itself" (p. 1338). The compulsion to repeat these triangles suggests something of the intensity of Trollope's interest in romantic and sexual attachments besides the conjugal one. There is also something of a preoccupation with bigamy in several of his novels.

Trollope's friend G. H. Lewes lived with George Eliot as lover and happy if not legal "husband." (He had separated from his wife, but having consented to her flagrant infidelity because of his liberal views, he was unable to divorce her legally.) In 1861, Lewes, then a new acquaintance of Trollope, wrote to him objecting to his cynical remarks about marriage at the end of *Framley Parsonage*. Trollope (1861) had suggested that anticipation is the greatest happiness in marriage. Here is the passage from the last chapter, which is ironically titled, "How They . . . Lived Happy Ever After":

> Can it be that a man is made happy when a state of anticipation is brought to a close? No, when the husband walks back from the altar, he has already swallowed the choicest dainties of his banquet. The beef and pudding of married life are then in store for him—or perhaps only the bread and cheese. Let him take care lest hardly a crust remain—or perhaps not a crust" [p. 629].[1]

---

1. There is a similar passage in *The Bertrams* in which Trollope (1859) contrasts the happiness of lovers' walks with what happens after the couple marries:
"We can still walk with our wives;—and that is pleasant too, very—of course. But there was more animation in it when we walked with the same ladies under other names. Nay, sweet spouse, mother of dear bairns, who hast so well done thy duty; but this was so, let thy brows be knit never so angrily. That lord of thine has been indifferently good to thee, and thou to him hast been more than good. Uphill together have ye walked peaceably laboring; and now arm-in-arm ye shall go down the gradual slope which ends below there in the green churchyard. 'Tis good and salutary to walk thus. But for the full cup of joy, for the brimming spring-tide of human bliss, oh give me back—! Well, well, well; it is nonsense; I know it; but

What Was Trollope Like?

Trollope wrote back to Lewes, stating that he was grateful for the "domestic and worldly happiness" he had been granted. I feel the addition of "and worldly" weakens the disclaimer. One should bear in mind that, as Mullen and Munson (1996) observe, most of the marriages in Trollope's fiction are happy; these are, however, generally marriages that are already established before the novel begins. (There are notable exceptions, for example, the Proudies in the Barsetshire series of novels.) Pope-Hennessy (1971), thinking of those marriages that resolve the plot of a novel, notes that "most of the novels close before the honeymoon" (p. 97).

In his letter replying to Lewes, Trollope invited him to dinner. Hall (1983a) quotes from what Lewes wrote in his journal after the visit: "Went down to Waltham to dine and sleep at Trollope's. He has a charming house and ground, and I like him very much, so wholesome and straightforward a man. Mrs. Trollope did not make any decided impression on me, one way or the other" (p. 147*n*).

Trollope started writing *Framley Parsonage* in 1859. He was then 45 and had been married to Rose for 15 years. He finished the book in its serial form for the *Cornhill Magazine* in June of 1860. Later that year, at his brother's house in Florence, he met the writer and actress Kate Field, an attractive, intelligent, intellectual American woman in her early 20s. Trollope was infatuated. Kate had strong views on the rights of women, and Trollope used her as a model for some features of his American women characters, with and without similar ideas. She liked famous people and being flirted with by older men. He continued to see her at intervals (in America and in Europe) and corresponded with her for most of the rest of his life. In his *An Autobiography* (Trollope, 1883) there is the following surprisingly emotional statement referring to Kate Field:

> There is an American woman, of whom not to speak in a work purporting to [be] a memoir of my own life would be to omit all allusion to one of the chief pleasures which has graced my later years. In the last fifteen years she has

---

may not a man dream now and again in his evening nap and yet do no harm?" (p. 358).

These remarks seem almost to have been addressed to Rose Trollope, the mother of two "dear bairns" when he wrote it.

Chapter 12

been, out of my own family, my most chosen friend. She is a ray of light to me, from which I can always strike a spark by thinking of her. I do not know that I should please her or do good to any one by naming her. But not to allude to her in these pages would amount almost to a falsehood. I could not write truly of myself without saying that such a friend has been vouchsafed to me. I trust she may live to read the words I have now written, and to wipe away a tear as she thinks of my feeling while I write them [pp. 316–317].

This heartfelt effusion is in sharp contrast to Trollope's reticence in the book about his feelings for other people, and especially to the way he writes of his wife (who remains almost as anonymous in the entire *Autobiography* as Kate is in the quoted paragraph) and of his marriage. The long attachment to the young American, which seems like that of a repressed, incest-inclined father,[2] probably never resulted in sexual contact, but it was apparently intense enough to arouse Rose's jealousy, although outwardly her relations with Kate were friendly. Sadleir (1945), in an editorial note to Trollope's *Autobiography*, says, "Though some of [Trollope's letters to her] are intimate and highly affectionate, there is no reason to suppose that their friendship was other than platonic" [p. 389]. This statement seems convincing in the light of what is known of both Kate and Anthony.

Trollope loved women—it shows in the obvious positive side of his ambivalence toward his wife and toward his mother in his life and in his portrayal of a variety of women in his novels. Many, including Henry James, have praised him as one of the best depicters of English girls and women in English literature. C. P. Snow (1975) thought he took his clever, energetic, and willful English women from characteristics of both his mother and his wife. Some of the attributes of Trollope's more passive heroines in his later novels were also probably borrowed from Florence Bland, Trollope's niece, the daughter of Rose Trollope's sister, whom the Trollopes

---

2. Compare Henry James's (1883) comment that "In his novels Trollope settled down steadily to the English girl. . . . He bestowed upon her the most serious, the most patient, the most tender, the most copious consideration. He is evidently always more or less in love with her. . . . But, . . . *if he was a lover, he was a paternal lover; as competent as a father who has had fifty daughters*" [pp. 1349–1350; italics added].

What Was Trollope Like?

adopted and took into their home when both of the girl's parents died. She became Anthony's amanuensis in his last years. Trollope was fond of her and left her money in his will, and she lived with Rose Trollope after Anthony's death.

Trollope's letters to his wife are always affectionate, and he had a high regard for her critical ability. She always read his books when he was writing them and copied his manuscripts before he sent them to the publishers. She wrote out a long list of events compiled from her journals to help him when he was writing his autobiography. Trollope valued her advice and once called her his second self. He wrote a letter to his son Henry about a forthcoming travel book on South Africa that the young man had been hired to edit: "Do you mean to put your name as Editor? If the book be good I should, and I should take Mamma's advice as to the goodness for she is never mistaken about a book being good or bad" (Hall, 1983b, p. 741). I think Trollope could love his wife tenderly, but I have the impression that sexual frustration and disappointment set in sometime early in the relationship; and, for the most part beneath consciousness, his dependence on her sometimes made her the object of the repressed hostility directed at his mother—part of a general hostility toward women that existed alongside his love for them.

Here is a letter written by Trollope to an unknown young lady in 1861, the year after he published *Framley Parsonage* and met Kate Field:

> My dearest Miss Dorothea Sankey,
> My affectionate & most excellent wife is as you are aware still living—and I am proud to say her health is good. Nevertheless it is always well to take time by the forelock and be prepared for all events. Should anything happen to her, will you supply her place—as soon as the proper period for decent mourning is over. Till then I am your devoted servant. Anthony Trollope [quoted in Hall, 1983a, p. 144].

The wise Hall, in a footnote to his collection of Trollope's letters, says: "Every informed student of Trollope considers the letter a joke; but in 1942 Sotheby's Catalogue called it 'one of the most extraordinary letters ever offered for sale,' and it provoked heated controversy in the press" (p. 144). It surely was meant to be a joke, but.... Perhaps here Trollope was unconsciously not being too different from the man Freud (1900) wrote about (I think the anecdote came from Heine) who said to his wife, "If one of us dies, I'll move to Paris" (p. 485).

An Autobiography, written when Trollope was 60, ends with a moving tribute (that shows a mixture of psychic pathology and psychic health) to his compulsive but gratifying activity as writer. His fiction especially provided a fulfillment in fantasy of his "castle-building" wishes through his passionate love for and identification with his created characters; this fantasy grew in intensity to comprise a compelling, compartmentalized inner world (charged with what Freud might have called "psychic reality"). It was a wonderful fulfillment, and yet it is very sad that he counted on this ardent involvement and activity more than on his actual loved ones for his future felicity. He wrote:

> For what remains to me of life I trust for my happiness still chiefly to my work—hoping that when the power of work be over with me, God may be pleased to take me from a world in which, according to my view, there can be no joy; *secondly, to the love of those who love me* and then to my books[3] [Trollope, 1883, p. 366, italics added].

There is much ambiguity in the italicized words. Trollope's statement is far from a simple declaration of loving his family. Perhaps he is feeling that he should return their love but is inhibited about it. But he also may be suggesting (consciously? unconsciously?) that he will love only those who he feels love him. If so, he is here under the neurotic shadow of the past, burdened with anger toward the family of his childhood during his years of life without mother.

---

3. He was, like his mother, both a passionate reader and a collector of books and read as extravagantly as he did everything else—he felt he had perhaps read more old English plays than anyone else alive.

Chapter 13

TROLLOPE'S LOVE FOR HIS CHARACTERS

The novelist has other aims than the elucidation of his plot.
—Anthony Trollope, *An Autobiography*

Trollope's passionate involvement (he calls it "intimacy") with his characters is revealed in an exuberant passage in *An Autobiography*. Trollope (1883), in giving a prescriptive model to would-be novelists, describes himself:

> He desires to make his readers so intimately acquainted with his characters that the creatures of his brain should be to them speaking, moving, living, human creatures. This he can never do, unless he knows these fictitious personages himself, and he can never know them unless he can live with them in the full reality of established *intimacy*. They must be with him as he lies down to sleep and as he wakes from his dreams. He must learn to hate them and love them. He must argue with them, quarrel with them, forgive them, *and even submit* to them. He must know of them whether they are cold-blooded or passionate, *whether true or false, and how far true and how far false*. The depth and breadth and the narrowness and shallowness of each should be clear to him. And, [here as] in our outer world, we know that men and women change—become worse or better as temptation or conscience may guide them. . . . It

is so that I have lived with my characters, and thence has come whatever success I have obtained. There is a gallery of them, and of all in that gallery I may say that I know the tone of the voice, and the color of the hair, every flame of the eye, the very clothes they wear. Of each man I could assert whether he would have said these or the other words: of every woman, whether she would then have smiled or so have frowned. When I feel that this *intimacy* ceases, then I shall know that the old horse should be turned out to grass [pp. 232–234; italics added].

Pope-Hennessy (1971) writes that "one is tempted to think that Trollope could not bring himself to marry [Lily Dale] to faithful Johnnie Eames because he was in love with her himself" (p. 20). Trollope loved his characters. His living with them in his mind was a passionate involvement, which intensified as he approached old age. He did not want to give up some of them, and he often peopled new novels with old characters. Trollope was in one of the periods of mild depression he suffered from during his last years when he was beginning the last of the Palliser series of novels, *The Duke's Children* (Trollope, 1880). In that book he announces the death of Lady Glencora Palliser (whom perhaps he loved even more than he did Lily Dale). I believe that loss contributed to his depression. In *An Autobiography*, Trollope (1883) says of Lady Glencora and her husband, Plantagenet Palliser, "By no amount of description or asseveration could I succeed in making any reader understand how much these characters with their belongings have been to me in my later life. I have used them for the expression of my political and social convictions. . . . They have served me as safety-valves by which to deliver my soul" (p. 180). Is it too fanciful to think of that last sentence as a declaration of Trollope's "castle-building" and literary activity as a means of partially undoing the traumata and neglect that I have called soul murder?[1]

---

1. His friend and first biographer, T. H. S. Escott, wrote, "Trollope's life was chronically saddened by recurrent moods of indefinable dejection and gloom" (quoted in Terry, 1987, p. 118). In his posthobbledehoy days, Trollope was, at least in public, characteristically full of energy and enthusiasm. He had tremendous physical stamina even in middle age and was given to strenuous hunting and traveling. In the last decade of his life he became

Lily Dale and Lady Glencora have a common trait: they are both attracted to men who are or turn out to be incapable of loving them, and both women are either initially (Glencora) or permanently (Lily) put off by good men who love them. This kind of masochism these feisty ladies share with other Trollope heroines, perhaps most notably (one might even say egregiously) by Clara Amendoz in *The Belton Estate* (Trollope, 1866a). I think Trollope's love for these forceful and intelligent women characters who tend to choose the wrong men was greatly determined by his feelings for his capable and managing mother in relation to her unfortunate choice in marrying his father. The admired women are varied versions of his mother. An unconscious identification with her would, I speculate, furnish some of the masochistic, passive, and homosexual trends that he struggled against with considerable success. At the same time, the "good" men—one of them is the hobbledehoy Johnny Eames—resemble Trollope himself and illustrate the heterosexual (father-replacing) side of the author's oedipal strivings. Sometimes the good men win in the end, but not Johnny Eames. (There are layers of complication here. I speculate that Trollope's having one of his favorite heroines, Lily Dale, masochistically persist in rejecting Eames not only represents competition for her with his alter ego figure but also is an instance of Anthony's masochistically expressing punishment for his oedipal rivalry toward a split-off fictional version of himself. Everyone in the oedipal triangle loses.)

Raban (1987) shows a deep appreciation of the importance of Trollope's relationships with the creatively transformed fictional

---

more depressed. The psychological readiness was supplemented by many bodily contributions to the fact of aging and the feeling of waning powers. Trollope developed deafness in one ear (at age 58); he also had increasing trouble with writer's cramp and experienced increasing difficulty riding horses. (He had several falls and had to give up fox hunting. This was at the time he was writing *An Autobiography*.)

"Once he had written his autobiography, he would have been content to die at any time. He was 'ready to go', and wanted no 'leisure evening of life', he wrote to his Australian friend, G. W. Rusden, in 1876 [when he was 61]. He dreaded only physical disability and that mental lethargy which is apt to accompany it. . . . 'No man dreads more than I do the time when life may not be enjoyable'" (Glendinning, 1992, p. 443).

He also wrote to Rusden of being done with making love.

Chapter 13

versions of the creatures from the novelist's castle-building fantasies. He also links Trollope's psychopathology to the motivation for his fiction. Trollope, the outsider rejected by his family and society, could fulfill his daydreams and have his revenge in his novels:

> Trollope himself had the character of a born loser. From childhood, he had learned to think of himself as someone to be despised. . . . [He] knew exactly what it was to be a failure, knew his failure could so easily creep up on a man from behind and silently garrotte him. He instinctively thought of success—at least social success—as a matter of arbitrary luck and hereditary money. For the wealthy, it was easy to be both popular and good. The Trollopes were neither. . . . [He] wrote in his *Autobiography*, "I have long been aware of a certain weakness in my character, which I may call a craving for love." He coveted popularity "with a coveting which was almost mean." He wanted desperately to shine—to revenge himself on the cruel dismissive judgements made on him all those years ago by his family and his schoolmasters. . . . In life Trollope cut an ungainly, donkeyish figure. When he was sent to the United States, his American hosts found his bluff clubland humour merely boorish. It was when he was alone with a pen and a ream of foolscap that Trollope was able to triumph. Writing in the early mornings, he anatomized the society which excluded him from its counsels and from the full warmth of its affection [p. 79].

In his writing, which he sometimes defensively denigrated, Trollope could be godlike, creating a controlled world in which he could love and hate, reward and punish freely. Raban calls the passionate directness "of a lover" to be found in Trollope's letters about literature a

> clue to the intensity and warmth of Trollope's fiction. Writing novels, he was able to experience an intimacy singularly lacking in his life outside fiction. His converse with his characters was pillow talk. He loved them, and said so. His letters, like his "roaring" talk at dinner, belong to

the injured and thwarted side of Trollope's life—the side that worked like the weights on a pressure cooker, to build up steam for the fiction within [p. 83].

Hall (1983a) notes the ardor also involved in Trollope's later (post-hobbledehoy) work for the post office: "Trollope fell in love with his work. It became a vocation, almost a passion, and he brought to it the same incredible energy he brought to novel writing" (p. xxii). Looking back in *An Autobiography*, Trollope (1883) remembered the time when he was checking the routes and the honesty of mail carriers in Ireland and in England. To do so he called "the ambition of my life.... It is amusing to watch how a passion will grow upon a man" (p. 87). He was depressed after he left the postal service in 1867, long after he had stopped being dependent on his salary there.

Trollope was addicted to writing. Henry James wrote:

It was once the fortune of the author of these lines to cross the Atlantic in [Trollope's] company, and he has never forgotten the magnificent example of plain persistence that it was in the power of the eminent novelist to give on that occasion. The season was unpropitious, the vessel overcrowded, the voyage detestable; but Trollope shut himself up in his cabin every morning for a purpose which ... could only be communion with the muse. He drove his pen as steadily on the tumbling ocean as in Montague Square [Hall, 1983b, pp. 666–667].

Trollope needed to control his resentment, with its potential for acquiring dangerous intensity, at least as much as his love, with its accompanying vulnerability to hurt. His predominant moderated masochism effectively neutralized and for the most part concealed the sadism so charged with the need for revenge for the neglect and humiliation of his childhood. Trollope's popularity as a novelist was revived during the turmoil and disorder of World War II. The mid-Victorian period seemed in retrospect to have been a time of order and comparative peace, and readers' nostalgia for the solid and dependable, especially in those who confined themselves to the Barsetshire series of novels, drew them to Trollope's fiction. One needs to read all of Trollope to realize how much murder, violence, crime, and madness there is in his fiction (see Mullen and Munson, 1996, pp. 520–521).

Brother Tom attests to the potential for violence when he describes Anthony's searching in a private desk in a post office for a valuable letter he thought the postmaster had stolen. When told that the key had been mislaid, he kicked the desk in "and there found the stolen letter" (T. A. Trollope, 1888, p. 179). Glendinning (1992) comments:

> [Trollope's] violent streak is reflected in his fiction—in murders, muggings, garrottings, in quarrels where a man is left with his head broken against a fireplace or slumped against railings on a dark street, in shootings and attempted stabbings by both men and women; in suicides; in physical brutality of brother to sister; in frequent authorial regrets that the days of duelling are no more. The violence in his novels is not the compensating fantasy of a peaceable man; it comes from the imagination of a man who knows what it is to see red [p. 173].

CONTROL

Several friends and observers have noted the extraordinary control Trollope had of his sleep. He was able to send himself to sleep instantly, sometimes for 10 or 20 minutes, and awake refreshed. (There are accounts of this practice to be found in Terry, 1987, p. 58.)

There was also the need to keep control of anality, specifically of the dirt and money that symbolized it. Dirt was associated with the helplessness of the schoolboy years; lack of money, with what in large part caused the helplessness.

> In my boyhood, when I would be crawling up to school with dirty boots and trousers through the muddy lanes, I was always telling myself that the misery of the hour was not the worst of it, but that the mud and solitude and poverty of the time would insure me mud and solitude and poverty through my life [Trollope, 1883, pp. 168–169].

Debt was also something to be dreaded and avoided. He was haunted by the example of his bankrupt father's shameful flight to Belgium—and by some of the experiences of his hobbledehoy days, when debts of about £20 grew by accumulated interest into one of over £200, and he was hounded by a moneylender who used to follow him into his office and make scenes, and "Sheriffs' officers with uncanny documents, of which I never understood anything, were common attendants on me.... The debts were not large, but I cannot think now how I could have lived, and sometimes have enjoyed life, with such a burden of duns that I endured" (p. 50). Aspects of these humiliating contacts appear in many of his novels.

Trollope was compulsive about money. "From his late twenties on he was a fanatical keeper of accounts. Money and the efficient management of money were to be central to his feelings of security" (Glendinning, 1992, p. 36). Other manifestations of the compulsiveness about money are to be found in and in relation to his novels. He almost always mentions the yearly incomes of the main characters, and in *An Autobiography* he lists the exact amount of money earned by every one of his books he had published, even including the shillings and pence.

Alongside this compulsivity, Trollope could also be realistic. He was not mercenary. Hall (1983a) writes of "his almost quixotic honesty and fairness in dealing with publishers" (p. xv). Indeed, his letters show that sometimes he was almost masochistic when offering to withdraw a manuscript or to accept lower fees when there appeared to be trouble for, or negative criticism from, a publisher. He offered to reimburse the publishers Chapman & Hall for the firm's losses when the last of his Palliser novels, *The Duke's Children* (Trollope, 1880), did not sell well. In a letter written in 1881, two years before his death, he countered a charge by his old friend John Tilley, who had been the husband of his dead sister Cecilia, "You say of me—that I would not choose to write novels unless I were paid. Most certainly I would—much rather than not write them at all" (Hall, 1983b, p. 773). He documents his contradictions, making it clear that he wrote out of emotional need and desire and not primarily for money.

His writing gave Trollope a feeling of control of his own psychic world, peopled by his own creations, that provided a feeling of satisfactory emotional freedom (guarded generally by his inner "rules" and "laws"). Whatever his problems with sexual identity, Trollope could, as a kind of bisexual Jehovah, be mother and father to his characters; he could both be them and make love to them. Henry James (1883) wrote that Trollope, in dealing with his American girl characters, "is full of good humour and of that fatherly indulgence, that almost motherly sympathy, which characterizes his attitude throughout toward the youthful feminine" (p. 1346). Raban (1987) writes: "Trollope wrote better about women than any male novelist in English. He understood their bitter sense of exclusion from the important centre of [19th century] society" (pp. 78–79). The last statement is certainly true; but so is one of Glendinning's (1992) about the ambivalence of Trollope's views about the rights of women: "[Sometimes] his terror of women abandoning the domesticity which sustained men overruled his intelligent sympathy" (p. 328).

Anthony Trollope clearly cared deeply for his wife and his two sons, although he seems also to have felt dissatisfied with them. In the end, his creative activity came to be more reliable and more meaningful than his outwardly successful roles in life as husband, paterfamilias, and famous author.

DISORDER

In the second volume of Trollope's *Collected Letters*, Hall (1983b) has included part of a commonplace book that Trollope began when he started to work at the post office. It has a section entitled "Order—Method":

> I am myself in all the pursuits (God help them) & practices of my life most disorderly and unmethodical—and the injury which this failing has occasioned is so near to utter ruin that I can but set myself as an example to others—as a buoy whereby other vessels may *afford* [sic] those sands on which my cargo was so nearly lost [p. 1027; italics added].

I feel that his slip—"afford" for "avoid"—and his resulting mixed metaphor show his contradictory feelings about order and disorder. The passage continues:

The first impression which a parent should fix on the mind of a child, is I think love of order—It is the reins by which all virtues are kept in their proper places—and the vices with whom the virtues run in one team, *are controlled* [p. 1027; italics added].

Of course, with the idea of order, which we try vainly to impose on a chaotic universe, one has at least the illusion of knowing what things are like, what the future will be like, what we ourselves are like. Trollope could excellently bring out the irrational and contradictory qualities in his fully portrayed characters. Trollope was perhaps aware that he did not know what he himself was like, although he needed to try to present a number of predictable personae in order to reassure others, but, above all, himself. He was wise enough and had suffered enough to grasp the disorder inherent in man's fate; and he could also be compelled by and even, spitefully and masochistically, enjoy disorder, frightening as it was. But in his fiction, the world and its disorder could be controlled.

Several years before his death and before the posthumous publication of *An Autobiography*, Trollope briefly summed up his life for a curious (unknown) correspondent: "I have written above 80 novels and novelettes, have written about almost all English speaking peoples, have written a life of Cicero, & memoirs of Caesar and Thackeray.[2] I have also been twice round the world, and was for 35 years in the post office.... I think I have answered all your questions" (Hall, 1983b, p. 933). He left out his run for a seat in

---

2. Thackeray was both friend and benefactor to Trollope. He died in the same year as Fanny Trollope; both losses were very hard for the 48-year-old Anthony. It is intriguing to speculate why Trollope was so interested in Cicero and Caesar. He wrote his biographical sketch of Cicero (one of his favorite Roman writers) after reading an attack on the Roman statesman and author, written by a man who had most unfavorably reviewed Trollope's book about Caesar. Trollope's excited dedication to the research involved in both classical biographies would certainly have returned him (now in the reassuring active role of mastery) to the texts of his schooldays. Trollope was fond of using classical quotations (mostly Latin) in his books. There was an identification with his father in Trollope's positive prejudices here (he was proud of his two Roman biographies and resented the lack of praise for them from scholars)—Thomas Anthony had been ardently devoted to classical literature. But there were also earlier threatening connections with Anthony's

Chapter 13

Parliament; but then he had lost, having come in third, at the bottom of the poll.

Here is a tribute from Henry James (1883), who, as a young man, wrote some hostile reviews of Trollope's novels but later in life came to admire him:

> The essence of [his] love of reality was his extreme interest in character. This is the fine and admirable quality in Trollope, this is what will preserve his best works. . . . If he was in any degree a man of genius (and I hold that he was) it was in virtue of [his] happy, instinctive perception of human varieties. His knowledge of the stuff we are made of, his observation of the common behavior of men and women, was not reasoned or acquired, not even particularly studied. All human beings deeply interested him, human life, to his mind, was a perpetual story. . . . If he was a knowing psychologist he was so by grace. . . . We care what happens to people only in proportion as we know what people are. Trollope's great apprehension of the real, which was what made him so interesting, came to him through his desire . . . to tell us what certain people were and what they did in consequence of being so [pp. 1333–1334].

The "happy, instinctive perception," being a psychologist "by grace" are gifts. Trollope made use of them to counter his traumatic and miserable childhood, but they are not a result of his psychic pathology.

---

childhood to counteract, such as rehearsing Latin grammar at the side of his razor-wielding father. There was also perhaps something Roman (ascetic, righteous, Republican Roman) in Thomas Anthony's character (reflected in Anthony's) that gave rise to admiration in the son, but this must have been alongside the fear of the Roman infanticidal father mentioned by Anthony in the letter to Tom that I have quoted.

Chapter 14

TROLLOPE'S DEATH

Now I stretch out my hand, and from the further shore I bid adieu to all who have cared to read any among the many words that I have written.
—Anthony Trollope's last written words
An Autobiography

In his last years, despite depression and ill health, Trollope continued to write and publish according to his customary schedule. This labor stopped suddenly when he suffered a stroke in 1882. He lingered on several months after the stroke occurred but never recovered enough to resume writing. The circumstances under which the stroke took place seem significant to me; this is my conjecture rather than certainty.

The stroke occurred in the late autumn of 1882 at a small family gathering at the home of Trollope's old friend and former brother-in-law, John Tilley (by that time thrice a widower). Trollope for some time had not been feeling fit. He had been warned that he was suffering from angina pectoris. That afternoon he had had a not uncharacteristic fit of rage at disorder thrust upon him: he engaged in a shouting-match with the leader of a German band that had disturbed him by playing outside his windows at a hotel where he was staying. At the Tilleys' he was still angry, and the family felt he was overexcited at dinner. Later that evening, it was decided that his Tilley niece would read aloud an amusing book about schoolboy and family life that had just been published, F. Anstey's (1882) *Vice-Versa, or a Lesson to Fathers*. Trollope had a very loud laugh that the family was used to, and he joined in the laughter with his customary obstreperousness. But after a time someone noticed that the loud low note of his clamor was no longer sounding, and the novelist was found slumped over in his chair—red-faced, speechless, and paralyzed on his right side. He survived for about five weeks. At first he seemed to be improving but then grew weaker. He never recovered his power of speech. I speculate that the content of the first chapters of Anstey's novel may have evoked a response of conflict-ridden emotional intensity involving all the disorder and early sorrow of his forlorn schooldays—rage at father and missing mother, longing in vain for empathy and loving care. The emotional turmoil, in counterpoint with his amusement and his vociferous laughing, may thus have provided too much of a strain for his vulnerable cerebral blood vessels.

Vice-Versa describes a magical exchange of bodies of a father and his schoolboy son during a Christmas school break. The mother is dead and the widower father is living in London with his three motherless children. His older son, Dick, now home for Christmas holidays, is about to return to boarding school. The situation resembles Anthony's horrible schoolday years with his father and without his mother at Harrow Weald. The selfish, uncaring, and unempathic father is depicted as being impatient to get rid of his son. Dick's conduct is much less subdued and more provocative than Anthony's was. Anstey (1882) describes him as just enough afraid of his father

> to prevent any cordiality between them and not enough to make him careful to avoid offence. . . . [The father] was one of those nervous and fidgety persons who cannot understand their own children, looking on them as objectionable monsters whose next movements are uncertain—much as Frankenstein must have felt towards his monster. He hated to have a boy about the house, and positively writhed under the irrelevant and irrepressible questions, the unnecessary noises and boisterous high spirits which nothing could subdue; his son's society was to him simply an abominable nuisance, and he pined for a release from it from the day the holidays began [pp. 5–6].

When Dick comes to say goodbye, the father hasn't have "the remotest idea of what to say to this red-haired solemn boy" (p. 5) who dreads going back to school. Since reproof is the easiest and most familiar way to communicate with his son, the father threatens him with punishment if he continues to misbehave at school. Dick expresses his wish to transfer from his present one, Dr. Grimstone's School; he would like to go to Harrow, where one of his friends is transferring. (The mention of his former and consciously hated school, the name potent with connotations of beating and rejection, surely affected Anthony.) The father refuses to consider the idea.

Dick had picked up from a tray and pocketed an Indian stone with a strange inscription on it, brought by a relative from India. To Dick, it looks like a talisman, and he wants to take it to school to impress his schoolmates. But the irascible father refuses permission and takes the stone in his own hand. He does not know that the ancient stone is indeed a talisman, endowed with the magical power to grant wishes. The exchange of bodies is brought about unexpectedly when the father voices a wish that follows the argument about Dick going back to Dr. Grimstone's. He first tells Dick that he considers the time at school the happiest time of life. Dick does not believe him.

> [The father] still had the stone in his hand as he sank back into his chair, smiling with a tolerant superiority. "Perhaps you will believe me," he said, impressively, "when I tell you, old as I am and much as you envy me, I only wish, at this very moment, I could be a boy again, like you. Going back to school wouldn't make me unhappy, I can tell you" [p. 19].

The body exchanges that ensue reverse the power situation. The transformed "adult" son can now take over the father's wish to get rid of the boy who was so reluctant to return to school. He can have his revenge by forcing his father (now in the son's body) back to the boarding school where he will be tormented and learn painfully to acquire empathy for what the boy had been living through.

For comparison, here is an observation about Trollope's father's incapacity for empathy from Tom Trollope's second wife, Frances's—not a surprising name for a wife of Tom's—biography of Fanny Trollope. She describes how Thomas Anthony wrote letters to his sons that were

> extraordinary from their minute and reiterated questions about every detail of their progress at Winchester. . . . He

Chapter 14

worries the boys unsparingly and unceasingly. No father could display more single-minded devotion to the welfare of his family than did Thomas Anthony Trollope. But he never put himself for a moment in the boy's place [quoted in Neville-Sington, 1997, p. 103].

Vice-Versa begins with a physical description of the father, Paul Bultitude, who (as his Trollopian name[1] connotes) is a large man: "a tall and portly person, of a somewhat pompous and overbearing demeanour; not much over fifty, but looking considerably older.... He was an elderly gentleman, too, of irreproachable character and antecedents" (pp. 3,5). This could be a description of Trollope himself. But it goes on to resemble his hot-tempered and impossibly unempathic father, who also was one of those "nervous and fidgety persons who cannot understand their own children." The story presented the potentially terrifying prospect for Anthony of returning in late middle age to his motherless schoolboy years of torment, persecution, and misery. Along with the terror, hearing about the triumph of the schoolboy who could send his father to face those miseries in his stead (part of Anstey's subtitle is "A Lesson to Fathers") could have mobilized intense guilt in the emotionally vulnerable elderly listener.

When Trollope (1883) was 60, he wrote: "Something of the disgrace of my schooldays has clung to me all through life (p. 17). He never could outlive the specters of disorder and early sorrow. But accomplishment and capacity for enjoyment continued, even when depression crept in during his last years of middle age. Following his stroke he was partly paralyzed, his speech and mental functioning were "almost completely" (Hall, 1993b, p. 514). impaired. He lingered on in a nursing home for a little over a month. At first he improved slightly, but he remained physically and mentally handicapped. He could not work. His autobiography, a completed novel, and a half-finished one were found in a drawer in his writing desk after his death.

---

1. Trollope had an unfortunate tendency to use impossible and too obviously comic names. I think few readers would respond with humor to his calling lawyers Mr. Allewinde or Mr. Gitemthruet or Mr. Neversay Die; or physicians Dr. Fillgrave, Dr. Rerechild, or Sir Omicron Pie. Trollope frequently uses names that belittle those characters espousing causes he detests: for example, militant feminists like Olivia Q. Fleabody, Ph.D. and Lady Selina Protest.

Chapter 15

TROLLOPE WITH MOTHER

If I were hanged on the highest hill,
Mother o'mine, O mother o'mine!
I know whose love would follow me still,
Mother o'mine, O mother o'mine!
—Rudyard Kipling, "Mother o'Mine"

Trollope, like most human beings who grow up with two parents, was profoundly influenced by both his mother and father and identified with both of them as he developed and matured—identifications that made up part of Anthony's identity and mental representation of himself. His mother seems to have been more meaningful to him than his father. She was a predominantly positive influence when she was present and able to attend to him, as well as someone longed for and despairingly resented when she was away or too busy to be attentive to his emotional and realistic needs.

Certainly he longed to love her and be loved by her. Anthony's love for his character Glencora Palliser (mentioned in chapter 13) can be seen as a displaced expression of his wish to love his mother and the loving side of his ambivalence toward her. I share Neville-Sington's (1997) conviction that the captivating yet difficult Lady Glencora represents Trollope's (1864) consciously willed decision to portray his mother. Here is the description of the character as she first appears in *The Small House at Allington*:

> The Lady Glencora was small of stature, and her happy round face lacked, perhaps, the highest grace of female

beauty. But there was ever a smile upon it, at which it was very pleasant to look; and the intense interest with which she would dance, and talk, and follow up every amusement that was offered her, was very charming [p. 661].

The physical description fits Fanny (and her well-known portrait by Hervieu), who loved dancing and (as the description goes on to mention) horses and riding horses.

The first chapter of *An Autobiography* (Trollope, 1883) is about his father and his school days. His mother is scarcely mentioned in it, and two of the four instances when the word "mother" is used have to do with her going to and returning from America, implicitly linking her with leaving Anthony behind. Another reference to her concerns the first separation from her, his birth. In chapter 2, titled "My Mother," he says of her early years with his father: "Her life, I take it, though latterly clouded by money troubles, was easy, luxurious, and idle, till my father's affairs and her own aspirations sent her to America" (pp. 22–23). He is somewhat grudging about her talents:

> She was an unselfish, affectionate, and most industrious woman, with great capacity for enjoyment and high physical gifts. She was endowed, too, with much creative power, with considerable humor, and a genuine feeling for romance. But she was neither clear-sighted nor accurate; and in her attempts to describe morals, manners, and even facts, was unable to avoid the pitfalls of exaggeration [pp. 32–33].

Even in his praise of her personality there is much ambiguity:

> Of the mixture of joviality and industry which formed her character, it is almost impossible to speak with exaggeration. The industry was a thing apart. . . . She was at her table at four in the morning, and had finished her work before the world had begun to be aroused. But the joviality was *all for others* [pp. 24–25; italics added].

The work, of course, was not housework but her writing. As to her joviality, Anthony was here consciously saying that she was not jovial for herself, but the words also can convey the meaning that the joviality was for others and not for him. He continues:

> She could dance with other people's legs, eat and drink with other people's palates, be proud with the lustre of other people's finery. Every mother can do that for her own daughters; but she could do it for any girl whose look, and voice, and manners pleased her [p. 25].

This joyful empathy was also extended to Anthony's three older brothers as well as to his sisters, but he did not feel it was there for him. Whatever Fanny felt about Anthony's wife, Rose, she treated her very well. Rose wrote about her mother-in-law after visiting her in Florence in 1853, praising her generosity and stating that she thought her the most charming old lady who ever existed. I wonder if Trollope may have had the fantasy that he would have been loved more if he had been his mother's daughter—if so, this fantasy would have contributed to his unconscious feminine identification. The passage from his autobiography continues: "Even when she was at work, the laughter *of those she loved* was a pleasure to her" (p. 25; italics added). But, one wonders, how much was Anthony able to see himself as someone Fanny loved? The paragraph goes on:

> She had much, very much, to suffer. Work sometimes came hard to her, so much being required—for she was extravagant, and liked to have money to spend; but of all people I have known she was the most joyous, or, at any rate, the most capable of joy [p. 25].

But, sadly, he could not feel convinced that she was joyous for or about him.

There is evidence of Anthony's malice toward his mother in the annotations he made at age 19 when copying out her long poem on the controversy over the burial of Allegra Byron, Byron's illegitimate daughter (see Super, 1988, p. 21). Fanny was deeply angry with Reverend Cunningham, an Evangelical minister at Harrow, who refused to set up a tablet to the child when she was buried in the churchyard. Some of Anthony's comments on Fanny's poem were quite hostile. Neville-Sington (1997) quotes three:

"these lines are bad," "twaddle, all this" and "perspicuity of style is by no means the merits of the poem" (p. 365). There is another occasion for anger toward his mother in relation to her novel, *Charles Chesterfield or the Adventures of a Youth* (F. Trollope, 1841). Fanny started to write this novel, which she began to publish in 1840, when she was in London nursing the sick Anthony, who was then 26. (This was the turning point in his hobbledehoy years that resulted in his actively arranging for his transfer to Ireland.) His mother had been aware of Anthony's wishes to be a writer since he was in his late teens. In the novel, which clearly seems to be about Anthony (see Neville-Sington, 1997. p. 289), Fanny describes a 19-year-old youth who, against his family's wishes, is determined to become a writer. His mother, however, is devoted to him and proud of her son's intellectual talents. Charles is described, in words Anthony is going to use about himself in his autobiography decades later, as "building all sorts of castles, possible and impossible, in the air" (quoted by Neville-Sington, 1997, pp. 190–191). Whatever joy Anthony found in this novel would have been nullified by its ending. The would-be author, after the frustration of many rejected manuscripts, feels himself a failure; he decides to stop writing, marries, and becomes a clergyman. This ending surely evoked bitter feeling in the man whose mother had first discouraged his ambitions to become one of the family writers and then reluctantly helped find him a publisher for his first novels but did not read them.

With his father there was more concentrated conscious hostility in his ambivalence. Anthony, as a boy, needed a good and a strong father as an object for identification to confirm his masculinity, one who could accept and tolerate the boy's hostility and rivalry. Here he was not well served; his father was a financial and emotional failure—easily hated and ridiculed and yet a frightening tyrant who could not control his outbursts of temper and was often ruled by whim. He was also most certainly perceived by his sensitive son as a tragic, vulnerable, and flawed figure—and was repeatedly so presented in various disguises in Anthony's fiction. When Anthony became a father himself he named his first-born Harry, after the dead brother who had been his father's favorite. I have mentioned that may conflict-ridden and contradictory feelings about his relations and identification with his father were greatly heightened when he was left alone with his father while the rest of the family remained in America. How could his mother have done this to his father and to him? Yet, at the same time the boy hated his father's miserliness, tyranny, and temper tantrums, while feeling sorry for him and guilty about his hatred. Why had his mother left him to go to America; and why hadn't his father prevented her leaving? There are frequent statements in his novels expressing the wife's duty not to desert her errant or failing husband.

ANTHONY'S MOTHER

Frances (Fanny) Trollope was born in 1779. She was the third-born of six children, three of whom died as infants. The two surviving siblings were her sister, Mary (three years older), and her brother, Henry (five years younger). Two children died between the births of Fanny and Henry. Death was a palpable presence in her early childhood, culminating with the death of her mother when Fanny was five. The resultant longing for mothering was probably tempered by a compensatory push for independence; she seems to have been generally well ahead in the competition for her father's attention with her less gifted older sister and her much younger brother. The young child suffered comparative neglect of the cultivation of traditional feminine domestic skills—this lack might well have been remedied by her mother's supervision if she had lived on.

The girl learned quickly and eagerly to speak and read Latin, French, and Italian. Fanny's comparative freedom of action as a young girl who could see to her own pleasures, education and needs was not interfered with by her fond father. This independence had profound effects on her developing character and seems to have helped make her a happy and self-confident child, a disposition she retained for most of the rest of her life. Her temperament must have involved overcompensation for traumatic loss, but it worked out well. In Bristol, where the family lived, Fanny was brought up in a lively intellectual, artistic, and social circle of friends and acquaintances of her father. Her life as a girl and young woman was full of balls and picnics, music and dancing, conversation about art and literature, and amateur theatricals—all of which she continued to cultivate and feel dependent

Chapter 15

on as a married woman and then as a widow in England and Europe. The theatrical presentations continued even when she was living in Cincinnati.

I repeat: Anthony's psychically central tie to his mother involved identification with her. This tie is most obvious in his being motivated to take up an identity as a literary man and a novelist. Aside from the display of her inherited talent, Fanny Trollope brought to her household a passion for intellectual activity. As a child she had the leisure and license to cultivate a lifelong fascination with reading. Neville-Sington (1997) points out that all Fanny's heroines are ardent readers (p. 8). So was her son Anthony, who also became a fervent collector of books.

In 1800, when she was 21, Fanny's father married again. Fanny, the central figure in her widower father's household, was apparently discontent to be ruled over by another woman. Three years after her father's second marriage, her brother, Henry, obtained a government job, and he and his two sisters moved out of their paternal home to live together in a house in London. It was there that she met her future husband, Thomas Anthony Trollope. They saw a lot of one another and corresponded often. Thomas Anthony could be charming and even humorous in his letters. Both Anthony and Tom admired and praised Fanny's part of the correspondence when they read her love letters after Fanny's death. Anthony (Trollope, 1883) wrote: "In no novel of Richardson's or Miss Burney's have I seen a correspondence at the same time so sweet, so graceful, and so well expressed" (p. 20).

Thomas Anthony was also blunt and honest about his deficiencies; and his letters show an obsessive concern about Fanny's health—probably a projection of his own hypochondriac propensities. But their letters also reveal mutual love. When they married, she was 29 and he was 35. Their first few years together were comparatively happy. But, as I have related, sometime after the birth of their first child Tom, Thomas Anthony's irritable disposition began to provoke failure with his clients and colleagues. And his health declined.

When, after the family all returned from America and Henry was told he needed to go to a warm climate to survive, Fanny had not enough money to follow the advice of the doctors. It was during the terrible years in Bruges after Thomas Anthony's flight from debtor's prison that Fanny had to awaken to do her writing at four in the morning in order to be with the family at breakfast. After that, most of her day was devoted to nursing the dying. Distress over the violent quarreling between Henry and Thomas Anthony made it sometimes necessary for Fanny, already working night and day, to take laudanum (tincture of opium), used as a sedative in the early 19th century as freely as aspirin is now. The drug's toxic qualities were ignored, as were calomel's.

Anthony, as a 19-year-old, appreciated how hard it was for her when both Henry and Thomas Anthony were dying:

> There were two sick men in the house, and hers were the hands that tended them. The novels went on, of course. We had already learned that they would be forthcoming at stated intervals—and they always were forthcoming. The doctor's vials and the ink bottle held equal places in my mother's rooms. I have written many novels in many circumstances; but I doubt much whether I could write one when my whole heart was by the bedside of a dying son. Her power of dividing herself into two parts, and keeping her intellect by itself clear from the troubles of the world, and fit for the duty it had to do, I never saw equaled [Trollope, 1883, p. 43].

Anthony too had this power of emotional isolation that permitted a compulsion to hold to work habits even under difficult circumstances.[1] And his novels, no less than his mother's, always came forth at "stated intervals."

There are many superficial similarities between mother and son. Both loved dancing and riding horses. Both were indifferent to appearance and careless about how they dressed. Both did their writing in a compulsive way and wrote in the early morning. Both were continuously active and productive, wont to start a new book as soon as an old one was finished.

The conscious or unconscious influence of his mother's books on Anthony is demonstrated by the frequent instances of likenesses and parallels between some of their fictional characters.

---

1. I think Jules Renard was addressing a similar defensive state when he wrote shortly before his death: "Between my brain and me there always remains a layer that I cannot penetrate" (quoted in Bouillier, 1990, p. 997; my translation).

Chapter 15

An example of such borrowing or echoing, pointed to by more than one critic or biographer, is the resemblance of the character of the hypocritical Reverend Cartwright, the eponymous "hero" of *The Vicar of Wrexhill* (F. Trollope, 1837) to that of the sanctimonious and dishonest clergyman Obadiah Slope in *Barchester Towers* (Trollope, 1857). Also both mother and son based many characters in many novels on aspects of the personality of their respective husband and father, Thomas Anthony Trollope. In *One Fault* (F. Trollope, 1840) Fanny depicted the monomania of a jealous, obsessive husband; this characterization was echoed in Anthony's portrait of Louis Trevelyan in *He Knew He Was Right* (Trollope, 1869b). Both fictional husbands had bad tempers and paranoid obsessions that were undoubtedly largely modeled on those of Thomas Anthony. Ransom (1995) points out the possible influence on Anthony's (Trollope, 1855) writing *The Warden* (begun in 1853) of the comic presentation of religious life and conflicts in his mother's recently published (F. Trollope, 1852) novel, *Uncle Walter*. She indicates the likeness of character that kindly Uncle Walter bears to Mr. Harding, Anthony's Warden. Also, Fanny Trollope set a precedent in her three novels about the widow Barnaby for many of Anthony's novels in which he repeated the use of the same characters—for example, in his Barsetshire and Palliser series.

I agree with Ransom's (1995) observation that Anthony was also influenced by his mother's style. A "Trollope style" that referred to both novelists was talked and written about in the mid-19th century. The central importance of the narrator and the free offering of her or his comments and opinions are common to both mother and son.

Anthony adopted his mother's prejudice against evangelical religion, both in his life and in his novels. Anthony had divided views on legal restrictions on women; he showed intuitive and indignant feelings but also could be antifeminist. Similarly, he felt in many situations both a sympathy and an identification with the underdog and yet a contradictory siding with and identification with the aggressor. This ambivalence is evident in his attitudes about the Irish and the Jews as well as in his views on women's political and family rights. Fanny too was subject to similar psychic splits; she was often both a Tory politically and emotionally and yet a sympathizer with, and a fervent believer in, liberal causes.

Both the archconservative Prince Metternich and the great Italian rebel Mazzini were her close personal acquaintances. Fanny Trollope was predominantly an enthusiastic exposer and a condemner of social abuses in her novels and travel books, especially in relation to the treatment of blacks in America and to the unfairness and cruelty doled out to women and children by the laws made for and by men. Her novels often had tendentious presentations of her views on specific social and religious questions—women's rights, the Poor Laws, Catholicism and the Oxford Movement; she described the plight of people condemned to the poorhouse and of children exploited day and night by the mill owners. This aspect of her writing made for much fellow feeling that enhanced the friendship between her and Charles Dickens. Fanny was able to present sexual situations, prostitution, and the plight of unmarried mothers and illegitimate children in her novels with an honesty and forthrightness that brought her much negative criticism. Her attitude was in marked contrast to the prudishness of most later Victorian fiction writing. Anthony continued her pattern with a similar indignant honesty in his novels, usually for but sometimes against liberal causes. He too could write tracts and lectures in his novels. His depiction of sexuality was presented in a more indirect fashion—the modification dictated partially, as I have noted, by the conventions insisted on by the publishers when novel reading had become an established family habit.

Anthony became aware of his mother as a professional writer and of her writing habits after her return from America when he was 15 years old. Ten years later, when she was already an established author, she still had the same writing routine. She wrote then to her son and companion Tom, asking him to be careful about expenses, since she had been forced out of her need for money to agree to her publisher's low offers of remuneration. "If you were sixty-two years old, and had to get up at four o'clock every morning to work for it, you would not wonder at my saying this" (quoted by Ransom, 1995, p. 148).

Anthony started to think of writing his first novel after the meaningful experience of his mother's nursing him through his disabling illness when he was in his mid-20s. At this time he repeated the experiences of his late teenage years of observing her writing habits at first hand—her astonishing productivity and

Chapter 15

industry and her early rising to do the writing. This time his admiring scrutiny that related to her taking care of *him* eventually bore the fruit of his own fiction, with his doing his writing using his own version of her compulsive work habits. After their brief period of closeness occasioned by her nursing him, she again left England to make frequent trips to write the travel books that were demanded of her by her publishers. Since Anthony was the only one of the surviving children who had a dependable salary, he was again left behind, while Tom (usually) and Cecilia (sometimes) were her companions. Anthony started to write his first novel in 1843, the same year that Fanny settled down to live with Tom in Italy; he was then 28, engaged to be married, and settled in Ireland.

The identification with Fanny as writer was an active and adaptive way of unconsciously holding on to the repetitively deserting mother. The still powerful unconscious assumption stemming from his childhood that there could be no life without mother was countered by the grown-up Anthony's attempt to keep a hold on her by becoming her, at least in his writing life.

Frances Trollope published her last book in 1856 at age 77. She became somewhat senile during her last few years and died at home in Florence at 84. In her last year, she wrote to Anthony a rare letter of praise. She first apologized for not having acknowledged his "precious packet" (apparently containing some of his own books) earlier and adds:

> But the degree of activity of which I have been wont to boast, and on which I have so often been complimented might have been accounted in my very best days as positive *idleness* to what you manifest. Tom and I agree in thinking that you exceed in this respect any individual whom we have ever known or heard of—and I am proud of being your mother—as well for this reason as for sundry others. I rejoice to think that you have considerably more than the third of a century to gallop through yet before reaching the age at which I first felt inclined to cry *"halte la!"* [quoted in Ransom, 1995, p. 215; italics added].

Here she was expressing her pride in being his mother in a way that seems heartfelt. Yet she specifies as her source of pride his industry and adds that there are also "sundry other" reasons. We cannot be sure how this praise affected Anthony. His mother does not praise him for being a good writer. I wonder whether he rankled at this omission and how extensive it was. There is no way of knowing if she read his books or commented on them if she did; or if she felt envious of his success when he became so popular and her reputation began to decline. She had, we do know, refused to read his first few novels.

Good parenting (in spite of the inevitability of its being unaccompanied by some that is deficient) is probably the most important influence we know on the mental health of a child. It does not follow that, however good it is, it is enough to save any individual child from neurotic conflict or even mental illness. At the beginning of this book, I emphasized the destructive and inhibiting effects on those people who remain with a deep and inflexible attachment to their parents. But how complicated and contradictory this kind of parental bond can be is illustrated by a consideration of Anthony Trollope's relationship to his mother. For him, alongside the damaging effects of the relationship with a mother who was not there for him at crucial times, one can see how his life with, without, and even *as* (and here I mean specifically his identification with her as a writer) his mother provided—in contrast to what appears to be true for Jules Renard—a support for both his life and his works. It is a paradox, but also a commonplace, that a child's *healthy* identification (strong and yet flexible, so that both can let go when necessary) with a parent contributes to that child's separate sense of identity in life and the use of his or her own creative talents in art.

PART III
CONCLUSION AND EPILOGUE

Chapter 16

CONCLUSION AND MORE LITERARY EXAMPLES

Das Ewig-Weibliche zieht uns hinan. [The eternal feminine leads us upward and on.]

—Johann Wolfgan von Goethe, *Faust*

In closing, I would like to state some general convictions about the mysterious sources of artistic and scientific creativity. I feel that creativity is inevitably related to psychopathology since we are all, being human, at least neurotic if not, one hopes, temporarily even sicker. Although most of us are not psychotic, I believe that we are all at least encumbered with what I have called (Shengold, 1995) the delusions of everyday life because our early psychic development leaves traces that, as Freud (1937) stated, resemble psychosis. Yet it is also my opinion that, whatever the complicated and ambiguous relationship of creativity to our psychic conflicts, drives, symptoms, traumata, and deficiencies may be, it makes no sense to base the sources of our talents and creative powers principally on pathology.

MUSING ON THE QUESTION, "IS THERE LIFE WITHOUT MOTHER?"—PHANTASMAGORIA OR WISDOM?

The mind arises out of the body. Freud (1941) said that the ego—the sense of identity, of I-ness—is first and foremost body ego.

Chapter 16

The newborn is preoccupied with sensations and perceptions from within its body and its body surface before there is differentiation between inside and outside. We begin as part of the mother's body, and the first unconscious fragments of the mind are taken up with the womb out of which we have come and the breast (or its equivalent) that feeds us. ("The breast is a part of me, I am the breast" [p. 299]).

Later these mental fragments begin to be separated out and are blended with and partially transformed into the cloaca/vagina and the phallus. Separation from the primal maternal bodily psychic presence (the eternal feminine as a bisexual primal parent) and the (relative and always incomplete) achievement of a separate identity comes slowly and is at first piecemeal. Even after this psychological birth, which takes place in the early years following the actual one, there is an almost complete dependence on the mothering figure—the first eventually externalized other who continues to be identified with, adding to the internal mother-as-primal parent presence (imago) in the mind. As psychic maturation proceeds and the dependence on the all-powerful, other, increasingly externalized presence shrinks, the father and others supplement and can partly replace the primal parental attachment.

The urgently needed, separated-out mother and father (or their functional substitutes) are the first objects of our love and our hate. They fill the world like gods. We focus on them initially all our anxieties and all our emotions. Once established outside the infant's mind and body, they continue to be taken in as part of the developing mind, which becomes modified by these identifications. These psychic internalizations have their own development and maturation, conceived of differently by psychoanalytic theorists (see Schafer, 1968). So identifications can be primitive or mature, and they can have pathological as well as healthy effects. The actual parental others are thus psychically assimilated—in inevitably subjectively distorted form—by evolving identificatory processes to become dynamic parts of our mental structure. It is one of the chief destructive effects of child abuse and soul murder that healthy, structure-building identifications are interfered with.

The mother and father outside our minds continue throughout childhood and adolescence to be vitally needed for nurturance and protection, love and care. Parents or parental substitutes are essential to help contain the child's innate, instinctually derived

Conclusion

emotions—especially rage, excitement, and anxiety—during and even after the time when the parental internalized images help form the child's own mental structures for self-regulation. (Imitation of and learning from the parents begins later.) The primal dangers of overstimulation and psychic obliteration are followed by a whole series of danger situations that center on loss of the parents and of parental care. To contend with the threats from within supplied by innate drives that center on conflicts over murder and incest, the child must have parental emotional modulation that can be accepted and internalized. For this to occur, the parents must be able to say "no" as well as "yes" to the child's urgent desires so that the child can become able to say "no" and "yes" to himself. Parental protection continues to be needed to ward off the dangers from the worlds outside the growing child's mind—the world of his body and the world external to his body, where disease and death lurk. The nature of external reality and the limitations of the human condition must be learned through parental example and guidance. Parental caring as well as parental care is needed to enable the child to love and therewith modulate hatred.

If one is to be able to care adequately about, as well as for, oneself, it is necessary to try to take over this inevitably inadequate parental care and caring even to the inevitably inadequate extent that is possible. This slow process proceeds over the prolonged span of time when physiological and mental mastery are beyond the child's capacities. Before old age (if we achieve it) brings us to our final shrinkage to nothingness, the adequacy of our mental and physical functioning is transitory and relative—almost never enough. We continue to depend on others, a need that increases with regression and awareness of our inadequacy. We can at best achieve for a while an intermittent, partial mastery of the human conditions within and outside. This mastery waxes and wanes; optimally it can be partly evoked by our conscious will. Similarly, we need to struggle to be able to care about others, and only intermittently can we transcend narcissism and achieve love. The optimal relatively stable attainment of a separate loving self, with the ability to care for oneself and for others, is constantly subject to regression due to trauma and loss.

And so we can never completely abandon the dependencies on and the need for parenting—especially from the unconscious psychic parental presences that remain subject to revivals through our lives. Some do better with these needs than others, at least for a while. We continue to need the inner parental presence for safety, identity, and containment of overwhelming emotional and physical pain. Some adults still feel an acute need for the physical presence of the parent. And those who have had to preserve and disguise (with mitigation or magnification, with denial or idealization) the bad aspects of bad parenting in order to hold on to the parent in their minds are frequently left with a lifelong burden of excessive sadomasochism. This burden is almost always hidden by the promise, conscious or unconscious, that the bad will—next time—be transformed into the good. We all, in varying degrees, never lose the capacity to feel—like the happy and satisfied infant at the breast (that shard of paradise that continues in our soul)—that there is no life without mother. Only a return to the primal parent or becoming a god could fulfill the promise of eternal bliss, and the promise itself can give some relief from pain. Most of us continue to cling to the illusory expectation in some way. But the idealized illusion is accompanied (in or out of consciousness) by fear of the primal parent as Satan promising eternal torment. Perhaps the wisest, who can come to some terms with death, find comfort in what Sophocles (n.d.) says at the end of *Oedipus Rex*:

> Make way for Oedipus. All people said,
>   'That is a fortunate man';
>   And now what storms are beating on his head!
>   Call no man fortunate that is not dead.
>   The dead are free from pain [p. 382].

I want to emphasize at the end of this book, as I did at the beginning, that, although my title says "Life Without Mother" and my clinical example is about a man who is tied to his mother, my generalizations have to do with mother as the chief carrier of the primal parent figure from earliest childhood.

    The mind is like a dynamic pentimento in relation to the parental figures who are so much a part of the basis for everyone's identity—no registration is lost and all can be regressed to and transformed at any given time. Modified editions can be easily imposed on the past ones. (These changes can be transient and flexible, as they are in health, or almost permanently or relatively fixed, as in character traits.) The primal parent imago marks the beginning of a series of registrations.

FATHERS

In the histories of Trollope and Renard, I have described two writers whose identifications with both mother and father were overwhelmingly powerful, setting their "characters"—for better and for worse. Their individual identificatory mixtures were complex and different. For those who continue as adults to remain haunted by parents and fixed internalized parental figures, it can be fathers rather than mothers who play the leading, or at least the leading pathological, role. Documentations of this can easily be found. I will cite two soul murder stories. The fine and emotionally wrenching autobiographical novel by Henry Roth (1934) about a childhood dominated by his paranoid father, *Call It Sleep*, and the father-as-God obsessed book—Schreber's (1903) *Memoirs of My Mental Illness*—made so much of in Freud's case history about him. Both books could be subtitled, "Is There Life Without Father?"

Finally, I want to repeat my impression that most of the difficult and resistant (but treatable) cases I have encountered in doing psychoanalysis and intensive psychotherapy seem to me to have been so because the patients were so terribly threatened by the loss of early emotional ties to their mental images of one or both parents.[1] I am simplifying their dilemma in the question, "Is there life without mother?" The patients I worked with turned out to have the psychological means to adapt, to accomplish in life, and, at least initially, to become involved in therapy. They either achieved—after great and long struggle—or turned out ultimately to lack, the motivation to separate from their parents. Some simply would or could not give up the mental compromises they had made that had allowed for some individual way of holding on (at least in their minds) to the parent or parents they wanted to get rid of but felt they could not live without. Such compromises

---

1. I am not referring to those people seen in the consulting room or in trials of therapy whose severity of mental illness rules out the possibility of forming any attachment to another human being; or who obviously need supportive rather than exploratory treatment; or who are seeking magical transformation from an all-powerful authority.

Chapter 16

can inhibit or even block aspects of maturation and the acquisition of separate identity. Clinging to a parent can impede caring about other people, make adult functioning forbidden and frightening, and interfere with achievement and creativity. All that is the pathological part of the makeup of those people. But compromises mean adaptation as well as maladaptation. The continuing mental ties to parents can sometimes also provide the matrix for some ability to love and care, some identity, some contribution to functioning well and playfully and to making use of creative talents. Both positive and negative effects can be seen as consequences of Trollope's lifelong psychic ties to and identifications with his mother and his father.

I have treated some patients who seemed to be almost addicted to their parents and yet used whatever amount of good care and caring—even scraps—furnished by or attributed to those parents to augment and help fashion their own superior intelligence and talents. The patients' own abilities had also, in many individually different ways, enabled them to achieve some separate identity and to, at least intermittently, keep at bay whatever was bad that was derived from the parents. These patients who appeared able, or actually became able, to profit from psychoanalytic treatment would react to it by becoming tempted to run, or actually running, away from analysis. Those few who needed to run away quickly from therapy seemed to me to belong in the category of patients whom Freud (1916b) characterized as being "wrecked by success"; failure and punishment meant a continuing masochistic tie with a parent that could or would not be given up. Alternatively, several patients became stalemated in therapy or analysis because their motivation for change was less than their need to continue on forever with the analyst, the new edition of the parent without whom they felt they could not survive. Several of them still seemed to have achieved, and I judged would probably retain after the treatment was terminated, considerable amelioration of their initial complaints. The continuing chief terrifying expectation for those people whose liberation in analysis was predominately successfully resisted seemed to be that of losing the parent. For such unfortunates who needed to continue the compulsion to repeat their past and cling to the relatively unmodified mental image of the early parent, other danger situations—even those connected with ear-

Conclusion

lier (overstimulation) and later childhood development (castration, death, fear of the conscience)—were all connected with and subsumed by parental loss. Phillips (1999) says, "All modern therapies are forms of bereavement counseling" (p. 14), but each of us has his or her own blend of bereavement. Fear of losing the parent on whom we are dependent is inevitable and omnipresent because of our inherent murderous tendencies.

It is my conviction that a review of the complicated and contradictory ways in which a person's parents are registered in the mind, centering on an exploration of love and hatred toward them, is a necessary part of every attempt to understand oneself and others. It follows that it is a necessary part of every psychoanalysis. The acquisition of a more flexible and complete capacity for self-observation—which involves being able to be responsibly aware of what is evil and ugly in ourselves as well as what is good—is an important part of therapeutic change. Self-observation includes being able to observe the parental part of oneself.

In lecturing about "life without mother" before various groups, I have been told in the subsequent discussion that I have been telling my audience something they already know. Often the tone used showed admiration and praise; but at least occasionally hostility and dismissal were being voiced by almost identical words. The importance of the parents *is* of course something most of us know about in a general way. Theories about dependency and pre-oedipal and oedipal attachments can be accepted and used in intellectual argument, but when we actually begin to feel the passionate sexual and aggressive conflicts, the intense anxiety-ridden mixtures of loving and hating, of lust and murder toward our parents, the possibility of life without mother (or father) is easily put out of mind.

I have dealt at length with Trollope and Renard and their struggles with fixations on their parents. I want to deal briefly with two other writers: Samuel Butler (1835–1902), who was a contemporary of both Trollope and Renard, and E. M. Forster (1879–1970), who was three years old when Trollope died and lived on to 1970. Their lives illustrate how varied the vicissitudes both of parental dependency and of the inhibitory influence of pathology on creativity can be.

Chapter 16

SAMUEL BUTLER

I have used excerpts from the 19th-century English writer Samuel Butler's *Notebooks* for several epigraphs for the chapters in this book. I had originally wanted to give this book the subtitle, "Parental Servitude," a term coined by Butler that also appears in the *Notebooks*, which he kept for a good part of his adult life (1874–1920; see Keynes and Hill, 1951, p. 202). I decided not to use the phrase in the subtitle because its meaning seemed too ambiguous—it could also connote servitude by parents—if isolated from some knowledge of Butler's life which I intend to supply here. The note reads:

> PARENTAL SERVITUDE. Some people seem compelled by unkind fate to parental servitude for life. There is no form of penal servitude much worse than this.

Butler was himself one of the people he described. I have elsewhere described the soul murder ambiance of his childhood (see Shengold, 1995). His servitude involved predominantly compulsive provocation and resistance rather than submission. Butler was finally liberated from his financial dependence on his father at the elder Butler's death when Samuel was 51. But even with his inheritance, Butler continued to complain obsessively about his parents and siblings. He was haunted by his childhood. The venom directed at his parents would pour out directly in his *Notebooks*[2] which he continued to write for the rest of his life. The *Notebooks* are also full of Butler's hostility, expressed in transferences onto successful parental figures: Mendelssohn, Dickens, Tennyson. Butler's books on evolution show a persecutory hatred of Charles Darwin, whom he accused of ignoring his forebears in the field— Charles's grandfather Erasmus Darwin and Lamarck—as well as

---

2. In the *Notebooks* (Keynes and Hill, 1951) we find the following note. It is not clear if this is fantasy or reality, but I believe it relates to his mother: SPIRITUALISM. "Promise me solemnly," I said to her as she lay on what I believed to be her death bed, "if you find in the world beyond the grave that you can communicate with me—that there is some way in which you can make me aware of your continued existence— promise me solemnly that you will never, never avail yourself of it." She recovered and never, never forgave me [pp. 16–17].

Butler's own writings. Darwin felt hounded by Butler and seems to have been almost physically afraid of him.

The obsessive hatred that accompanied Butler's "parental servitude" appears in slightly fictionalized form in his novel and masterpiece, *The Way of All Flesh*, a bitter review of how he had registered his upbringing. He had started writing it in 1873 (at age 38) and continued to work on it for decades. The novel was nearly finished when Eliza Savage, his close friend of 15 years, died in 1885. Their intense friendship cooled toward its end when the lifelong bachelor Butler was fighting the realization that he would never be able to be physically attracted toward her despite and because of the feelings of tenderness he had for her. (Sex and tenderness did not go together for Butler.) He consciously hated his mother, whose influence on him may have been even greater than that of his father, and probably never had sexual contact with a woman he could care for. He struggled against the positive and loving feeling he had for Miss Savage, started to neglect her, and felt very guilty when she died. Most of their contact had taken place through their letters, but in her last years Butler ran away even from these. She had served as his literary conscience; and the last third of his last novel, deprived of her delicate and tactful supervision, is a definite falling off from the great first two-thirds. It was published in its probably rather incomplete form the year following Butler's death in 1903.

Butler perhaps exaggerated the isolation and parental persecution of his childhood as fictionalized in *The Way of All Flesh*—as Jules Renard probably did in his novel *Poil de Carrote*. Yet both men, whatever the "facts," were clearly expressing the emotional truth of their inner convictions based on what they felt had happened to them.

E. M. FORSTER

E. M. Forster was brought up in a household of dominating women, itself dominated by his mother. His father, who may also have been predominantly homosexual (his son was exclusively so), died shortly after he was born. Beauman (1993) makes a convincing case that Lily Forster was well aware of and resented her young husband's attachment to a cousin, Ted Streatfield, to whom he was very close and who he insisted go with him and his wife on their first trip to the Continent. Lily apparently disposed of every written trace of Streatfield, but Beauman feels that she shared some intimations about her husband's errant sexuality with her son. Forster may have had the unconscious fantasy that his powerful mother had destroyed his bad father. Beauman point out that there are no good fathers in Forster's novels. There are not that many good mothers either.

Forster hated his mother and he loved her. She had a consuming curiosity about every detail of his life; as he belatedly matured, he stopped confiding everything and began to conceal much from her. Lily Forster seems to have been threatened by any meaningful contact her son had with others, tried to estrange him from friends, subtly encouraged his failings, and coddled him like a child long after he was grown up and a graduate of Cambridge. Yet she seemed also to want him somehow to be masculine and independent (for an excellent and sensitive view of the mother–son relationship, see Beauman, 1993). Lily made her only child the center of her world and was capable of hints that seemed to reproach him for interfering with her prospects of remarrying (which she appears to have shown no signs of desiring). He continued writing letters to her addressed to "Dear Mummy" into his middle age.

Forster in middle age wrote about his mother to his friend J. R. Ackerley, "Although my mother has been intermittently tiresome for the last thirty years, cramped and warped my genius, hindered my career, *blocked and buggered up my house*, and *boycotted my beloved, I have to admit that she has provided a sort of rich subsoil where I have been able to rest and grow*" (quoted in Furbank, 1978, p. 217; italics added). And despite his feeling "blocked and buggered up" by his mother in his writing and in his sexuality, Forster lived with her until he was 66. But Forster here does employ the metaphor of an enriching matrix by attributing benefits that accompanied the constricting parental bind. Certainly Fanny Trollope, though not physically healthy most of the time, functioned in a similar way for Anthony. (She also, in contrast to Lily Forster, offered him a model for his career as a writer.)

May Buckingham, a friend whose husband, Bob Buckingham, was a policeman and the boycotted "beloved" of Forster's middle and old age, was aware that Forster was in love with her husband,

Conclusion

but perhaps did not allow herself to know about their sexual connection. Forster had met Buckingham in 1930, when he was 51 and Buckingham 28. Buckingham was, according to Beauman (1993) bisexual. Beauman remarks that Buckingham was "*the* great love of his life as [Forster] would always consider it, which would last, despite Bob's marriage, until Morgan's [Forster was often called by his middle name Forster] death forty years on" (p. 347).

May Buckingham wrote of the famous writer who had befriended the couple (1979): "[Robert and I] were guided and educated by loans and gifts of books. When [Forster's] Mother[3] died in 1945 I feel that in some ways I took her place. He always came to stay with us whenever he was unwell from then on and always spent his birthday with us" (p. 183).

Something of Forster's complex and contradictory view of his mother can be seen in a paragraph from a short story with a homosexual theme. The story, "The Other Boat," was begun in 1913 as an attempt at a novel that was abandoned. It was taken up again, and a homosexual love affair added to it, in 1957. It was probably the last serious piece of fiction that Forster produced. (He had a writer's block in relation to fiction and stopped writing novels after his (first) great commercial success, with *A Passage to India* [1924]. It was a best seller as well as being acclaimed by critics. But his reputation as a great novelist for the general public, at least in America, rested on that one book until interest was revived in his earlier novels by the publication of Lionel Trilling's critical study of his work in 1943. He continued, although after considerable inner struggle, to be able to write essays and biographies but wrote no more major works in his later years despite his retention of his intellectual powers up to his death at 91. His loss of creativity as a novelist of genius can be seen as an instance of being "wrecked by success." This conclusion is seconded in Furbank's official biography of Forster (1977) which I read subsequent to forming it.

There had been an earlier but more modest financial reward after the publication of *Howard's End* (1911). That novel received the highest critical praise for Forster's novels so far published, even being hailed as a great novel by more than one reviewer. But,

---

3. The capitalization of Mother is Mrs. Buckingham's. The relationship had for Forster a kind of *idealized ménage-à-trois*, with a complaisant mother looking after, or at times away from, her "son" and his lover.

Chapter 16

although this flash of fame marked a turning point in Forster's life, attracting new friends and providing opportunities to go abroad (to India), it was also followed by a long period of anxiety and of paralysis in his writing. Furbank (1977), noting Forster's reactions of inhibition and "superstitious" foreboding, comments:

> He showed symptoms, I think, of the psychology which Freud describes in his paper "Those Wrecked by Success" (p. 191). Furbank quotes from a letter Forster wrote to a friend in 1913: "You ask me about my work. I feel you too sympathetic to keep silent. I am dried up. Not in my emotions, but in their expression. I cannot write at all" [p. 249].

Forster wrote a note in his diary in 1924 after the considerable financial success of *A Passage to India*: "Have pains in my heart, so that I may not be able to carry vegetables home.... Too much good luck and too late. I cannot live up to it" (Furbank, 1977, p. 130).

The successful creativity that distanced the dependency on his mother evoked the need for punishment. Although Forster lived on for another 47 years and wrote some brilliant nonfiction, he found himself unable to write another novel.

The fragment from 1913 that is the first part of "The Other Boat" (Forster, 1972) describes a mother and her children on board a ship returning home to England from India. Lionel is her eldest son. The first part ends with a furious outburst by Mrs. March, the mother of the story's hero, Lionel, against a young but rich half-caste boy from India (nicknamed Cocoanut) who has been playing with her children. Mrs. March, a stickler for correctness like Lily Forster, says she would not have allowed her children to play with the clever and somewhat effeminate but unruly and mischievous child whose dusky complexion shows "a touch of the tar-brush" if they were on the way to India, "but it doesn't matter on the voyage home" (p. 203). She is terrified of sunstroke and becomes alarmed when she sees the children playing on deck in the strong sun without their head coverings. She blames this lapse on Cocoanut and screams at the children. As she tries to pick up her youngest son, Baby, "Another mishap occurred. A sailor—an Englishman—leapt out of the hatchway with a piece of chalk and drew a little circle round her where she stood. Cocoanut screamed, 'He's caught you. He's come'" (p. 206).

She had trespassed on the seamen's quarters. There is a custom that, if "caught," they have to pay by contributing some money that gets distributed among the crew. Terrified, Mrs. March "fell into a sort of trance. She stared at the circle stupidly, unable to move out of it, while Cocoanut danced round her and gibbered" (p. 206).

The sudden appearance of the sailor seems to have been taken as a kind of confrontation with brutal masculine sexuality resulting in the sexually repressed woman's falling into a defensive "trance."[4] But when she recovers, her fury is felt and voiced not at the sailor but at the jeering Cocoanut, who had yelled, "He's caught you. He's come." She turns on him with unusual heat. "You never play any game properly and you stop the others. You're a silly idle useless *unmanly* little boy" (pp. 206–207).

We learn later in the story that, when her youngest child became ill and died months later in England, she felt this was a result of the exposure to the sun and blamed it on Cocoanut. In the ending written many years later, Lionel—now in his early 20s and an Army Captain and hero who had killed and been wounded by blacks in desert warfare—writes a letter home to his mother. He tells her that Cocoanut is one of the passengers but does not tell her that he is sharing a cabin with him. He later regrets having posted the letter. Cocoanut, now a late adolescent who is very rich, had, unbeknownst to Lionel, managed through friends in the Purser's office to arrange for a double cabin with Lionel on the overcrowded ship. Lionel is ashamed to be housed with a "wog" but he likes Cocoanut and accepts the arrangement. The youth seduces the slightly older man after plying him with champagne. They fall into a kind of mutual love. Cocoanut wants it to last forever, but Lionel is engaged to a girl in England and does not see what he is doing and enjoying as a serious matter. The two

---

4. We know she is repressed because, when Lionel thinks about how much sexual pleasure he is feeling with Cocoanut, he reproaches his mother for how ashamed of his own body he had been: "His preceptors had condemned carnality or had dismissed it as a waste of time, and his mother had ignored its existence in him and all her children; being hers, they had to be pure" (pp. 216–217).

youths do not mix outside the cabin. Homosexuality was a crime and disgrace in England.

Cocoanut is still a spoiled child used to getting what he wants. He arranges to leave the cabin door unbolted, expecting that they will be sleeping together in the morning and that Lionel will be disgraced, be dismissed from the Army, and come back to India to work for him and live with him forever. When Lionel discovers that the door is unbolted and why, after the two have had intercourse and he realizes that Cocoanut has tried to keep him up all night in order to be caught, he is furious. He goes up on deck and decides to quit the cabin despite still feeling love for Cocoanut. He will henceforth sleep on deck, where some of the officers, including Lionel's Colonel, have put down bedding because of the heat. Cocoanut responds to Lionel's awkward goodbye and his refusal to kiss him by biting him. Lionel loses control and strangles the naked youth. He then kisses the closed eyes of the corpse, goes on deck, and commits suicide by diving into the sea, "naked and with the seeds of love on him" (p. 233). When Lionel's superior officer finds the strangled naked body, he and the ship's doctor, who has examined Cocoanut's body, know what has transpired. But the Colonel writes Mrs. March, assuring her

> that her son's death had been accidental whatever she heard to the contrary; that he had stumbled overboard in the darkness during a friendly talk they had had together on deck. . . . Mrs. March thanked [him] for writing but made no comment. She also received a letter from Lionel himself—the one that should have been intercepted in the post—and she never mentioned his name again [p. 34].

With this sting in the tail, the story that couples love with murderous hatred ends. Forster gave Mrs. March both the perception of what her son was really like (alongside her denials) and the hatred of male homosexuality that his mother, Lily Forster, had carried over from her husband to him. This bitter paragraph is the last mention of a mother in Forster's fiction, and the second half of the story is the only really good piece of fiction that Forster was able to write after *A Passage to India*.

Beauman (1993) reports that in 1957, just after finishing "The

Conclusion

Other Boat," the 78-year-old Forster wrote in his commonplace book—a work not intended for publication—[5]

> that he thought *Howard's End* "my best novel and approaching a very good novel" [but] he did not care for it because it had "not a single character in it for whom I care. In *Where Angels* Gino, in [*Longest Journey*] Stephen, in [*Room with a View*] Lucy, in [*Passage to India*] Aziz . . . And Maurice and Alec . . . And *Lionel* and *Cocoa*" [p. 369; italics added].

So he regarded the story he had just completed as containing favorite characters that probably represented different aspects of himself—aspects sexually and emotionally rejected by his mother, who would have disapproved of all the listed characters that he liked from his novels.

Two years later Forster, nearing 80, wrote in his commonplace book, shortly before he gave up writing in it: "Mother's Birthday. Her age would be 110. I suppose bones and some muck still remain from her. I have bought her some flowers" (quoted in Beauman, 1972, p. 371). This, apparently the last written mention of Mother, seems full of ambivalence. He is certainly thinking of her, but it does not sound as if he is looking forward to joining her. Yet one wonders, was he fantasizing about an afterlife, a religious idea he consciously had ceased to believe in, *with* or *without* Mother?

---

5. A type of diary, According to Funk & Wagnall's, "a book containing a methodical collection of notes and passages."

EPILOGUE
Multiple Personalities

There is as much difference between us and ourselves as between us and others.
— Michel de Montaigne, *Essays*

There is a similarity between the creation of characters in a pathological entity and those imagined in fiction—both show a mixture of creativity and personal pathology. To illustrate: I was invited to be a commentator on a 1999 presentation by Dr. Ian Graham of the Toronto Psychoanalytic Society of a long-term treatment of a woman afflicted with "multiple personality disorder." This diagnostic designation refers to people such as those publicized in the popular written accounts and movies like *The Three Faces of Eve* and *Sybil*. The syndrome has evoked a large and controversial literature that ranges from passionate defense of its existence and widespread occurrence to a denial of its validity, its existence even being attributed to conscious or unconscious suggestion by credulous therapists.

In such patients, it is reported, there is a widespread use of an individually varying array of psychic defenses, including transient or fixed vertical ego or personality splits, shifts in consciousness, isolation, and denial. These defensive mixtures are frequently labeled "dissociation" in the psychiatric writings about child abuse, multiple personality disorders, and satanic cult syndromes. I am convinced that some such dissociation exists to some degree in all of us and that its individually varying presence is not in itself pathognomonic of any specific diagnosis. I have never seen a case of a person with multiple personalities, although I have treated one patient who seemed to approach the description of a dual personality (like Dr. Jekyll and Mr. Hyde), but he did not possess the completely separate personality boundaries that have been described. The patient suffered from, and had defended himself from unbearable knowledge and affects with, a failure in the synthesizing function of his mind—a kind of intermittent short circuit. I hope some day to write up that case history. I do not feel I have enough experience to contribute anything but suspension of disbelief in both the possibility of the spontaneous (idiopathic or noniatrogenic) origin of multiple personality syndrome or of its existence as a reaction to overwhelming trauma in childhood. Dr. Graham and his patient have written and are to publish an account of her life and treatment. I have read the manuscript of a convincing and sensible book (that I recommend to the reader) about both dissociation and multiple personalities by Ira Brenner (submitted). On the other hand, many people whom I respect dismiss the pathological entities of multiple personality disorder and satanic-abuse victimization, currently widely publicized in America, as due almost entirely to suggestion or autosuggestion. I have not enough experience here to have any conviction one way or another.

Dr. Graham's presentation in Toronto furnished direct experiential visual evidence of the pathological phenomena involved. He showed a fascinating videotape that featured the transformation—and sometimes the literal collapse, when babies were involved—into various "alters" (alter ego "characters") that were called up by the therapist. Body posture, facial expressions, voices were all completely differentiated. I was most impressed by the dedication of Dr. Graham to his work and the honesty of his presentation (which both showed how difficult the task was and demonstrated his good character and devotion to his patient that made good work, but not a final resolution of the patient's symptoms, possible). I was most grateful for the direct view his video afforded of the intriguing and bizarre phenomena I had previously only read about; there could be no doubt that the symptoms existed, whatever their origin. I think that the manuscript, written largely by his patient, is a most valuable source of important questions (rather than answers) about the syndrome that should prove helpful to those studying the syndrome and its treatment.

The alter "characters" emanating from and embodied in the single human being seem to me to be the products of a particular kind of pathological vertical splitting of identity that gives rise to distinct and somewhat caricature-like entities in people who suffer from or develop some deficiency of mental integration. (These are in contrast to the chaotic fractures without personality boundaries that one sees with ego splitting in other pathological conditions like schizophrenia; or the more common, transient vertical ego splits that exist in all of us—for example, one can find oneself asking, "Why am I acting like a son-of-a-bitch today?"). These alters can, I believe, be like the flat and comparatively predictable characters of Dickens and perhaps also more infrequently resemble the more rounded and complex characters of other novelists. Being able to create such characters involves more than pathology. Such ability seems to me also to demonstrate a kind of creativity akin to that of a good actor who "becomes" the character he is portraying or to that of the fiction writer who fashions personalities in his writings. Actors and writers alike make (conscious and unconscious) use for this purpose of (projected) aspects of their own identity and of the identities of others whom they have observed, blended and recorded in their minds; so do the creators of multiple personalities.

What struck me as relevant to what I had been writing about for this book was the description of the reluctance of people who have the faculty and misfortune to develop these bizarre, identity-splitting defenses against overwhelming stimulation to give up their "alters." The individual characters fight for their lives and identities; the host/creator is in conflict and can, and I believe inevitably does, strongly fear and resist destroying them by integration. Dr. Graham's patient had peopled her inner world with characters that represented split-off, contradictory aspects of herself and perhaps of others at various ages. She was thereby holding on to her past, and her identifications with the important people in her past, but in a fashion that was full of unconscious conflict and maladaptation to reality. I was reminded specifically of Trollope's neurotic but sublimated and adaptive conflicts. In his passionate involvement with his characters, he resembled the patient—and yet without breaking with reality. He felt love and hate for them as separate entities, and they allowed him catharsis—to express and discharge his love and his hate in an active and adaptive way when he was fashioning their fictional lives. I thought of Trollope's fondness for using favorite characters in novel after novel, of his reluctance to give them up, which was compatible with his giving in occasionally to impulses to get rid of them. Anticipating his own death, he had dreaded most of all the prospect of having to give up creating new characters.

There is a holding on to the past as well as to the present by creatively projecting mental representations of self and others both onto delusional entities and onto fictional characters. (I am emphasizing the resemblances and not the obvious differences here—the artist [unlike the patient] can, relatively speaking, retain and enjoy control. Sublimation does not involve a break with external reality.)

There are links of creativity to pathology in my comparison of writers to multiple personality patients, but, to reiterate, there is in neither category an explanation for the creativity by the pathology. We are left with the mystery of why some people who suffer the unbearable "too-much-ness" of physical and psychological abuse and neglect become psychologically disabled, some become creative, and some can be both.

References

Anstey, F. (1882), *Vice-Versa or A Lesson To Fathers*. London: John Murray, 1954.
Beauman, N. (1993), *E. M. Forster. A Biography*. New York: Knopf, 1994.
Blake, W. (1804), Milton. A poem. In: *Poems and Prophecies by William Blake*, ed. M. Plowman. London: J. M. Dent & Son, pp. 1945, 109–161, 1945.
––––– (1808), Annotations to Sir Joshua Reynolds's Discourses. In: *Blake: Complete Writings*, ed. G. Keynes. London: University Press, 1966, pp. 445–479.
Bogan, L. & Roget, E., ed. & trans. (1964), *The Journal of Jules Renard*. Excerpts. New York: George Brazillier.
Bouillier, H. ed. (1990), *Journal* [of J. Renard]. Paris: Robert Lafont.
Brenner, I. (submitted), *The Dissociation of Trauma: Theory, Phenomenology, and Technique*.
Brodie, F. (1967), *The Devil Drives*. London: Eyre & Spottiswoode.
Buckingham, M. (1979), Some reminiscences. In: *E. M. Forster. A Human Exploration*, ed. G. K. Das & J. Beer. New York: New York University Press, 1979, pp. 183–185.
Butler, S. (1903), *The Way of All Flesh*. New York: Macmillan, 1925.
Cooper, A. (1993), Paranoia: A part of most analyses. *J. Amer. Psychoanal. Assn.*, 41:423–442.
Edel, L. (1985), *Writing Lives. Principia Biographica*. New York: Norton.
Edwards, P. (1980), Introduction to *An Autobiography* by Anthony Trollope, ed. M. Sadleir & F. Page. Oxford: Oxford University Press, 1950, pp. v–xviii.
Fliess, R. (1942), The metapsychology of the analyst. *Psychoanal. Quart*, 11:211–227.
––––– (1956), *Erogeneity and Libido*. New York: International Universities Press.
Forster, E. M. (1924), *A Passage to India*. New York: Harcourt, Brace, 1927.
––––– (1972), The other boat. In: *The Life to Come and Other Short Stories*. London: Penguin, 1984, pp. 202–234.
Forster, J. (1874), *The Life of Charles Dickens*. New York: Doubleday, Doran, 1928.

References

Franklin, B. (1732), *Poor Richard's Almanack. Benjamin Franklin's Best Sayings*, ed. D. Walley. Kansas City, MO: Hallmark, 1967.

——— (1771), The autobiography. In: *Benjamin Franklin*. New York: Library of America, 1987, pp. 1305–1495.

Freud, S. (1896), Further remarks on the neuro-psychoses of defense. *Standard Edition*, 3:158–188. London: Hogarth Press, 1962.

——— (1900), The interpretation of dreams. *Standard Edition*, 4 & 5. London: Hogarth Press, 1953.

——— (1908), Creative writers and day-dreaming, *Standard Edition*, 9:141–153. London: Hogarth Press, 1959.

——— (1909), Analysis of a phobia in a four-year-old boy. *Standard Edition*, 10:3–147. London: Hogarth Press, 1955.

——— (1911), Psychoanalytic notes on an autobiographical account of a case of paranoia (dementia paranoides). *Standard Edition*, 13:3–79. London: Hogarth Press, 1958.

——— (1916), Those wrecked by success. *Standard Edition*, 14:315–331.

——— (1916–1917), Introductory lectures on psycho-analysis. *Standard Edition*, 15. London: Hogarth Press, 1961.

——— (1919), "A child is being beaten." *Standard Edition*, 17:177–204. London: Hogarth Press, 1955.

——— (1928), Dostoevsky and parricide. *Standard Edition*, 21:177–196. London: Hogarth Press, 1961.

——— (1937), Analysis, terminal and interminable. *Standard Edition*, 23:216–253. London: Hogarth Press, 1964.

——— (1941), Findings, ideas, problems. *Standard Edition*, 23:299–300. London: Hogarth Press, 1964.

Furbank, P. N. (1977), *E. M. Forster: A Life*, New York: Harcourt Brace Jovanovich.

Gitelson, M. (1973), *Psychoanalysis: Science and Profession*. New York: International Universities Press.

Glendinning, V. (1992), *Anthony Trollope*. New York: Penguin.

Gubrich-Simitis, I. (1998), Nothing about the totem meal. On Freud's notes. In: *Freud: Conflict and Culture—Essays on his Life, Work, and Legacy*, ed. M. Roth. New York: Knopf, pp. 17–31.

Guichard, L, (1971), *Avertissement* to "*La Bigote*" by Jules Renard. In: *Jules Renard. Oeuvres*, Vol. 2. Paris: Gallimard, pp. 823–829.

Hall, N. J. (1983a), *The Letters of Anthony Trollope, Vol. 1*. Stanford, CA: Stanford University Press.

——— (1983b), *The Letters of Anthony Trollope, Vol. 2*. Stanford, CA: Stanford University Press.

——— (1991), *Trollope. A Biography*. Oxford: Clarendon Press.

Harvey, G. (1991), Introduction to *The Bertrams* by A. Trollope, ed. A. Harvey. Oxford: Oxford University Press.

Holroyd, M. (1994), *Lytton Strachey. The New Biography*. New York: Farrar, Straus & Giroux.
Ibsen, H. (1896), John Gabriel Borkman, trans. W. Archer. In: *Works of Henrik Ibsen*. New York: Himebaugh & Browne, undated, pp. 179–349.
James, H. (1883), Anthony Trollope. In: *Essays, American and English Writers*. New York: Library of America, 1984, pp. 1330–1354.
Jarrell, R. (1958), The taste of the age. In: *Kipling, Auden and Others*. New York: Farrar, Straus & Giroux, 1980, pp. 290–30.
——— (1985), *Randall Jarrell's Letters*, ed. M. Jarrell. Boston, MA: Houghton, Mifflin.
Keynes, G. & Hill, B., eds. (1951), *Samuel Butler's Notebooks*. New York: Dutton.
Kris, E. (1953), *Psychoanalytic Explorations of Art*. London: Allen & Unwin.
Lamb, C. (1833), Sanity of true genius. In: *The Complete Works And Letters of Charles Lamb*. New York: Modern Library, 1935.
Lerner, L. (1967), Introduction. In: *The Last Chronicle of Barset*. London: Penguin, 1986, pp. 9–24.
Lewin, B. (1948), The nature of reality, the meaning of nothing, with an addendum on concentration. *Psychoanal. Quart.*, 17:524–526.
Lovell, M. (1998), *A Rage to Love: A Biography of Richard and Isabel Burton*. New York: Norton.
Masson, J., ed. & trans. (1985), *The Complete Letters of Sigmund Freud to Wilhelm Fliess*. Cambridge, MA: Harvard University Press.
McLynn, F. (1993), *Snow Upon the Desert*. London: Murray.
Miller, J. H. (1987), *The Ethics of Reading*. New York: Columbia University Press.
Montiero, G., ed. (1996), *Conversations with Elizabeth Bishop*. Jackson: University Press of Mississippi.
Mullen, R. (1992), *Anthony Trollope: A Victorian in His World*. London: Duckworth.
——— & Munson. J. (1996), *The Penguin Companion to Trollope*. London: Penguin Books.
Neville-Sington, P. (1997), *Fanny Trollope: The Life and Adventures of a Clever Woman*. London: Penguin.
Orwell, G. (1948), *Nineteen Eighty-Four*. New York: Harcourt, Brace.
Phillips, A. (1999), *Darwin's Worms*. New York: Basic Books.
Pope-Hennessy, J. (1971), *Anthony Trollope*. Boston: Little, Brown.
Prater, D. (1995), *Thomas Mann: A Life*. Oxford: Oxford University Press.
Raban, J. (1987), Trollope. In: *For Love and Money*. London: Pan Books, pp. 73–83.
Ransom, T. (1995), *Fanny Trollope. A Remarkable Life*. Stroud, Eng.: Allan Sutton.

Renard, J. (1864–1910), *Correspondance*, ed. L. Guichard. Paris: Flammarion, undated.

────── (1894a), *Poil de Carotte*. Paris: Maxi Poches, 1993.

────── (1894b), *Poil de Carotte*, trans. R. Manheim. New York: Walker, 1967.

Renard, J. (1909), La bigote. In: *Jules Renard. Oeuvres*, Vol. 2. Paris: Gallimard, 1971, pp. 838–895.

Roper, W. (1535?), The life of Sir Thomas More, Knight. In: *A Treasury of Biography*, ed. E. Johnson. New York: Howell, Soskin, 1941, pp. 43–52.

Roth, H. (1934), *Call It Sleep*. Paterson: Pageant Press, 1960.

Sadleir, M. (1945), *Trollope. A Commentary* (rev.) London: Oxford University Press.

Schafer, R. (1968), *Aspects of Internalization*. New York: International Universities Press.

Schreber, D. P. (1903), *Memoirs of My Mental Illness*, ed. & trans. J. Macalpine & R. A. Hunter. London: Dawson, 1955.

Shengold, L. (1963), The parent as sphinx. *J. Amer. Psychoanal. Assn.*, 11:725–751.

────── (1989), *Soul Murder*. New Haven, CT: Yale University Press.

────── (1991), *"Father, Don't You See I'm Burning?" Reflections on Sex, Narcissism, Symbolism, and Murder: From Everything to Nothing.* New Haven, CT: Yale University Press.

────── (1995), *Delusions of Everyday Life*. New Haven, CT: Yale University Press.

────── (1999), *Soul Murder Revisited*. New Haven, CT: Yale University Press.

Snow, C. P. (1975), *Trollope. His Life and Art*. New York: Charles Scribner's Sons.

Sophocles (n.d.), King Oedipus, trans. W. B. Yeats. In: *Greek Plays in Modern Translation*, ed. D. Fitts. New York: Dial, 1947, pp. 345–382.

Spence, D. (1982), *Narrative and Historical Truth*. New York: Norton.

Super, H. (1988), *The Chronicler of Barsetshire. A Life of Anthony Trollope*. Ann Arbor: University of Michigan Press.

Terry, R. C., ed. (1987), *Trollope. Interviews and Recollections*. New York: St. Martin's Press.

Thackeray, W. (1848), *Vanity Fair*. London: Penguin, 1994.

Toesca, M. (1977), *Jules Renard*. Paris: Albin Michel.

Trilling, L. (1943), *E. M. Forster*. Norfolk CT: New Directions.

────── (1945), Art and literature. In: *The Liberal Imagination*. New York: Viking, 1950, pp. 160–180.

Trollope, A. (1855), *The Warden*. London: Everyman's, 1998.

────── (1857), *Barchester Towers*. London: Penguin, 1999.

────── (1858), *The Three Clerks*. New York: Dover, 1981.

References

——— (1859), *The Bertrams*. Oxford: Oxford University Press, 1991.
——— (1860), *Castle Richmond*. New York: Dover, 1984.
——— (1861), *Framley Parsonage*. London: T. Nelson & Sons, undated.
——— (1864), *The Small House at Allington*. London: Thomas & Sons, 1914.
——— (1866a), *The Belton Estate*. New York: Oxford University Press, 1986.
——— (1866b), *Nina Balatka*. Manchester, NH: Ayer, 1982.
——— (1867), *The Last Chronicle of Barset*. London: Penguin. 1986.
——— (1868), *Linda Tressel*. Manchester, NH: Ayer, 1981.
——— (1869a), *Phineas Finn*. London: Oxford University Press, 1962.
——— (1869b), *He Knew He Was Right*, ed. F. Kermode. London: Penguin, 1996.
——— (1870), The panjandrum. In: *Later Short Stories*, ed. J. Sutherland. London: Oxford University Press, pp. 136–173, 1995.
——— (1875), *The Way We Live Now*. London: Chapman & Hall.
——— (1877), Why Frau Frohmann raised her prices. In: *The Complete Short Stories, Vol. 5. The Journey to Panama and Other Stories*. London: Trollope Society, undated, pp. 1–66.
——— (1879a), *Thackeray*. New York: Harper & Brothers.
——— (1879b), *John Caldigate*. London: Oxford University Press, 1993.
——— (1880), *The Duke's Children*. London: Oxford University Press, 1913.
——— (1881), *Dr. Wortle's School*, ed. M. Iralauh. London: Penguin, 1993.
——— (1883), *An Autobiography*, ed. M. Sadleir & F. Page. Oxford: Oxford University Press, 1950.
Trollope, F. (1832), *Domestic Manners of the Americans*. New York: Dodd, 1901.
——— (1837), *The Vicar of Wrexhill*. London: Alan Sutton, 1995.
——— (1840), *One Fault*. London: Richard Bentley.
——— (1841), *Charles Chesterfield or the Adventurer*. London: Henry Colburn.
——— (1852), *Uncle Walton*. London: Henry Colburn.
Trollope, T. A. (1888), *What I Remember, Vol. 1*. New York: Harper & Brothers.
Vidal, G. (1990), Maugham's half and half. In: *Sexually Speaking: Collected Sex Writings*, ed. D. Wiese. New York: Cleis Press, 1999, pp. 155–179.
Wilson, E. (1929), Philoctetes: The wound and the bow. In: *The Wound and the Bow: Seven Studies in Literature*. New York: Oxford University Press, 1947, pp. 272–295.
Woolf, V. (1932), The art of biography. In: *Collected Essays*. New York: Harcourt, Brace & World, 1990, pp. 221–228.

Index

A
abuse, child, 62, 89–90
  most destructive effect, 25
abuser, need to hold on to one's, 58. *See also* identification, with aggressor
aggression, 27–28. *See also* murderous rage
  turned inward. *See* masochism
ambivalence, 47, 52, 156, 176
Anstey, F., 169–171
art and artists, 5. *See also* creativity
Auden, W. H., 36

B
Beauman, N., 194, 195, 197, 200
biographers
  current and historical "truth" and, 5, 9
  limited knowledge, 5
  psychoanalysts contrasted with, 5–6
biographical biases, 5–7
biography, 148
  fiction and, 6–7
  writing, 3–4
    difficulty of, 3
Bishop, E., 13
Blake, W., 140
Bogan, L., 19
Bonaparte, M., 17
Bouillier, H., 41, 44, 48, 57, 179n
Burton, I., 8
Burton, R., 8
Butler, S., 193–195

C
child abuse. *See* abuse, child
Cooper, A., 16
creativity. *See also under* daydreaming; Trollope, A.
  analysts on, 11–14
  artistic, 11–16
  psychopathology and, 16–21, 61, 161–162, 187, 193, 203, 206
  sources, 183, 187

D
daydreaming, 131–132
  in service of creativity and sexuality, 118–120
death, 58, 64, 177
delusions
  of everyday life, 16, 34, 187
  of having had concerned loving parent, 25
  quasi-delusions, 34
Delusions of Everyday Life (Shengold), 18n
dependence, 61–62, 97, 193
Dickens, C., 65–66, 82, 134, 149, 181
dishonesty, 148–149
dissociation, 203, 204

E
Edel, L., 6
Edwards, P., 63
empathy and imagination, 18

Index

F
father-son conflict and hostility, 90. *See also* oedipal dreams; *specific individuals*
father(s), 191–193
  life without, 191
Field, K., 155
Fitzgerald, O., 122–123
Fleiss, R., 17, 29
Forster, E. M., 193, 195–201
Forster, J., 66
Franklin, B., 110–111
  The Autobiography, 111–115
  obsessive-compulsiveness, 112–113
free association, 5
Freud, S., 16–18, 32, 118, 120n, 124, 158, 187–188, 192
  on creativity, 11–12
  letter to L. Strachey, 9
Furbank, P. N., 196, 198

G
Gitelson, M., 13
Glendinning, V., 68–70, 76, 79, 87, 96, 106, 118, 123, 124, 140, 148, 165, 166
God, 32
good object/parent, loss of, 25, 27
Gray, P., 17, 18
Gregory, W., 88
Grubrich-Simitis, I., 102
Guichard, L., 55, 56

H
Hall, J. N., 62, 73, 87, 90, 98, 122, 126, 130, 152, 153, 155, 157, 165–167
Harvey, G., 136
Hill, B., 194
Holroyd, M., 4, 6, 9
homosexuality and bisexuality, 195–197, 199–200
  in Trollope's writings, 121–124

I
Ibsen, H., 83
  on soul murder, 24, 83
identification
  with aggressor, 25, 45, 48, 54, 58, 86, 90, 98
  with parent, 188, 191. *See also under* Trollope, A.
  healthy, 183, 188
  partial, 18–19
imagination
  empathy and, 18
  powers of, 20
imagos, 7

J
James, H., 105, 153, 156, 156n, 163, 166, 168
Jarrell, R., 15–16

K
Keynes, G., 194
Kris, E., 11, 17
Kronenberger, L. 36

L
Lamb, C., 13
Lewes, G. H., 154–155
Lewin, B., 34
loss of parent and parental love, 25, 27, 193. *See also* separation; Trollope, A., losses
love, 36
love-death, 58
Lovell, M. S., 8, 15, 53n

M
male development and masculinity, 64
Mann, T., 127–128
masochism, 25, 45, 54, 90, 98, 161
Masson, J. M., 102
merger, 58n
Miller, J. H., 119, 120, 124
Monteiro, G., 13

mother. *See also specific topics*
  life without, 187–191, 193. *See also under* Trollope, A., mother
  "Is there life without mother?", 26–27, 31–32, 54, 58, 75. *See also* Renard, parents and childhood
Mullen, R., 97, 133, 134, 148, 149, 155, 164
multiple personality disorder, 203–206
Munson, J., 97, 133, 134, 148, 149, 155, 164
murder, 27–28
murderous rage/aggression, 45, 58, 81–82, 193

N
Neville-Sington, P., 79, 80, 97n, 126n, 131n, 144n, 172, 173, 175–176
1984 (Orwell), 25
"nothing," 34, 35

O
obsessive-compulsiveness, 128, 141. *See also under* Franklin; Trollope, A.
oedipal dreams, 51
Oedipus Rex, 190
Orwell, G., 25

P
paranoia, 19, 145–146
  "combinatory," 18
  of everyday life, 16–17
parent. *See also specific topics*
  primal, 29–32, 191
    clinical illustration, 32–36
    defined, 29
    resistance to idea of bad/pathological, 27
Phillips, A., 193
poetry, 15, 41, 48

Pope-Hennessy, J., 79, 97, 127, 150
Prater, D., 128
primal mental representations, 30. *See also* parent, primal
primary-process thinking, 17
psychoanalysis
  applied, 11, 21. *See also specific topics*
psychobiography, 3
psychological health, 12–14
psychopathology of everyday life, 16–18, 28. *See also* delusions, of everyday life

R
Raban, J., 149–151, 166
Ransom, T., 77, 94, 180–182
regression in service of ego, 17
Renard, A-R., 39, 41–46, 52–55
  death, 55
Renard, F., 39, 41, 44, 46, 52–53, 55
Renard, J., 19, 26, 39–49, 149
  childhood and family dynamics, 39–49
  soul murder, 49–50
  illness and death, 56–58
  maternal seduction, sadomasochistic incestuous impulses, and, 50–59
  personality, 44–45, 48
  self-reflections, 19
  writings, 179n
    The Bigoted Woman (*La Bigote*), 55, 56
    Journal, 41, 44, 48, 57
    Poil de Carotte (autobiographical novel), 39, 40, 42, 44–47, 49, 50, 52, 55–59, 195
Renard, Marie, 53
Renard, Maurice, 41, 44, 53
repetition compulsion, 25, 192–193
Roget, E., 19
Roth, H., 191

Index

S

Sadleir, M., 67, 78, 83, 88
sadomasochism, 108. *See also*
    identification, with aggressor;
    masochism; Renard, maternal
    seduction
Schreber, D. P., 191
separation, traumatic, 48, 75, 83
separation-individuation, 31,
    187–192
Shakespeare, W., 8
    Richard III, 8
Shengold, L., 9, 12, 23, 29, 34,
    47–49, 96, 194
slips of tongue. *See* psychopathology
    of everyday life
Snow, C. P., 15, 64, 74, 90, 98, 156
Sophocles, 190
soul murder, 12, 23–25, 28, 108,
    160, 188
    as destroying capacity for joy, 83
    Renard and, 49–50
    splitting and, 47
soul murder victims, 27
    ambivalence toward perpetrator,
        47
splitting, 47, 205. *See also*
    Trollope, A., conflicting/
    contrary views and mental
    splits
Strachey, L., 3–7, 9–10
sublimation, 17, 19
Super, H., 175

T

talents, and psychopathology,
    16–21
Terry, R. C., 81, 86, 106, 151, 164
Toesca, M., 41, 45
traumatic separation, 48, 75, 83
Trilling, L., 12
Trollope, A. *See also specific topics*
    alone in London, 93–94
    anal offensiveness, 91
    anger and conflicting fantasies,
        124–127
    biographers and biographies, 74,
        80–81, 90, 149–150, 167n
    brother (T. Adolphus Trollope)
        and, 79–80, 85–91
    compared with other writers,
        65–66, 82, 101–102, 113,
        127–128, 134, 146, 149, 156
    conflicting/contrary views and
        mental splits, 150–151, 180,
        205. *See also* ambivalence
    control, 164–166
    creativity
        daydreaming and, 117–119,
            124–125
        ghost-laying function, 134
    decision to become writer, 94
    education and schooling, 71,
        77, 85–91, 151, 164, 172,
        174
        beatings at school, 86, 87, 91
    father (T. Anthony Trollope) and,
        66–72. *See also* Trollope, T.
        Anthony
    neglect and verbal abuse,
        89–90
    finances, 67–68, 83, 89, 92,
        97–98, 164–165
    guilt, 82
    identification with his parents,
        97, 98, 124, 161, 173, 176,
        178, 191
    illnesses and death, 96, 97, 161n,
        169–172
    losses, 64, 80, 92–93
    Mann and, 127–128
    marriage and family, 62,
        152–158, 166, 176, 182
    masochism, 82, 91, 161, 163
    mother (F. Trollope) and, 72–78,
        177–183
        on A. Trollope, 86
        life without, and motivation
            for writing, 80–84
        return of, 91–93
        writing and, 74, 99–100, 127,
            181, 183

Index

murderous rage and its vicissitudes, 81–82, 89, 91
need for distance from deep emotion, 153
obsessive-compulsiveness, 89, 91, 97–98, 102, 105, 107, 110, 113, 125, 126, 165
   feelings about order and disorder, 166–169, 172
personality, 147–152. *See also specific topics*
sense of humor, 149
sexuality, 93, 117–119, 124–127, 166
turning points, 95–99
on writer's gifts and powers, 19–20
writing style, 108–109, 180
anonymity, 107
writing(s), 67, 67n, 101, 182
   An Autobiography, 3, 14–15, 26, 63, 66, 71, 74, 75, 80, 82, 90, 91, 98, 99, 102, 109, 117–121, 130, 131, 134, 150, 152–153, 158–160, 174–175
   Barchester Towers, 100, 152
   The Belton Estate, 161
   The Bertrams, 67n, 105, 133, 135–138, 146
   Castle Richmond, 122–123
   disorder and provocation in, 107–110
   Dr. Wortle's School, 130
   The Duke's Children, 123–124, 160
   Framley Parsonage, 129, 132, 154, 155, 157
   He Knew He Was Right, 141, 180
   homosexuality and bisexuality in, 121–124
   involvement with his characters, 159–168
   John Caldigate, 63n
   Lady Anna, 106
   The Last Chronicle of Barsetshire, 129, 130, 132–134
   letters, 126n, 151, 152, 157, 162–163, 166–168
   method of, 101–107, 110
   "The Panjandrum," 118
   "penetration" in, 105
   The Small House at Allington, 129, 130, 132, 173–174
   The Three Clerks, 109, 130
   Trollope on his own, 102
   The Warden, 65–66, 99–100, 180
   The Way We Live Now, 82, 136
   "Why Frau Frohmann Raised Her Prices," 139–146
Trollope, C. (sister), 64, 93
Trollope, F. (mother), 79, 80. *See also* Trollope, A., mother; *specific topics*
   biography of, 171
   characters in A. Trollope's novels who resemble, 140–141, 173–174
   illness and death, 92, 178
   marriage, 72, 73, 75–76, 78, 178
   writing(s), 81, 102
      A. Trollope and, 74, 181, 183
      diary, 81
      Domestic Manners of the Americans, 64–65, 81, 91–92, 97
      letters, 76–77
      One Fault, 180
      The Vicar of Wrexhill, 144n
Trollope, T. Adolphus (brother), 79–80, 85–91
Trollope, T. Anthony (father). *See also* Trollope, A., father
   characters in A. Trollope's novels who resemble, 133
   illness and death, 93–94, 178
   letters to his sons, 171–172
   neurological problems, 69–70
"Trollopian sin," quintessential, 148

V
vulnerability, 61

W
Warren, R. P., 15

Wilson, E., 12
Woolf, V., 6–7
Wright, F., 76–77